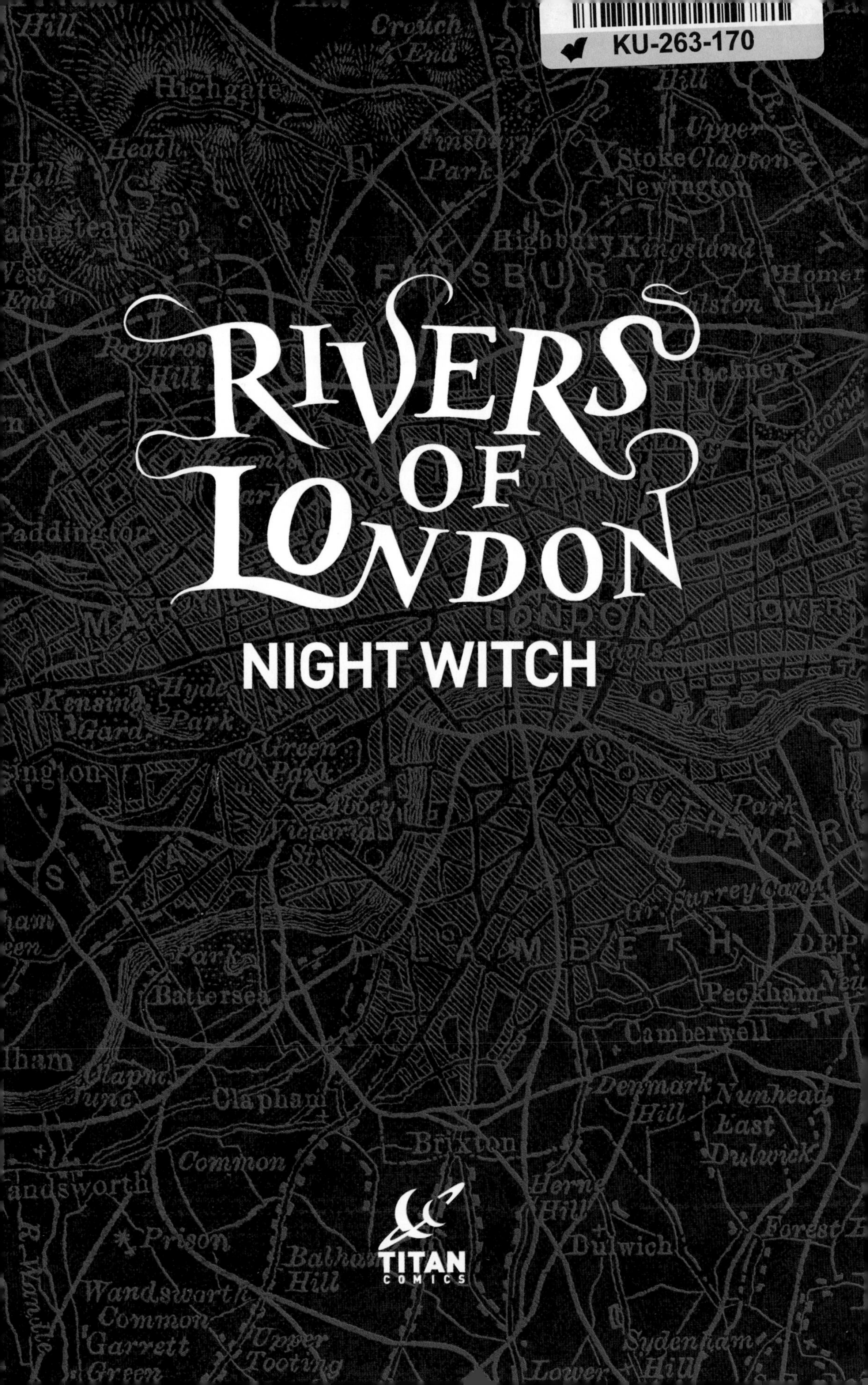
Crouch End
Highgate
Heath
Hampstead
Finsbury Park
Stoke Newington
Upper Clapton
Highbury
Kingsland
FINSBURY
Dalston
Hackney
Paddington
LONDON
Hyde Park
Green Park
Abbey
Victoria St.
SOUTHWARK
Surrey Canal
LAMBETH
Battersea
Peckham
Camberwell
Clapham
Denmark Hill
Nunhead
East Dulwich
Brixton
Common
Wandsworth
Herne Hill
Prison
Dulwich
Balham Hill
Wandsworth Common
Garrett Green
Upper Tooting
Sydenham Hill

RIVERS OF LONDON

NIGHT WITCH

TITAN COMICS

RIVERS OF LONDON: NIGHT WITCH
ISBN: 9781785852930

TITAN COMICS

EDITOR STEVE WHITE
DEPUTY EDITOR JESSICA BURTON
SENIOR DESIGNER ANDREW LEUNG

Senior Comics Editor Andrew James
Titan Comics Editorial Lizzie Kaye, Tom Williams
Production Supervisors Jackie Flook, Maria Pearson
Production Assistant Peter James
Production Manager Obi Onuora
Art Director Oz Browne
Senior Sales Manager Steve Tothill
Senior Marketing & Press Office Owen Johnson
Marketing Manager Ricky Claydon
Commercial Manager Michelle Fairlamb
Publishing Manager Darryl Tothill
Publishing Director Chris Teather
Operations Director Leigh Baulch
Executive Director Vivian Cheung
Publisher Nick Landau

Published by Titan Comics
A division of Titan Publishing Group Ltd.
144 Southwark St.
London
SE1 0UP

A CIP catalogue record for this title is available from the British Library.

First edition: November 2016

10 9 8 7 6 5 4

Printed in Spain.
Titan Comics.

WWW.TITAN-COMICS.COM

Become a fan on Facebook.com/comicstitan

Follow us on Twitter @ComicsTitan

RIVERS OF LONDON

NIGHT WITCH

WRITTEN BY
BEN AARONVITCH & ANDREW CARTMEL

ART BY
LEE SULLIVAN

COLORS BY
LUIS GUERRERO

LETTERING BY
ROB STEEN

Titan
COMICS

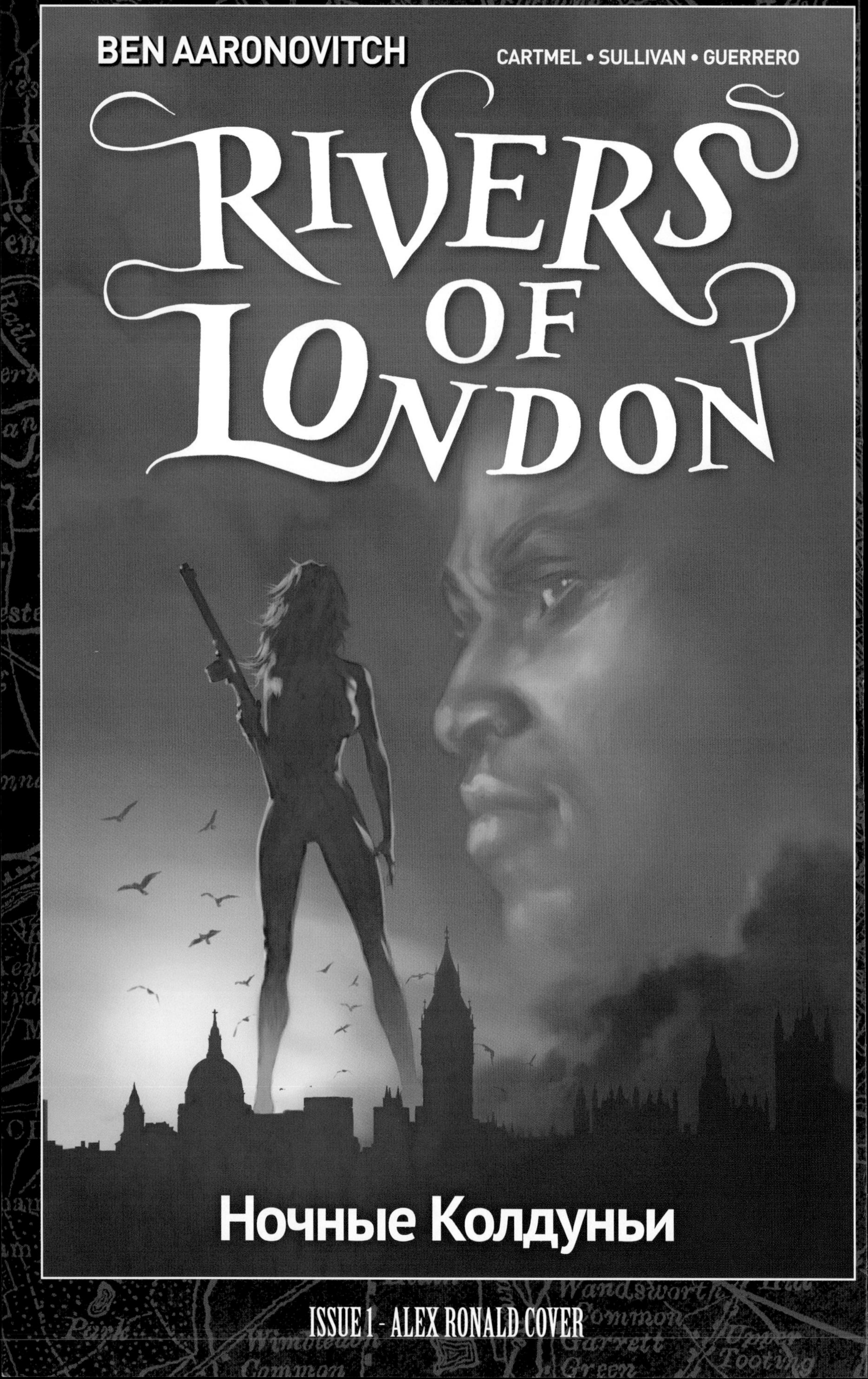
BEN AARONOVITCH
CARTMEL • SULLIVAN • GUERRERO
RIVERS OF LONDON
Ночные Колдуньи

ISSUE 1 - ALEX RONALD COVER

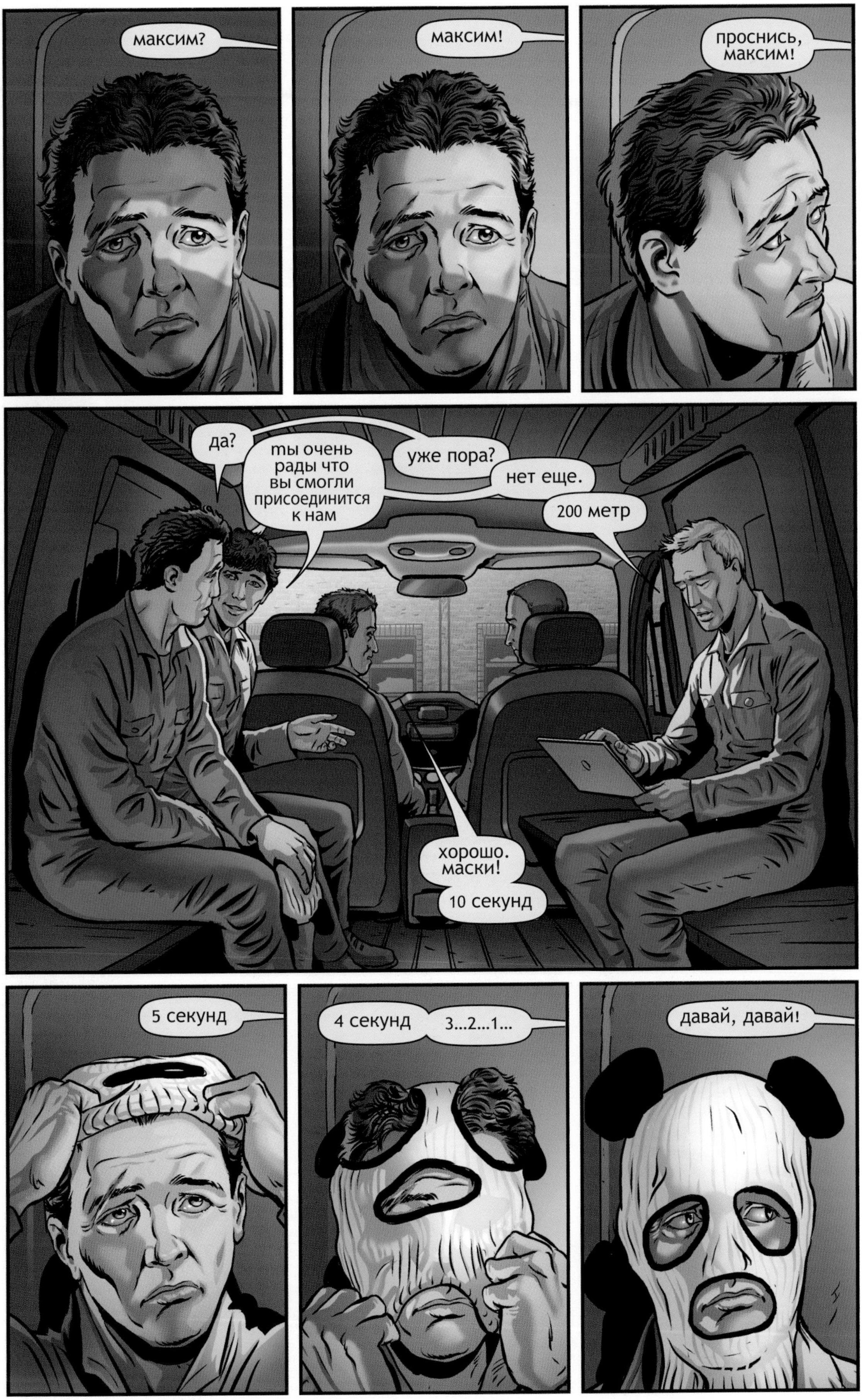
максим?
максим!
проснись, максим!
да?
ты очень рады что вы смогли присоединится к нам
уже пора?
нет еще.
200 метр
хорошо. маски!
10 секунд
5 секунд
4 секунд
3...2...1...
давай, давай!

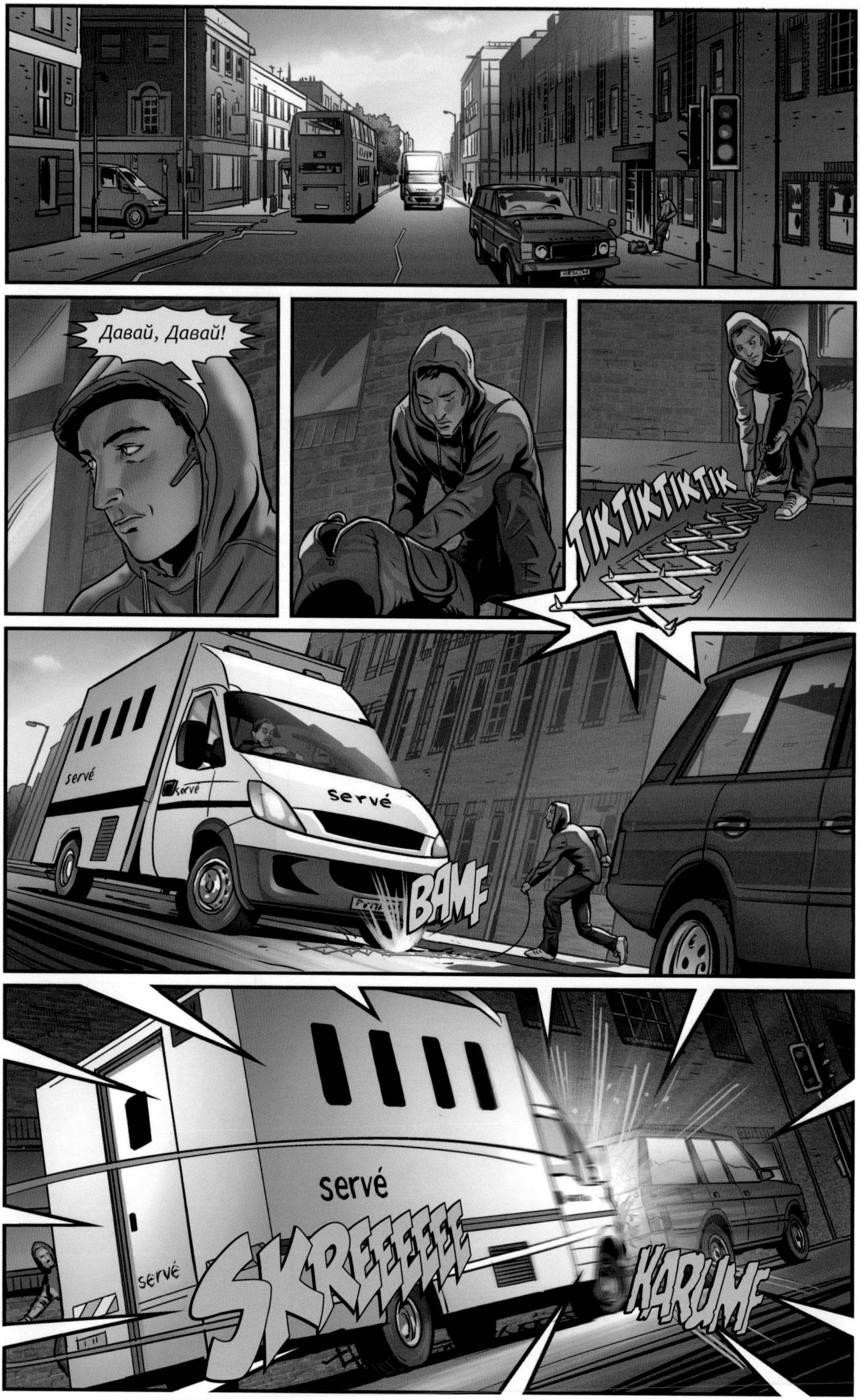
Давай, Давай!
TIKTIKTIKTIK
servé
servé
servé
BAMF
servé
servé
SKREEEEEE
KARUMF

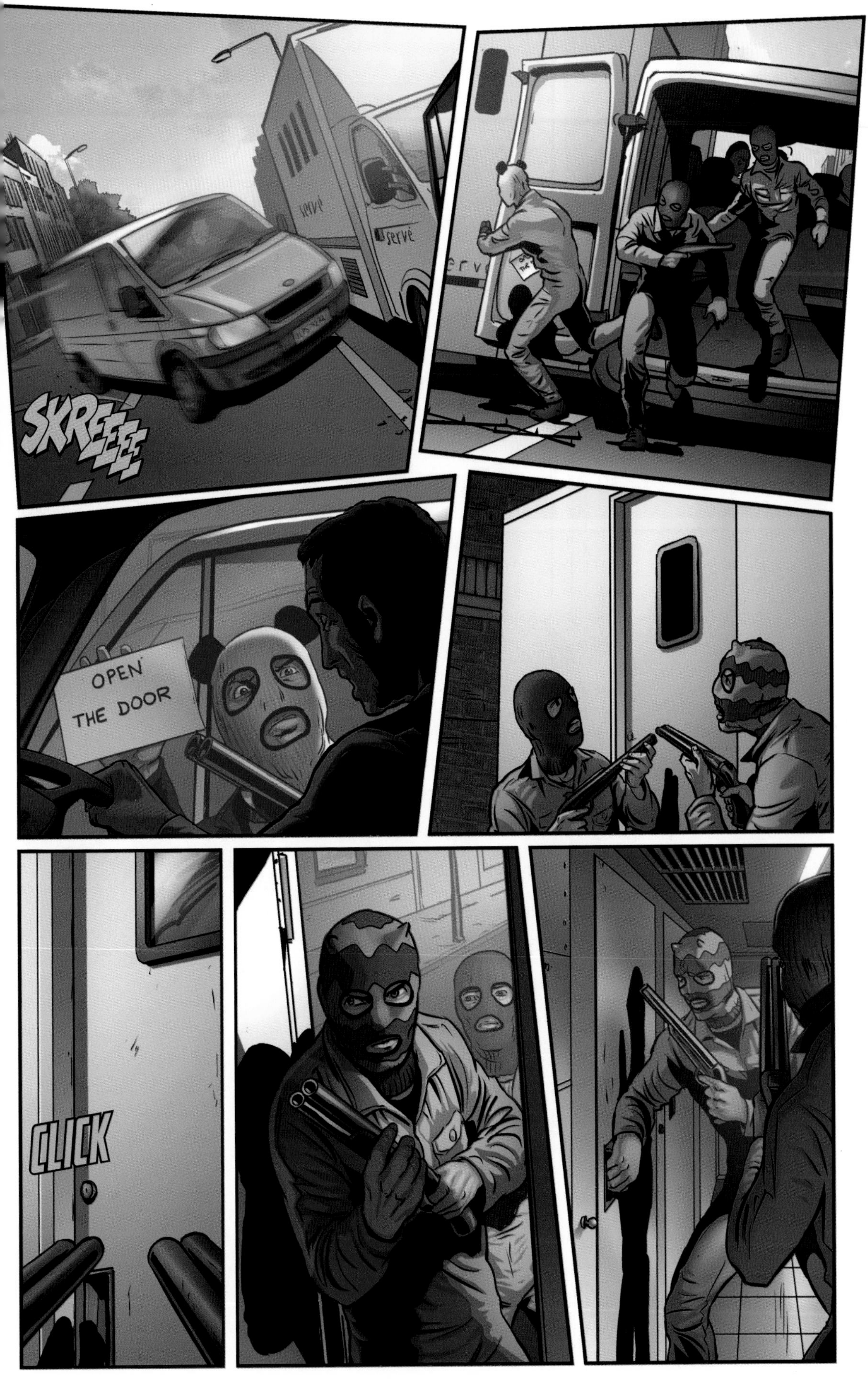
SKREEEEE
OPEN THE DOOR
CLICK

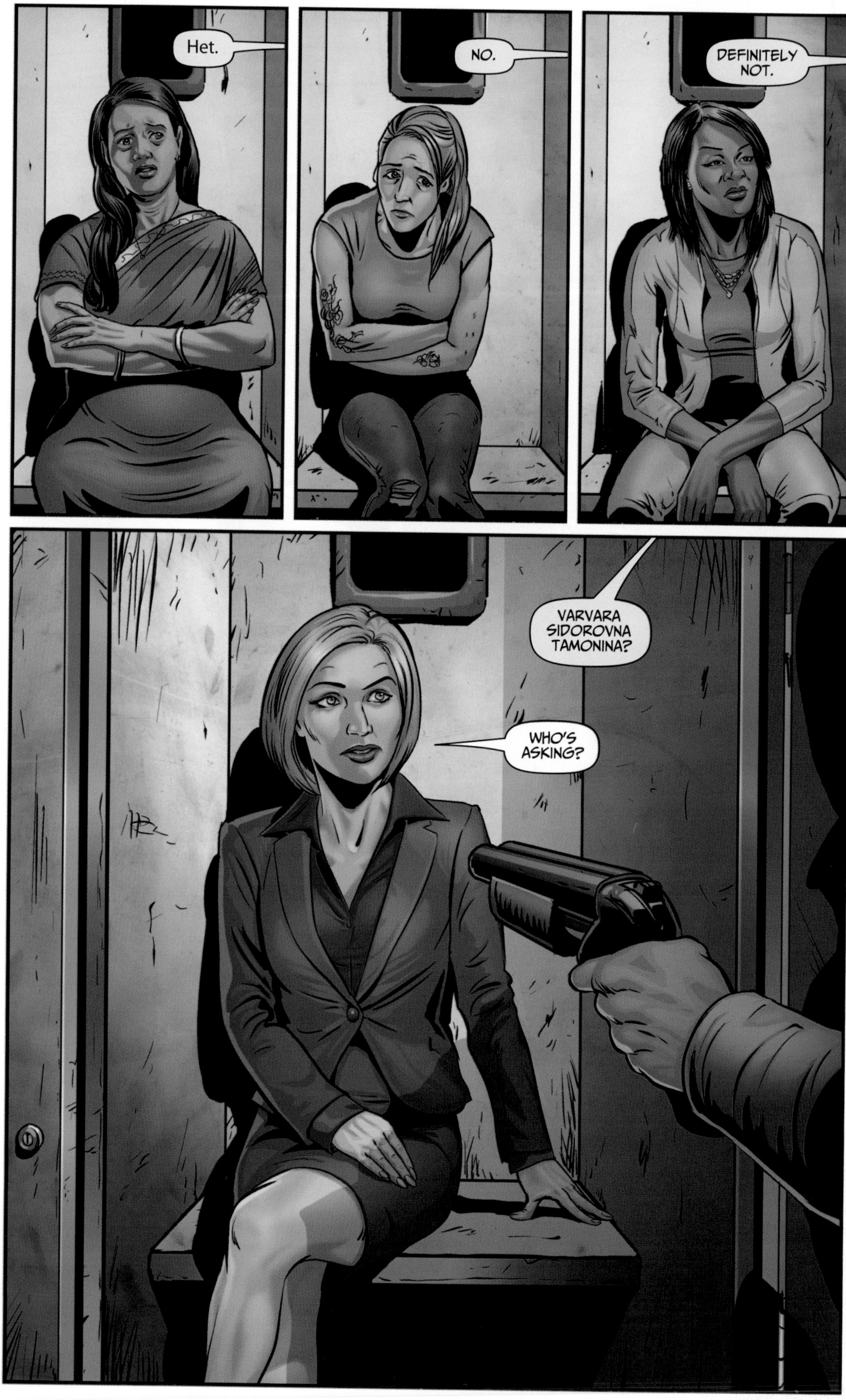
Het.
NO.
DEFINITELY NOT.
VARVARA SIDOROVNA TAMONINA?
WHO'S ASKING?

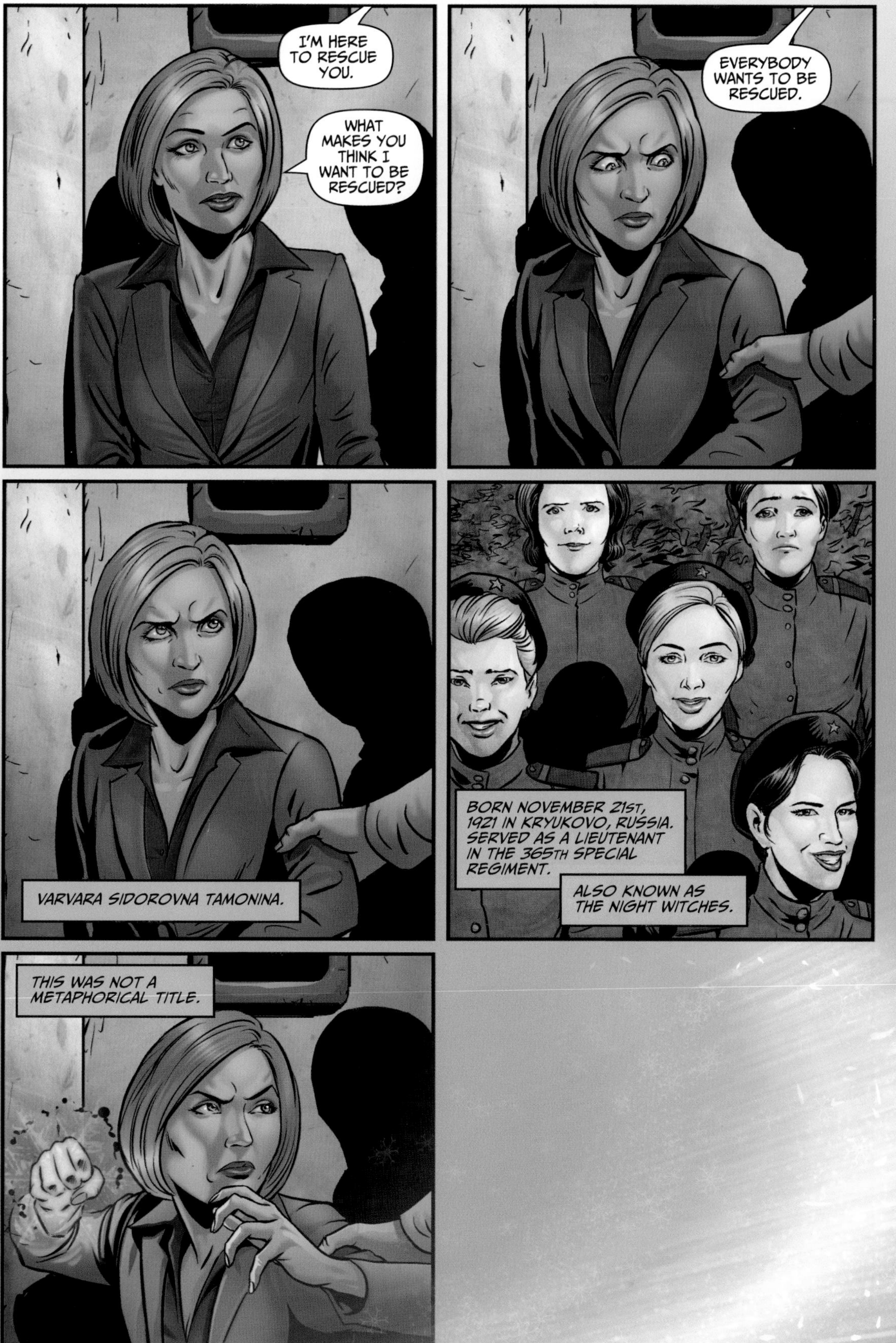
I'M HERE TO RESCUE YOU.
WHAT MAKES YOU THINK I WANT TO BE RESCUED?
EVERYBODY WANTS TO BE RESCUED.
VARVARA SIDOROVNA TAMONINA.
BORN NOVEMBER 21ST, 1921 IN KRYUKOVO, RUSSIA. SERVED AS A LIEUTENANT IN THE 365TH SPECIAL REGIMENT.
ALSO KNOWN AS THE NIGHT WITCHES.
THIS WAS NOT A METAPHORICAL TITLE.

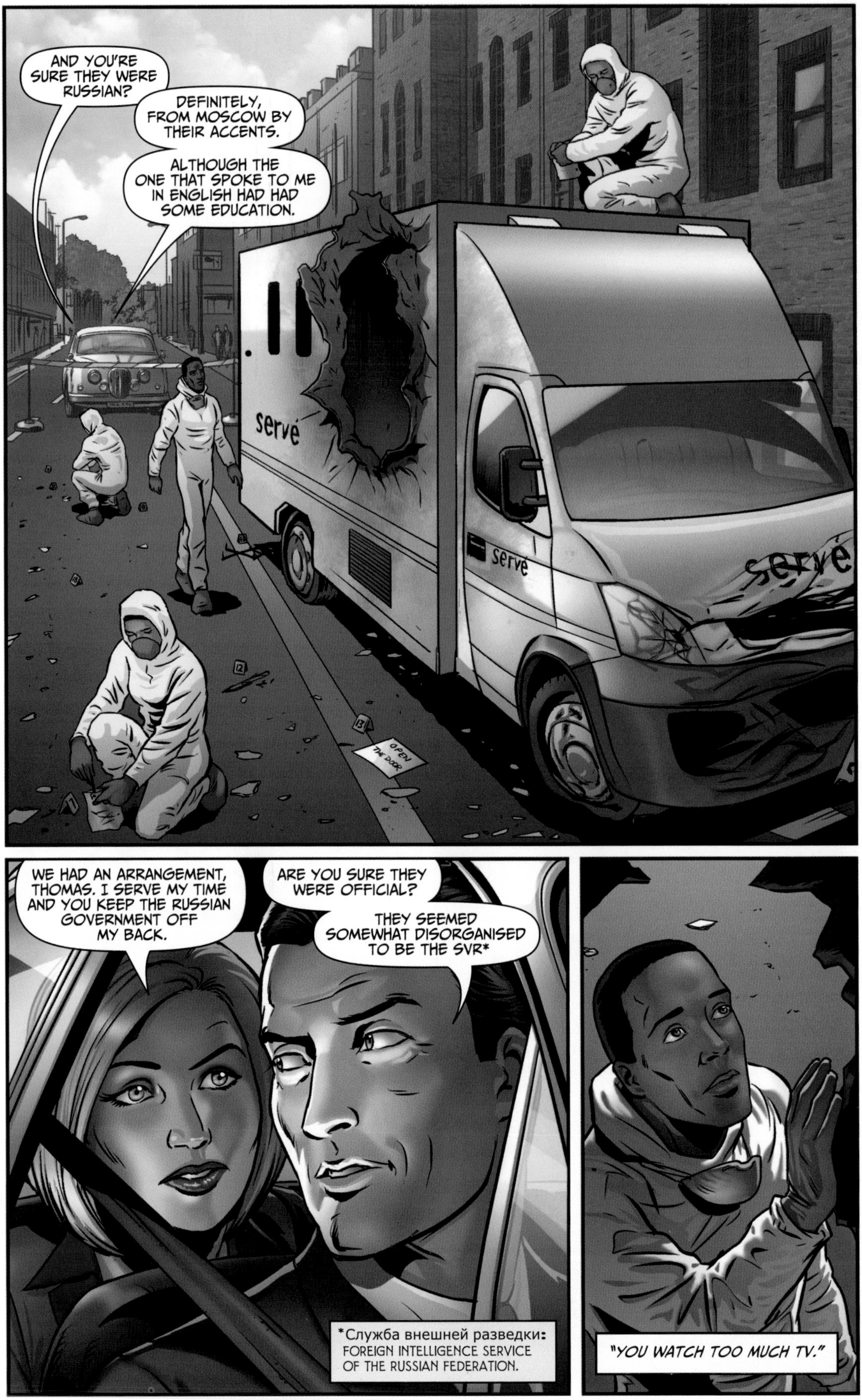
AND YOU'RE SURE THEY WERE RUSSIAN?
DEFINITELY, FROM MOSCOW BY THEIR ACCENTS.
ALTHOUGH THE ONE THAT SPOKE TO ME IN ENGLISH HAD HAD SOME EDUCATION.
servé
servé
servé
OPEN THE DOOR
WE HAD AN ARRANGEMENT, THOMAS. I SERVE MY TIME AND YOU KEEP THE RUSSIAN GOVERNMENT OFF MY BACK.
ARE YOU SURE THEY WERE OFFICIAL?
THEY SEEMED SOMEWHAT DISORGANISED TO BE THE SVR*
*Служба внешней разведки: FOREIGN INTELLIGENCE SERVICE OF THE RUSSIAN FEDERATION.
"YOU WATCH TOO MUCH TV."

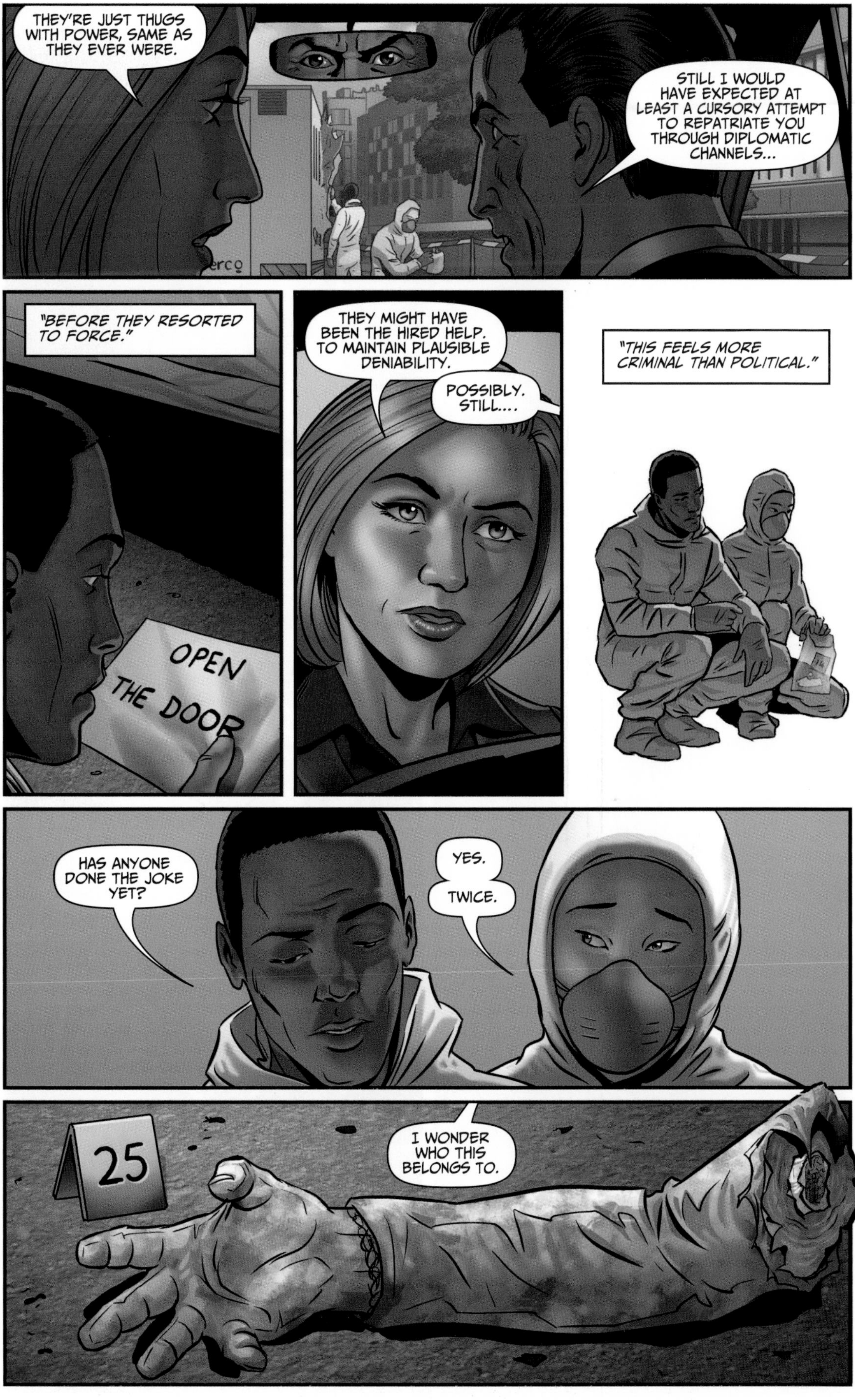
THEY'RE JUST THUGS WITH POWER, SAME AS THEY EVER WERE.
STILL I WOULD HAVE EXPECTED AT LEAST A CURSORY ATTEMPT TO REPATRIATE YOU THROUGH DIPLOMATIC CHANNELS...
"BEFORE THEY RESORTED TO FORCE."
OPEN THE DOOR
THEY MIGHT HAVE BEEN THE HIRED HELP. TO MAINTAIN PLAUSIBLE DENIABILITY.
POSSIBLY. STILL....
"THIS FEELS MORE CRIMINAL THAN POLITICAL."
HAS ANYONE DONE THE JOKE YET?
YES.
TWICE.
25
I WONDER WHO THIS BELONGS TO.

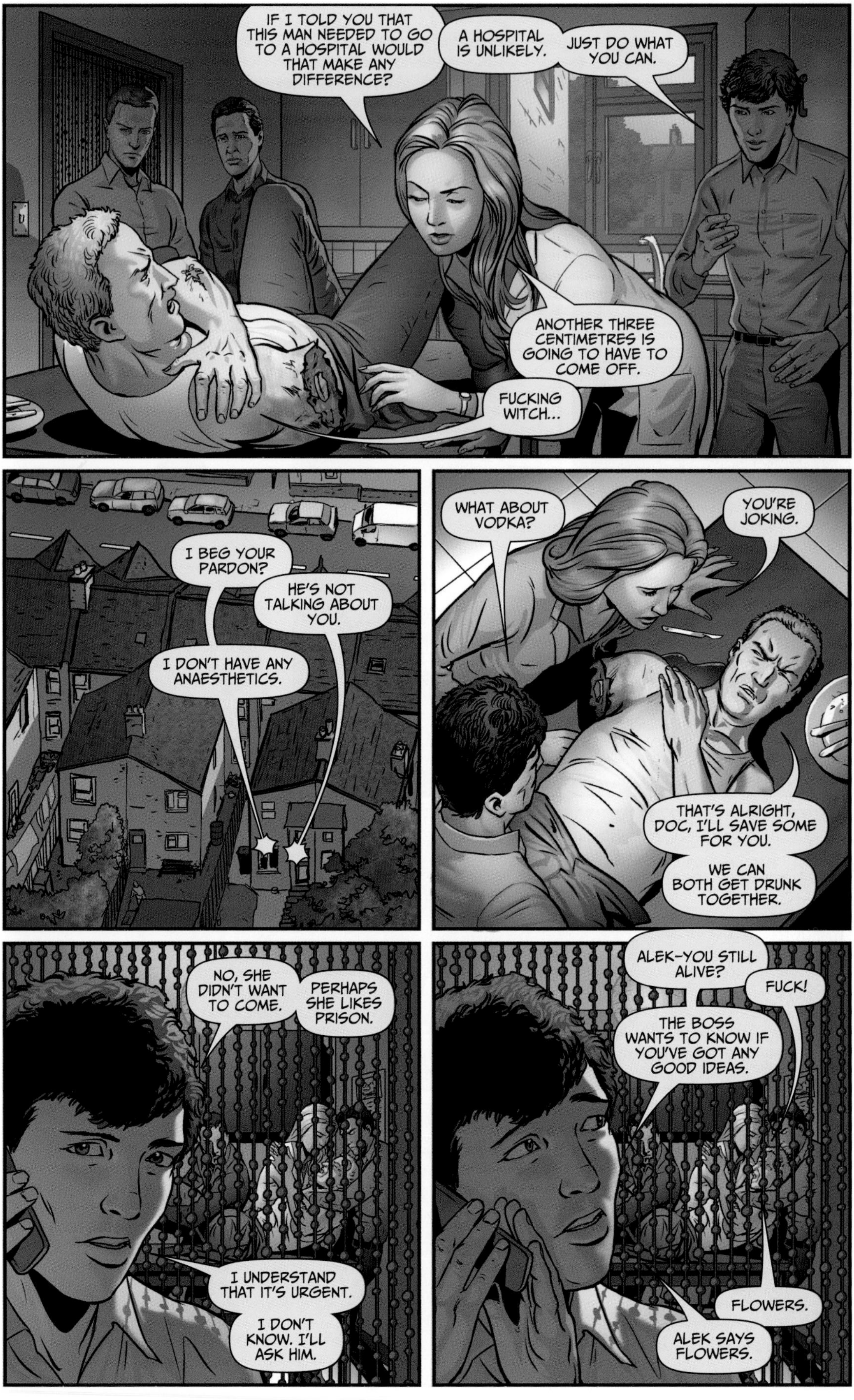
IF I TOLD YOU THAT THIS MAN NEEDED TO GO TO A HOSPITAL WOULD THAT MAKE ANY DIFFERENCE?
A HOSPITAL IS UNLIKELY.
JUST DO WHAT YOU CAN.
ANOTHER THREE CENTIMETRES IS GOING TO HAVE TO COME OFF.
FUCKING WITCH...
I BEG YOUR PARDON?
HE'S NOT TALKING ABOUT YOU.
I DON'T HAVE ANY ANAESTHETICS.
WHAT ABOUT VODKA?
YOU'RE JOKING.
THAT'S ALRIGHT, DOC, I'LL SAVE SOME FOR YOU.
WE CAN BOTH GET DRUNK TOGETHER.
NO, SHE DIDN'T WANT TO COME.
PERHAPS SHE LIKES PRISON.
I UNDERSTAND THAT IT'S URGENT.
I DON'T KNOW. I'LL ASK HIM.
ALEK-YOU STILL ALIVE?
FUCK!
THE BOSS WANTS TO KNOW IF YOU'VE GOT ANY GOOD IDEAS.
FLOWERS.
ALEK SAYS FLOWERS.

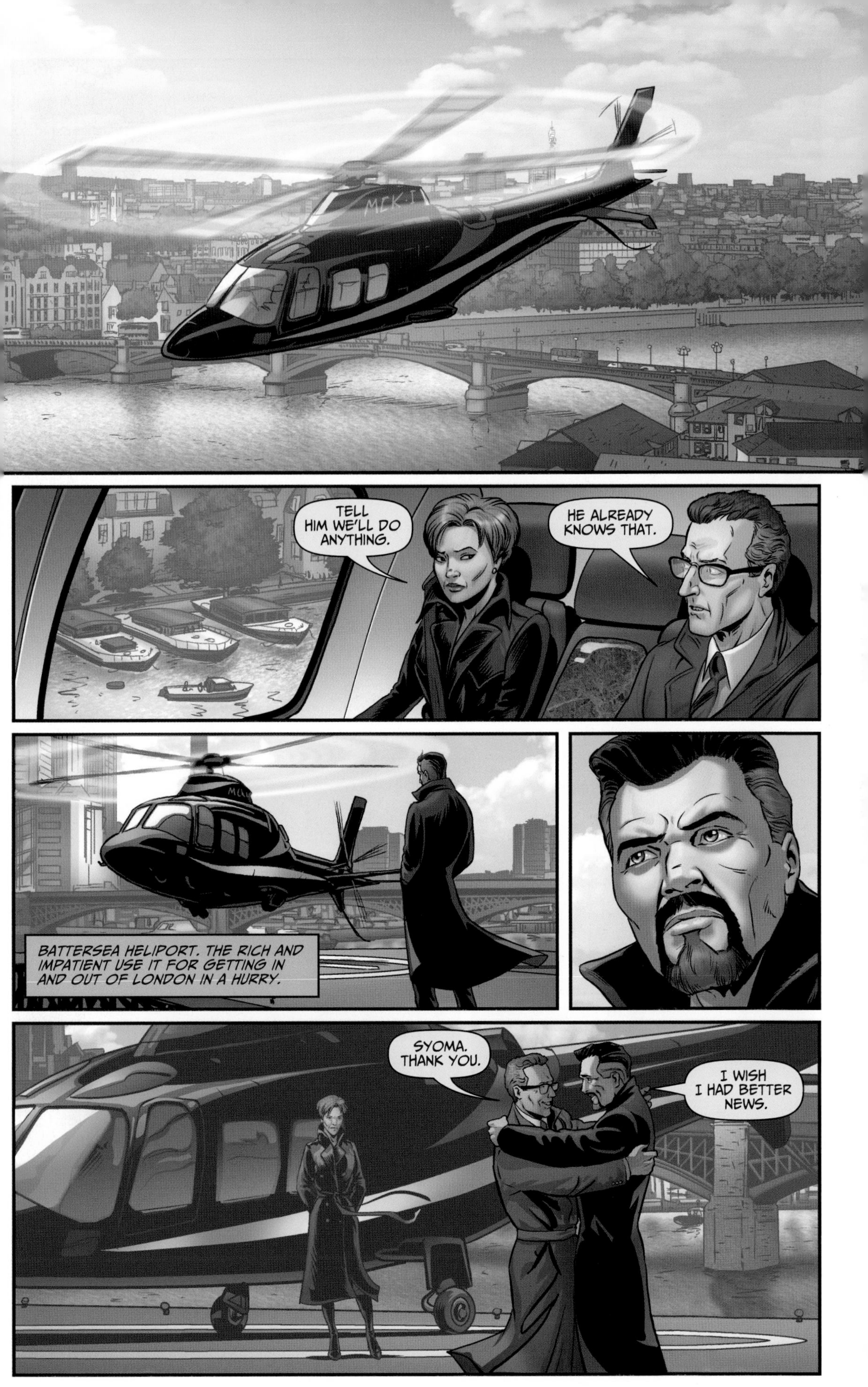
TELL HIM WE'LL DO ANYTHING.
HE ALREADY KNOWS THAT.
BATTERSEA HELIPORT. THE RICH AND IMPATIENT USE IT FOR GETTING IN AND OUT OF LONDON IN A HURRY.
SYOMA. THANK YOU.
I WISH I HAD BETTER NEWS.

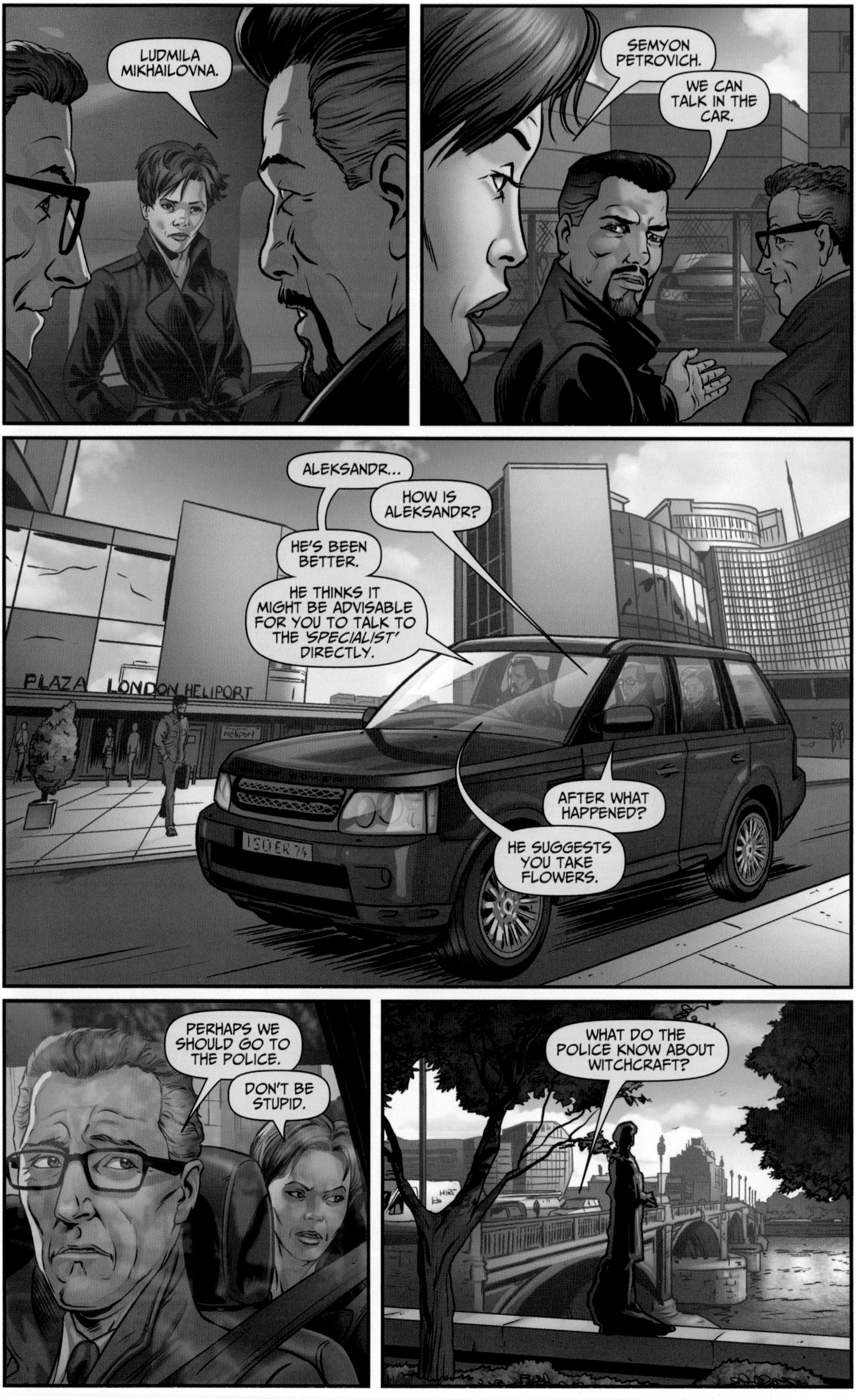
LUDMILA MIKHAILOVNA.
SEMYON PETROVICH.
WE CAN TALK IN THE CAR.
ALEKSANDR...
HOW IS ALEKSANDR?
HE'S BEEN BETTER.
HE THINKS IT MIGHT BE ADVISABLE FOR YOU TO TALK TO THE 'SPECIALIST' DIRECTLY.
PLAZA LONDON HELIPORT
AFTER WHAT HAPPENED?
HE SUGGESTS YOU TAKE FLOWERS.
PERHAPS WE SHOULD GO TO THE POLICE.
DON'T BE STUPID.
WHAT DO THE POLICE KNOW ABOUT WITCHCRAFT?

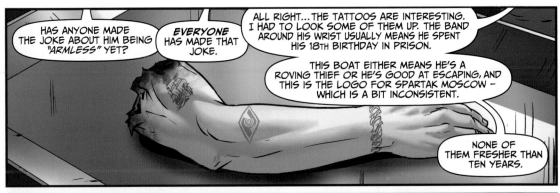

HAS ANYONE MADE THE JOKE ABOUT HIM BEING "ARMLESS" YET?

EVERYONE HAS MADE THAT JOKE.

ALL RIGHT... THE TATTOOS ARE INTERESTING. I HAD TO LOOK SOME OF THEM UP. THE BAND AROUND HIS WRIST USUALLY MEANS HE SPENT HIS 18TH BIRTHDAY IN PRISON.

THIS BOAT EITHER MEANS HE'S A ROVING THIEF OR HE'S GOOD AT ESCAPING, AND THIS IS THE LOGO FOR SPARTAK MOSCOW – WHICH IS A BIT INCONSISTENT.

NONE OF THEM FRESHER THAN TEN YEARS.

SO, NOT THE RUSSIAN GOVERNMENT THEN.

DR ABDUL HAQQ WALID, CRYPTOPATHOLOGIST.

NOT UNLESS THEIR DRESS CODE IS SLIPPING.

SO THE QUESTION IS, WHAT DOES THE RUSSIAN MOB WANT WITH OUR VARVARA?

SHE HAS HAD RATHER A CHEQUERED PAST.

THE MOTIVE COULD RELATE TO THAT.

REVENGE PERHAPS – OR A PAST DEAL THAT WENT BADLY?

THERE'S SOMETHING I WANT TO KNOW, THOUGH.

IF VARVARA IS PULLING THERMAL ENERGY OUT OF THE ENVIRONMENT, WHERE IS IT GOING?

IS THAT ENTIRELY RELEVANT TO THE MATTER AT HAND?

YOU COULD USE AN INFRARED CAMERA AND SEE IF YOU CAN SPOT A THERMAL BLOOM.

IT WOULD HAVE TO BE AT A DISTANCE OR WE'D LOSE THE CAMERA.

BUT THAT'S THE POINT--IT'S A TEST WE CAN DO FROM A DISTANCE.

GENTLEMEN.

DO YOU THINK WE CAN PICK UP A CAMERA ON EBAY?

GENTLEMEN!

THE RUSSIANS HAVE A FEARSOME REPUTATION FOR VIOLENCE AND TENACITY.

I THINK WE CAN EXPECT THEIR NEXT STEP TO BE A DANGEROUS ESCALATION.

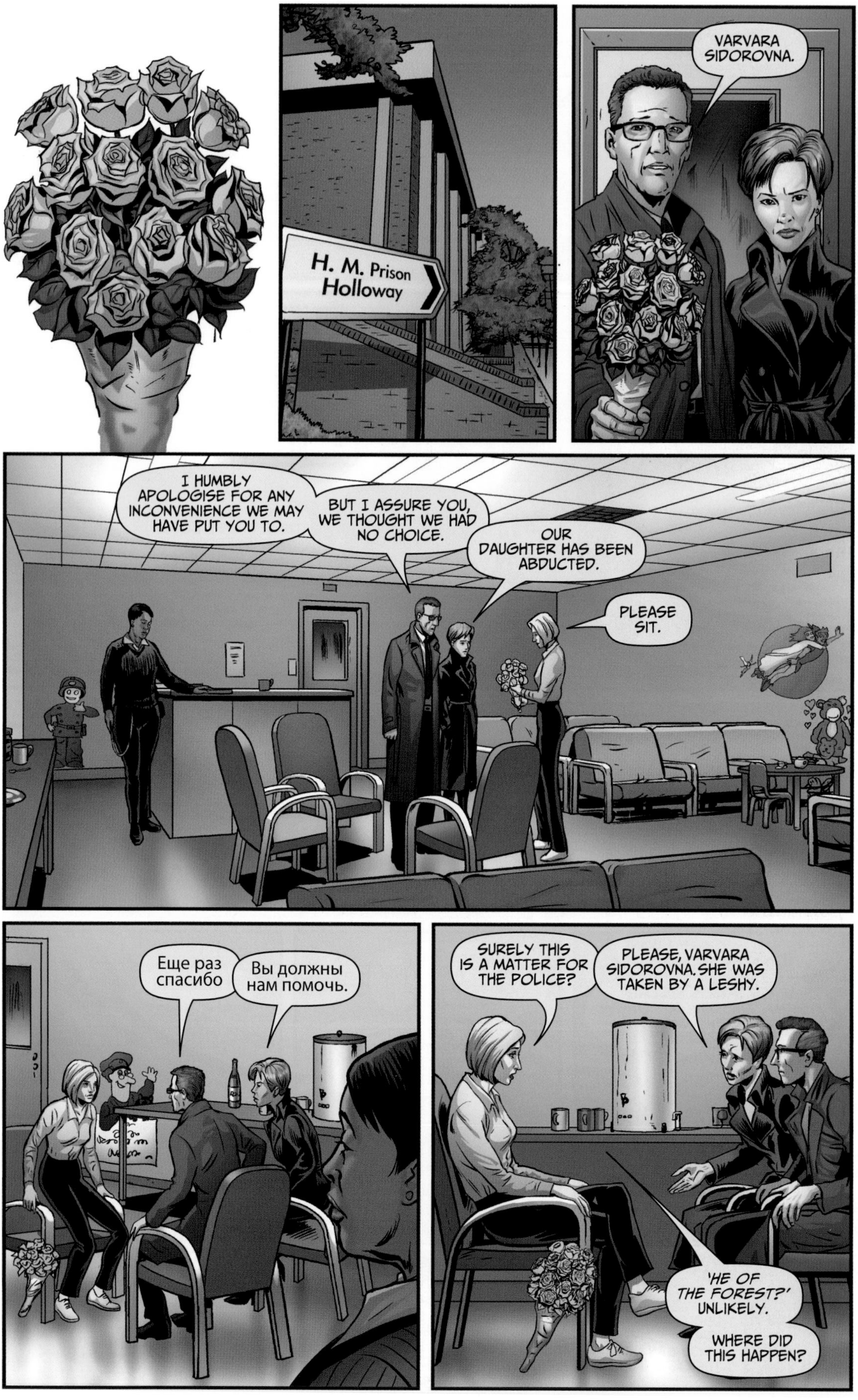
H. M. Prison
Holloway
VARVARA SIDOROVNA.
I HUMBLY APOLOGISE FOR ANY INCONVENIENCE WE MAY HAVE PUT YOU TO.
BUT I ASSURE YOU, WE THOUGHT WE HAD NO CHOICE.
OUR DAUGHTER HAS BEEN ABDUCTED.
PLEASE SIT.
Еще раз спасибо
Вы должны нам помочь.
SURELY THIS IS A MATTER FOR THE POLICE?
PLEASE, VARVARA SIDOROVNA. SHE WAS TAKEN BY A LESHY.
'HE OF THE FOREST?' UNLIKELY.
WHERE DID THIS HAPPEN?

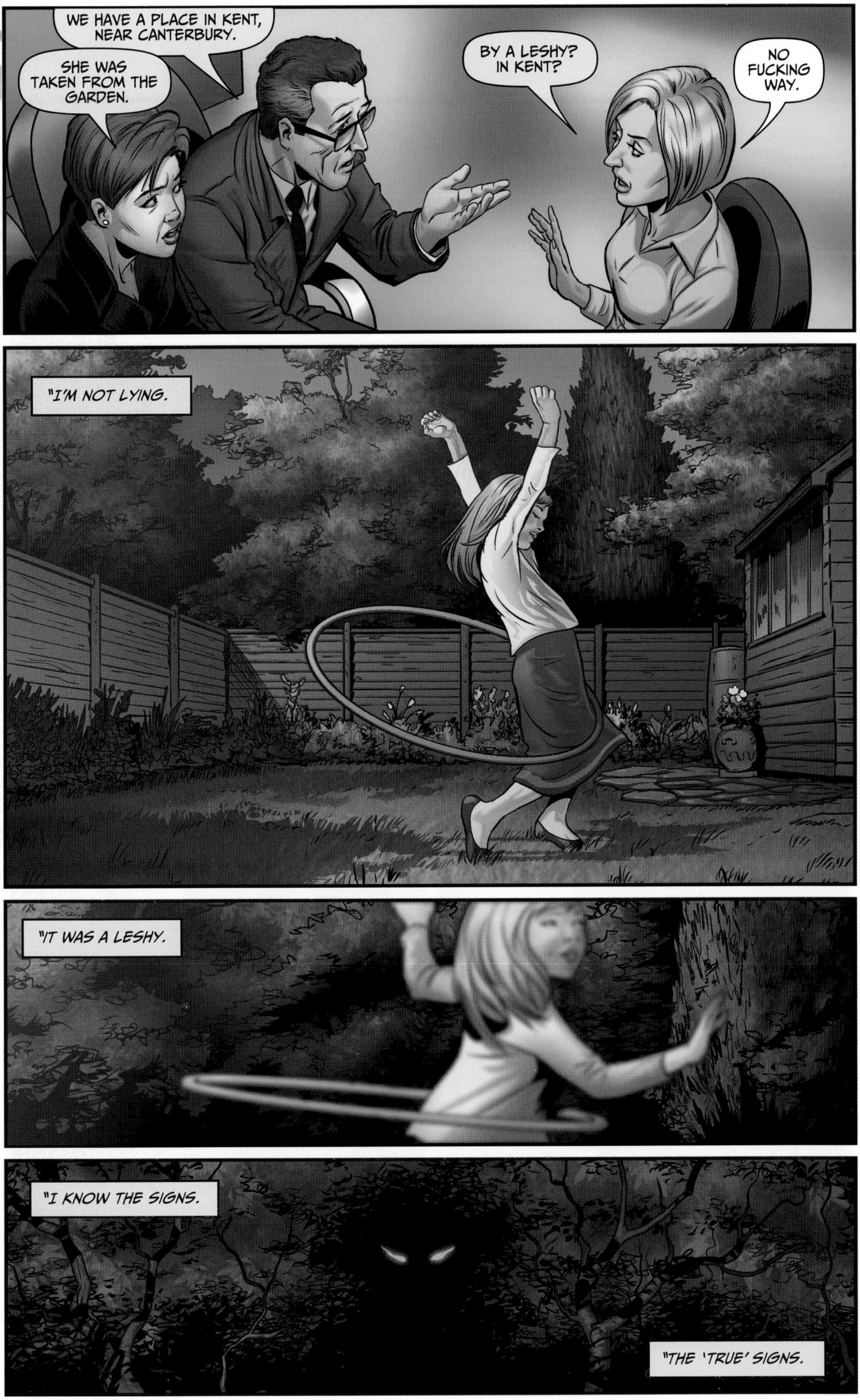
WE HAVE A PLACE IN KENT, NEAR CANTERBURY.
SHE WAS TAKEN FROM THE GARDEN.
BY A LESHY? IN KENT?
NO FUCKING WAY.
"I'M NOT LYING.
"IT WAS A LESHY.
"I KNOW THE SIGNS.
"THE 'TRUE' SIGNS.

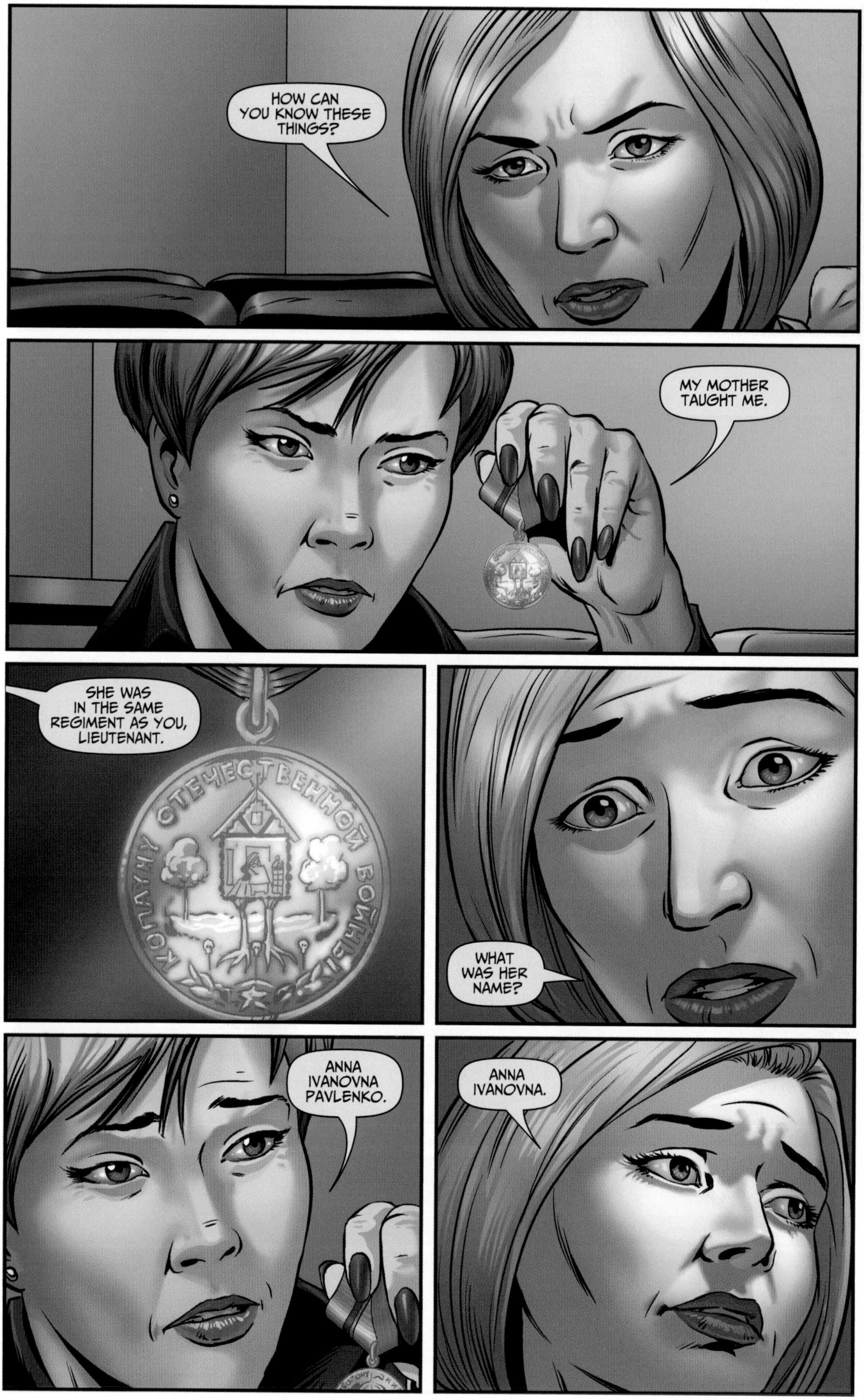
HOW CAN YOU KNOW THESE THINGS?
MY MOTHER TAUGHT ME.
SHE WAS IN THE SAME REGIMENT AS YOU, LIEUTENANT.
WHAT WAS HER NAME?
ANNA IVANOVNA PAVLENKO.
ANNA IVANOVNA.

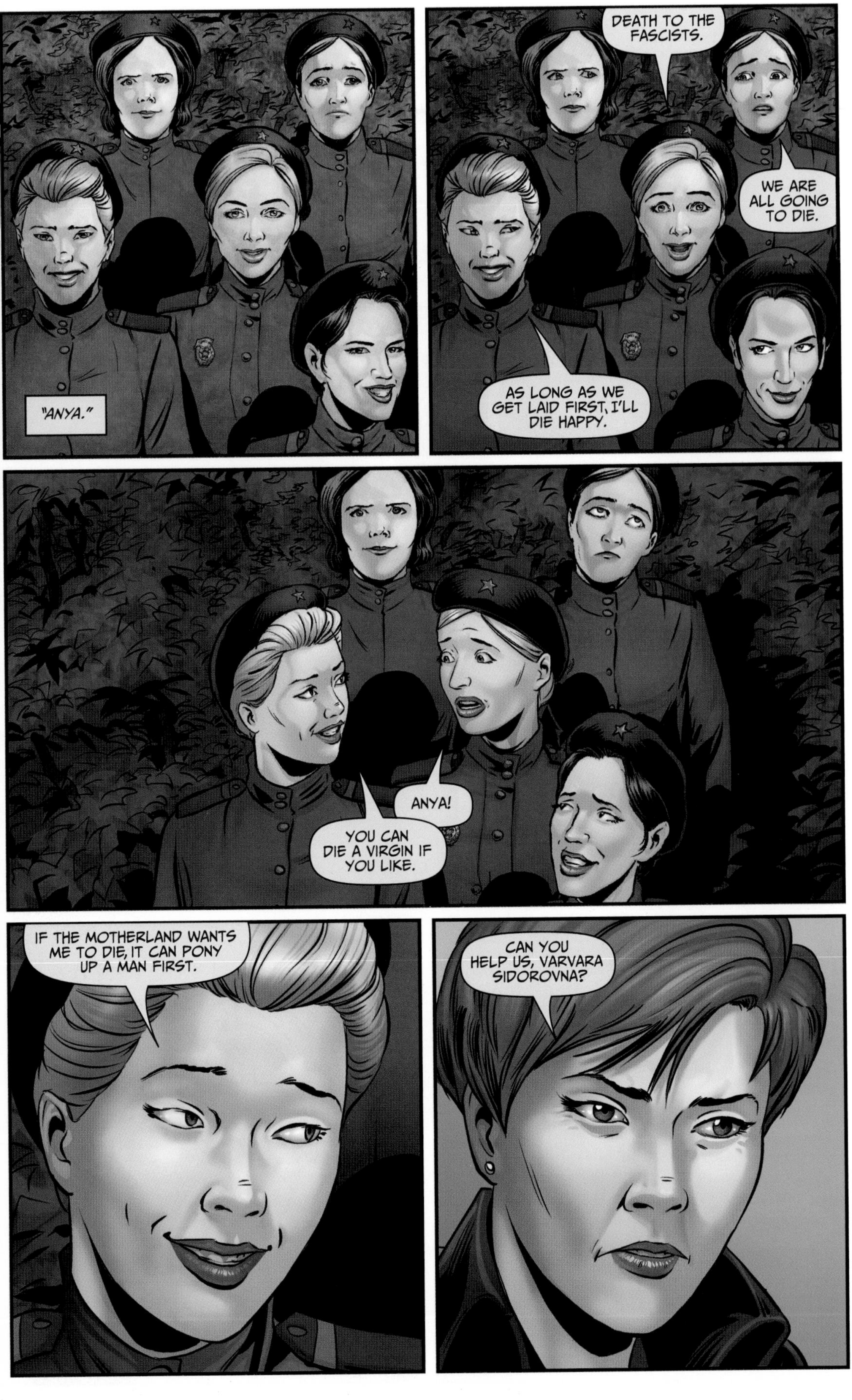
"ANYA."
DEATH TO THE FASCISTS.
WE ARE ALL GOING TO DIE.
AS LONG AS WE GET LAID FIRST, I'LL DIE HAPPY.
ANYA!
YOU CAN DIE A VIRGIN IF YOU LIKE.
IF THE MOTHERLAND WANTS ME TO DIE, IT CAN PONY UP A MAN FIRST.
CAN YOU HELP US, VARVARA SIDOROVNA?

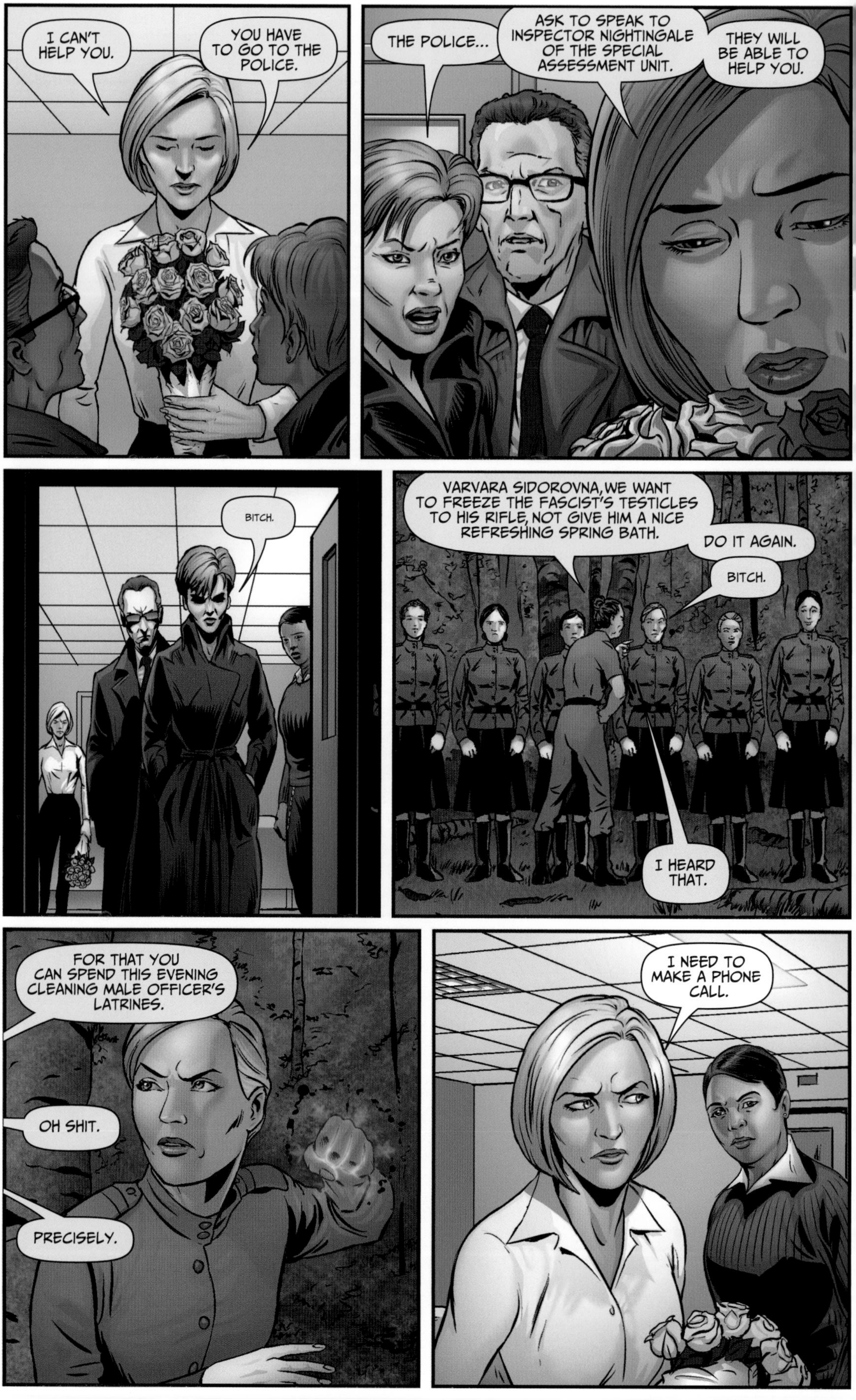
I CAN'T HELP YOU.
YOU HAVE TO GO TO THE POLICE.
THE POLICE...
ASK TO SPEAK TO INSPECTOR NIGHTINGALE OF THE SPECIAL ASSESSMENT UNIT.
THEY WILL BE ABLE TO HELP YOU.
BITCH.
VARVARA SIDOROVNA, WE WANT TO FREEZE THE FASCIST'S TESTICLES TO HIS RIFLE, NOT GIVE HIM A NICE REFRESHING SPRING BATH.
DO IT AGAIN.
BITCH.
I HEARD THAT.
FOR THAT YOU CAN SPEND THIS EVENING CLEANING MALE OFFICER'S LATRINES.
OH SHIT.
PRECISELY.
I NEED TO MAKE A PHONE CALL.

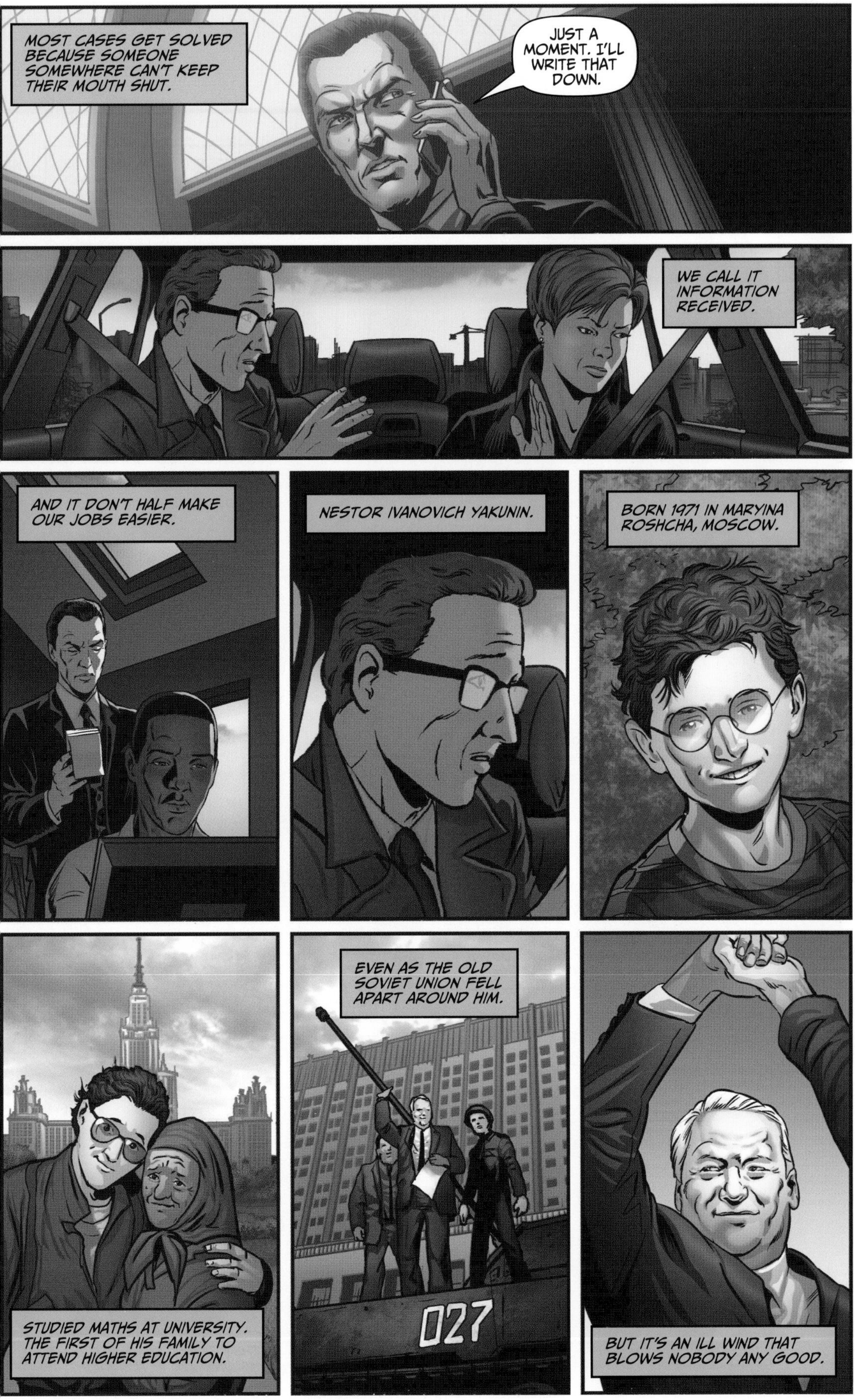
MOST CASES GET SOLVED BECAUSE SOMEONE SOMEWHERE CAN'T KEEP THEIR MOUTH SHUT.
JUST A MOMENT. I'LL WRITE THAT DOWN.
WE CALL IT INFORMATION RECEIVED.
AND IT DON'T HALF MAKE OUR JOBS EASIER.
NESTOR IVANOVICH YAKUNIN.
BORN 1971 IN MARYINA ROSHCHA, MOSCOW.
STUDIED MATHS AT UNIVERSITY. THE FIRST OF HIS FAMILY TO ATTEND HIGHER EDUCATION.
EVEN AS THE OLD SOVIET UNION FELL APART AROUND HIM.
027
BUT IT'S AN ILL WIND THAT BLOWS NOBODY ANY GOOD.

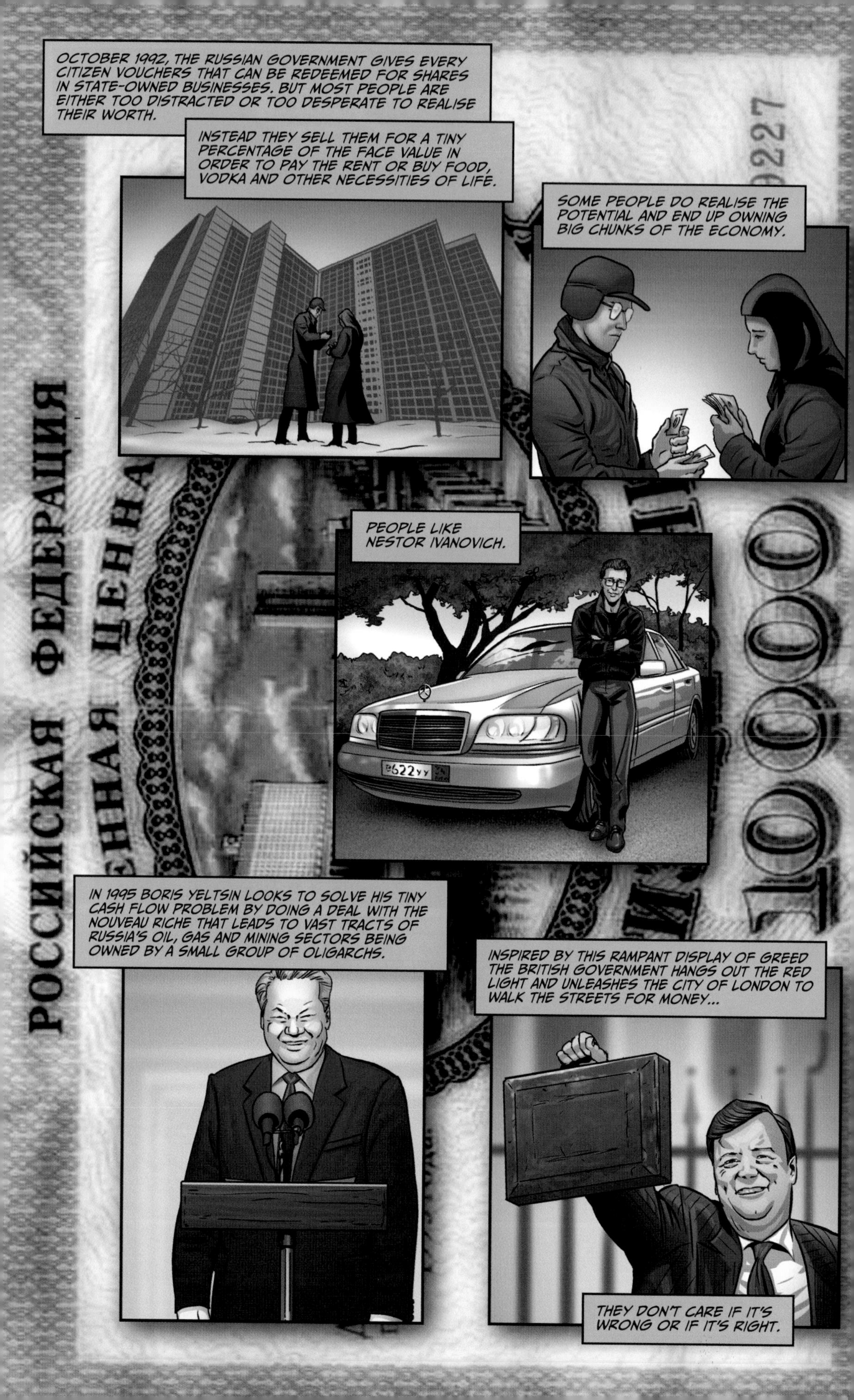
OCTOBER 1992, THE RUSSIAN GOVERNMENT GIVES EVERY CITIZEN VOUCHERS THAT CAN BE REDEEMED FOR SHARES IN STATE-OWNED BUSINESSES. BUT MOST PEOPLE ARE EITHER TOO DISTRACTED OR TOO DESPERATE TO REALISE THEIR WORTH.
INSTEAD THEY SELL THEM FOR A TINY PERCENTAGE OF THE FACE VALUE IN ORDER TO PAY THE RENT OR BUY FOOD, VODKA AND OTHER NECESSITIES OF LIFE.
SOME PEOPLE DO REALISE THE POTENTIAL AND END UP OWNING BIG CHUNKS OF THE ECONOMY.
PEOPLE LIKE NESTOR IVANOVICH.
IN 1995 BORIS YELTSIN LOOKS TO SOLVE HIS TINY CASH FLOW PROBLEM BY DOING A DEAL WITH THE NOUVEAU RICHE THAT LEADS TO VAST TRACTS OF RUSSIA'S OIL, GAS AND MINING SECTORS BEING OWNED BY A SMALL GROUP OF OLIGARCHS.
INSPIRED BY THIS RAMPANT DISPLAY OF GREED THE BRITISH GOVERNMENT HANGS OUT THE RED LIGHT AND UNLEASHES THE CITY OF LONDON TO WALK THE STREETS FOR MONEY...
THEY DON'T CARE IF IT'S WRONG OR IF IT'S RIGHT.
РОССИЙСКАЯ ФЕДЕРАЦИЯ

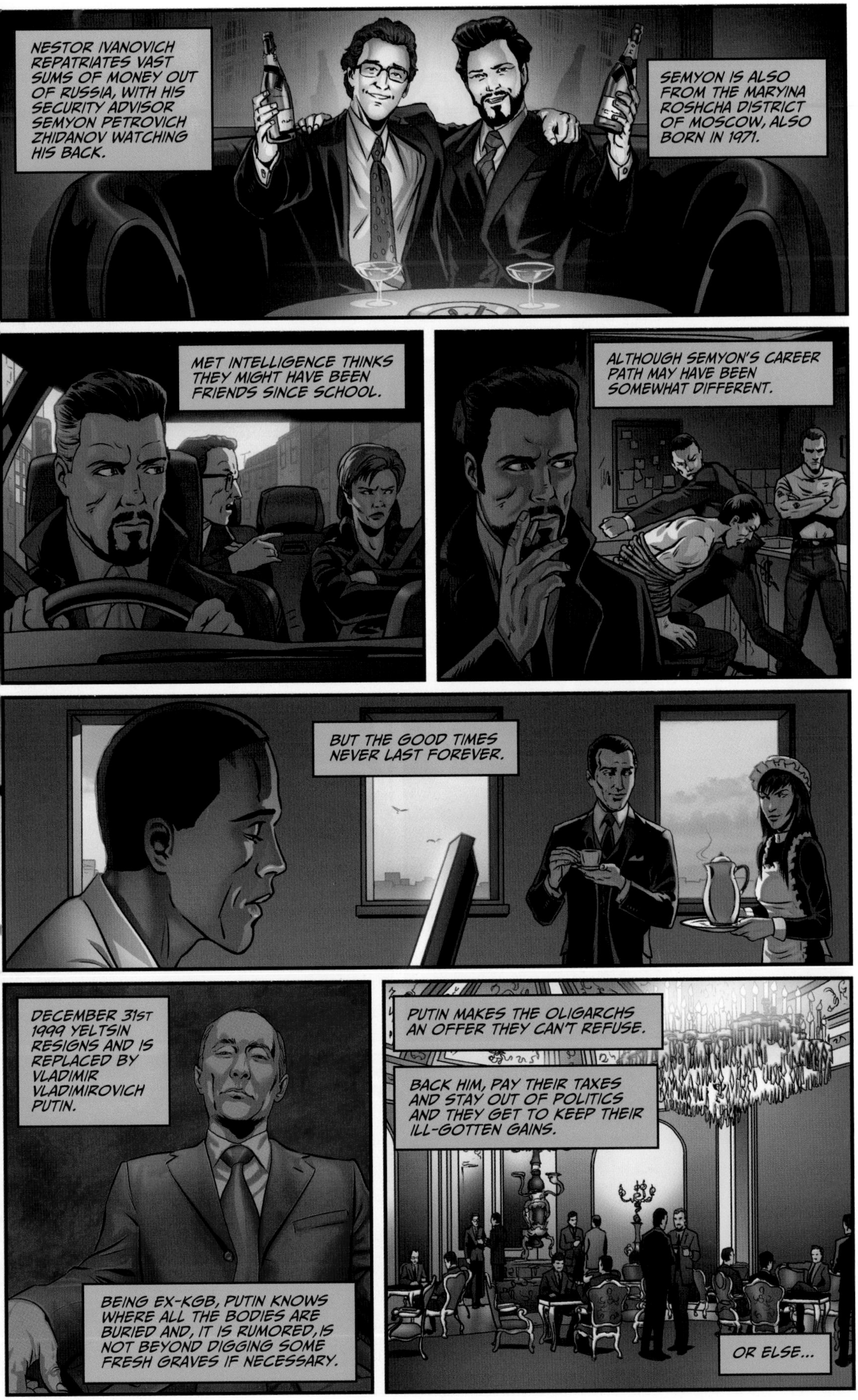
NESTOR IVANOVICH REPATRIATES VAST SUMS OF MONEY OUT OF RUSSIA, WITH HIS SECURITY ADVISOR SEMYON PETROVICH ZHIDANOV WATCHING HIS BACK.
SEMYON IS ALSO FROM THE MARYINA ROSHCHA DISTRICT OF MOSCOW, ALSO BORN IN 1971.
MET INTELLIGENCE THINKS THEY MIGHT HAVE BEEN FRIENDS SINCE SCHOOL.
ALTHOUGH SEMYON'S CAREER PATH MAY HAVE BEEN SOMEWHAT DIFFERENT.
BUT THE GOOD TIMES NEVER LAST FOREVER.
DECEMBER 31ST 1999 YELTSIN RESIGNS AND IS REPLACED BY VLADIMIR VLADIMIROVICH PUTIN.
BEING EX-KGB, PUTIN KNOWS WHERE ALL THE BODIES ARE BURIED AND, IT IS RUMORED, IS NOT BEYOND DIGGING SOME FRESH GRAVES IF NECESSARY.
PUTIN MAKES THE OLIGARCHS AN OFFER THEY CAN'T REFUSE.
BACK HIM, PAY THEIR TAXES AND STAY OUT OF POLITICS AND THEY GET TO KEEP THEIR ILL-GOTTEN GAINS.
OR ELSE...

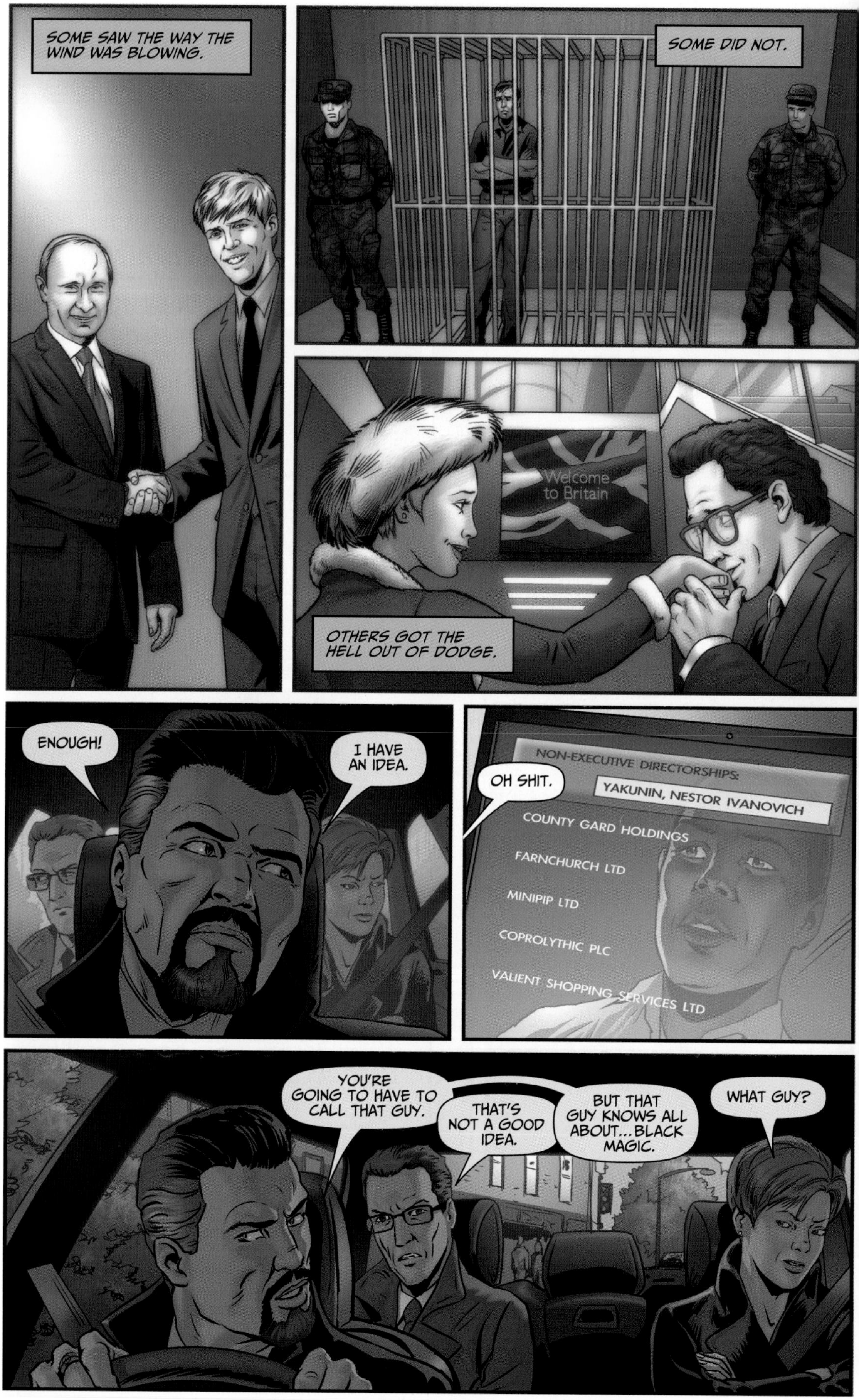
SOME SAW THE WAY THE WIND WAS BLOWING.
SOME DID NOT.
Welcome to Britain
OTHERS GOT THE HELL OUT OF DODGE.
ENOUGH!
I HAVE AN IDEA.
OH SHIT.
NON-EXECUTIVE DIRECTORSHIPS:
YAKUNIN, NESTOR IVANOVICH
COUNTY GARD HOLDINGS
FARNCHURCH LTD
MINIPIP LTD
COPROLYTHIC PLC
VALIENT SHOPPING SERVICES LTD
YOU'RE GOING TO HAVE TO CALL THAT GUY.
THAT'S NOT A GOOD IDEA.
BUT THAT GUY KNOWS ALL ABOUT...BLACK MAGIC.
WHAT GUY?

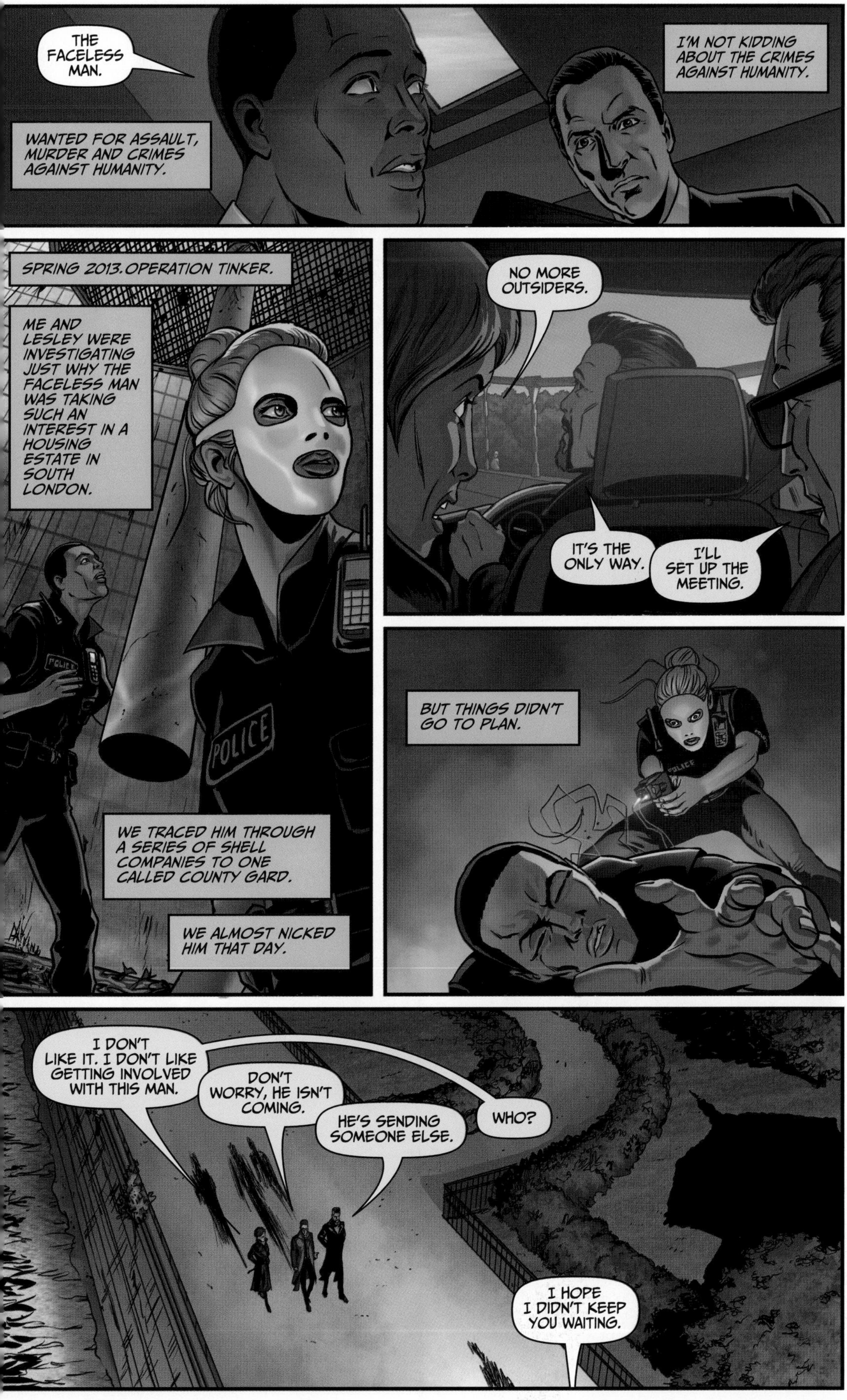
THE FACELESS MAN.
WANTED FOR ASSAULT, MURDER AND CRIMES AGAINST HUMANITY.
I'M NOT KIDDING ABOUT THE CRIMES AGAINST HUMANITY.
SPRING 2013. OPERATION TINKER.
ME AND LESLEY WERE INVESTIGATING JUST WHY THE FACELESS MAN WAS TAKING SUCH AN INTEREST IN A HOUSING ESTATE IN SOUTH LONDON.
POLICE
POLICE
WE TRACED HIM THROUGH A SERIES OF SHELL COMPANIES TO ONE CALLED COUNTY GARD.
WE ALMOST NICKED HIM THAT DAY.
NO MORE OUTSIDERS.
IT'S THE ONLY WAY.
I'LL SET UP THE MEETING.
BUT THINGS DIDN'T GO TO PLAN.
POLICE
I DON'T LIKE IT. I DON'T LIKE GETTING INVOLVED WITH THIS MAN.
DON'T WORRY, HE ISN'T COMING.
HE'S SENDING SOMEONE ELSE.
WHO?
I HOPE I DIDN'T KEEP YOU WAITING.

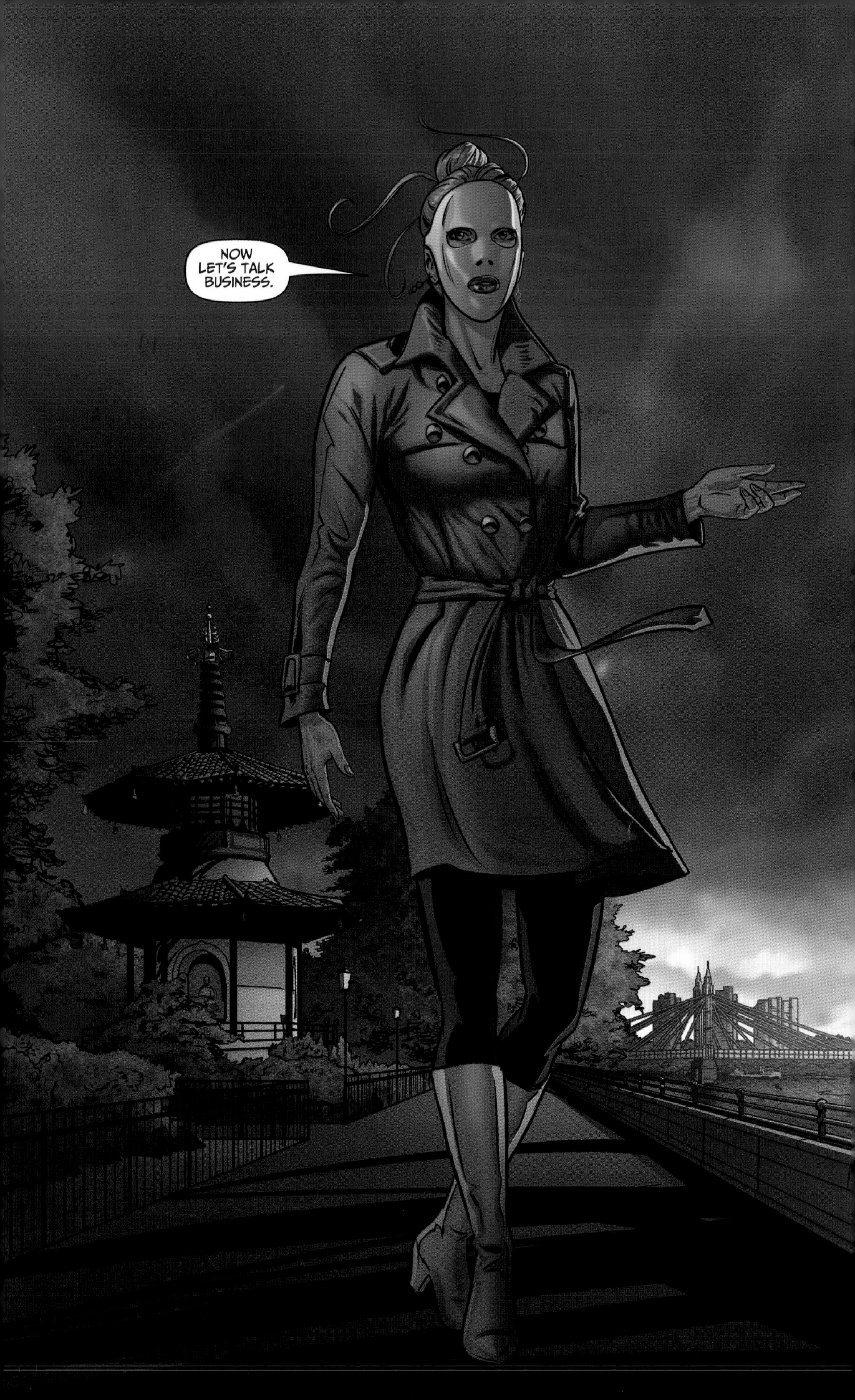
NOW LET'S TALK BUSINESS.

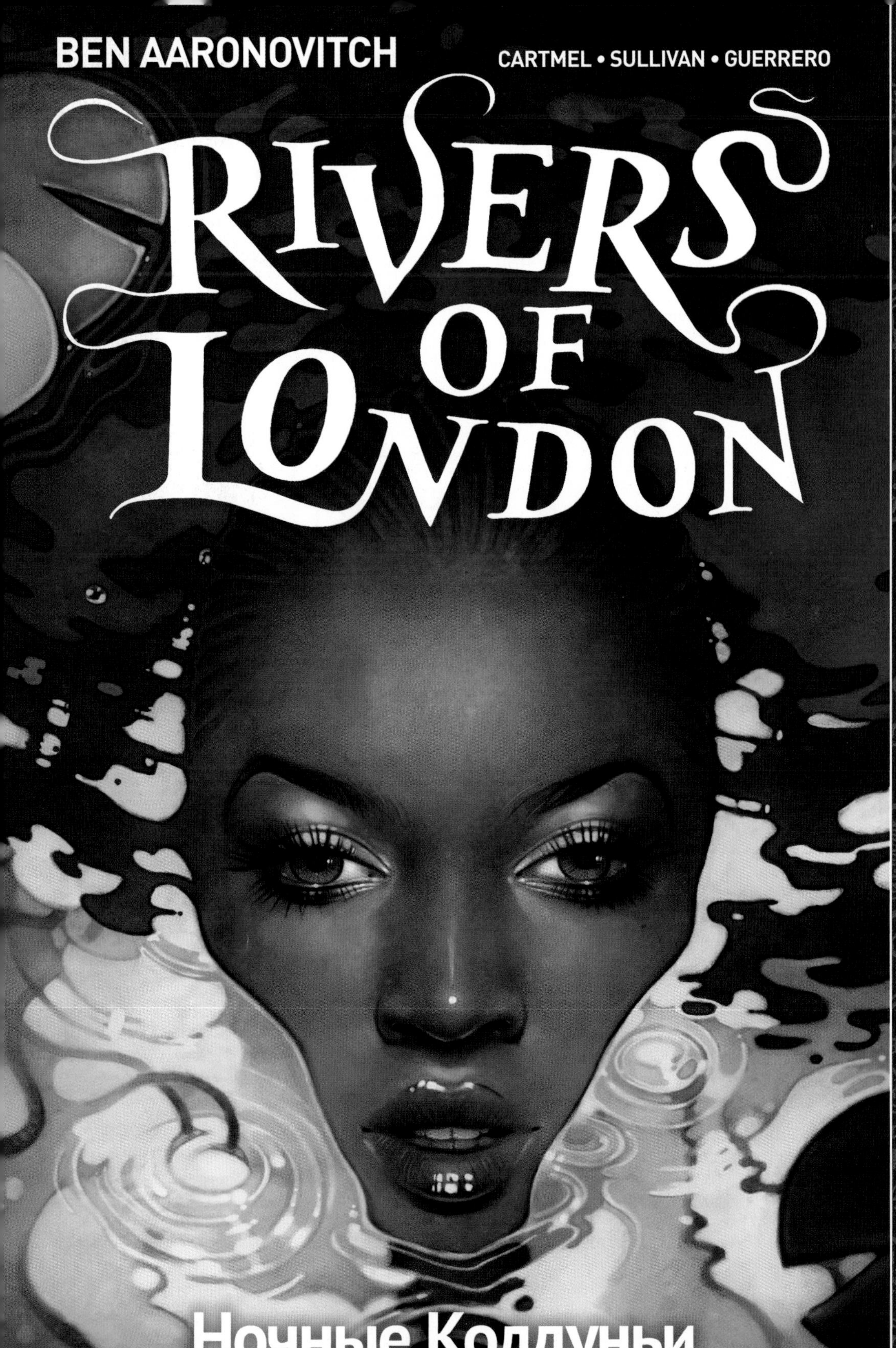
BEN AARONOVITCH
CARTMEL • SULLIVAN • GUERRERO
RIVERS OF LONDON
Ночные Колдуньи

ISSUE 2 - ANNA DITTMANN COVER

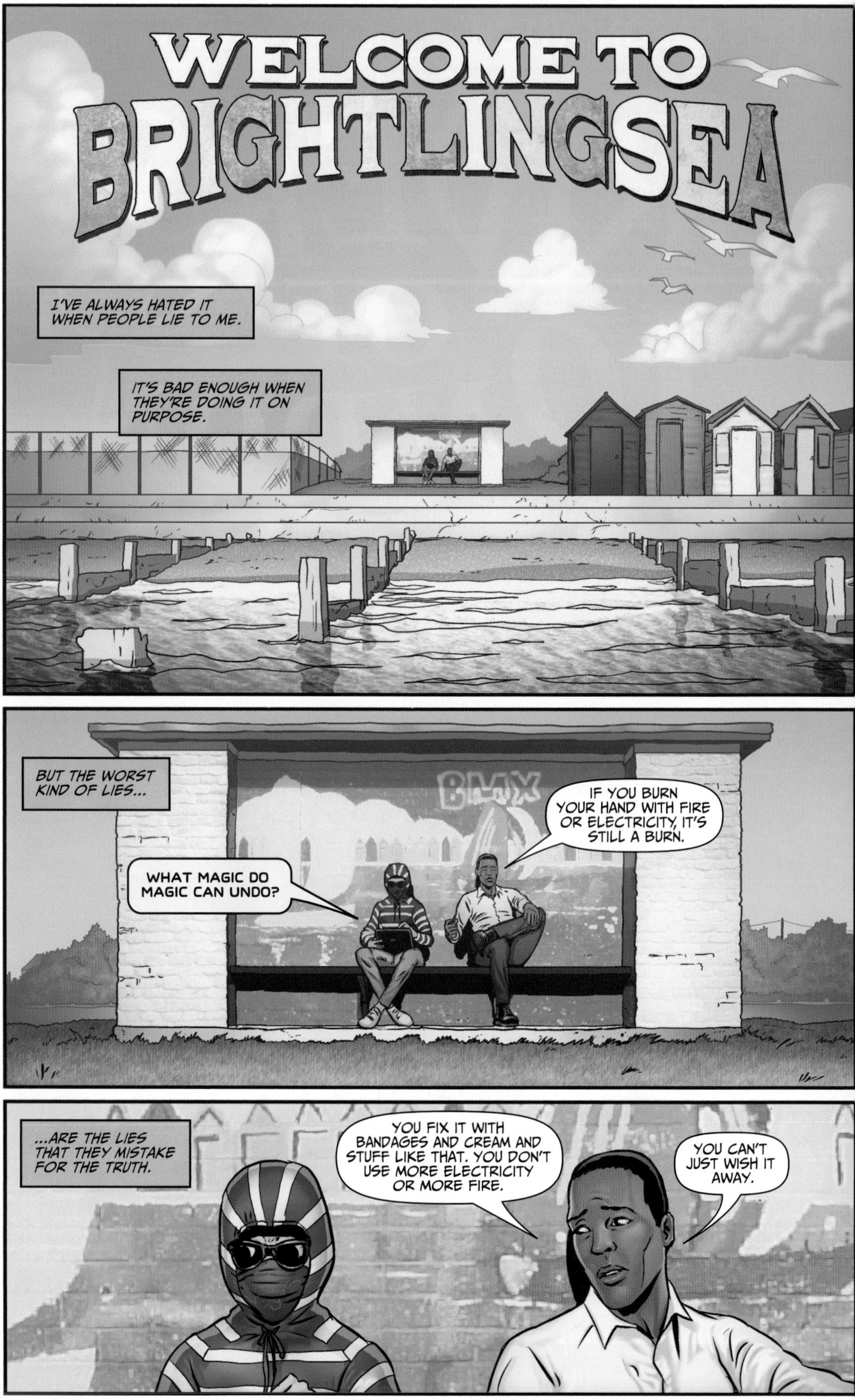
WELCOME TO
BRIGHTLINGSEA
I'VE ALWAYS HATED IT WHEN PEOPLE LIE TO ME.
IT'S BAD ENOUGH WHEN THEY'RE DOING IT ON PURPOSE.
BUT THE WORST KIND OF LIES...
BMX
IF YOU BURN YOUR HAND WITH FIRE OR ELECTRICITY, IT'S STILL A BURN.
WHAT MAGIC DO MAGIC CAN UNDO?
...ARE THE LIES THAT THEY MISTAKE FOR THE TRUTH.
YOU FIX IT WITH BANDAGES AND CREAM AND STUFF LIKE THAT. YOU DON'T USE MORE ELECTRICITY OR MORE FIRE.
YOU CAN'T JUST WISH IT AWAY.

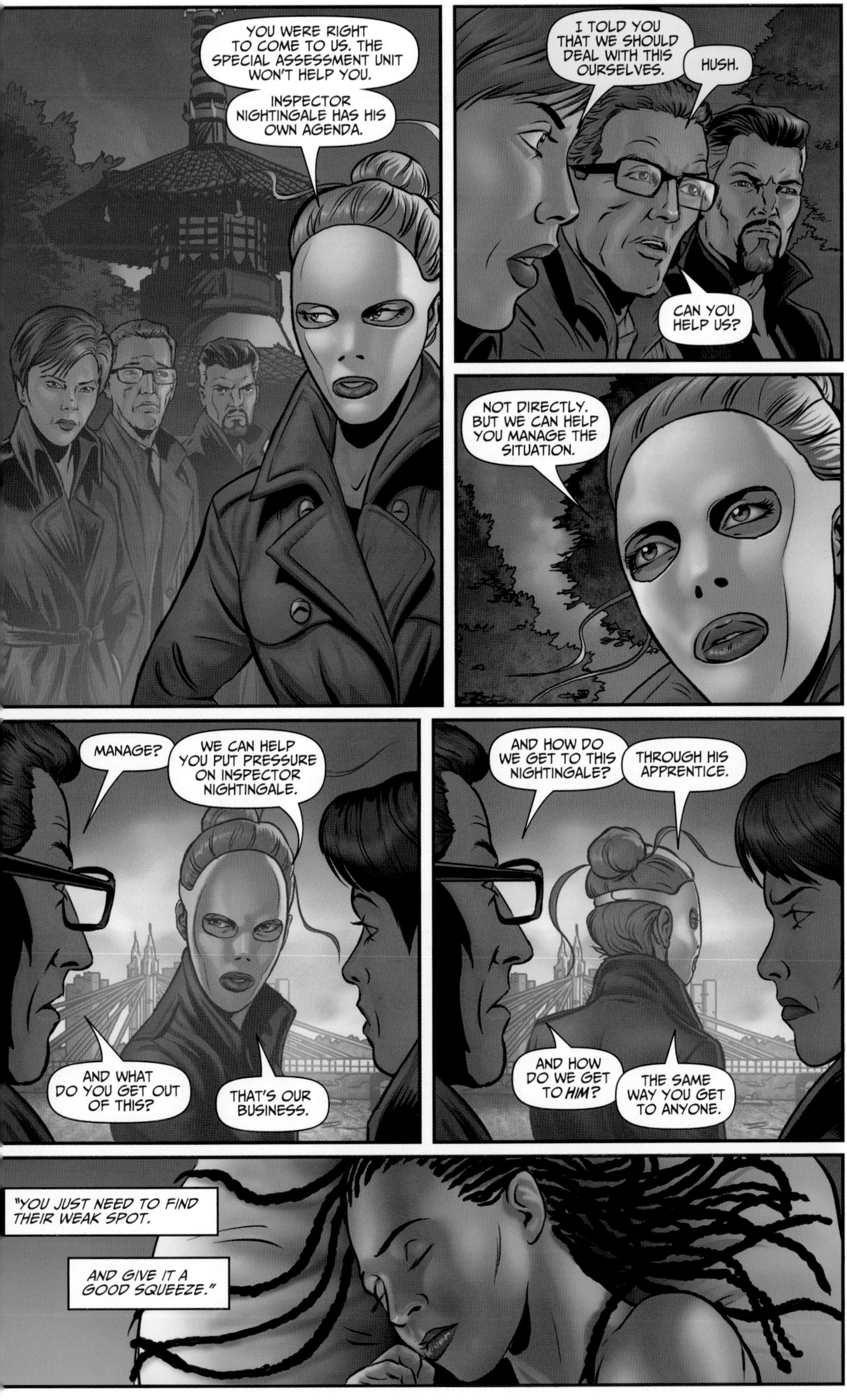
YOU WERE RIGHT TO COME TO US. THE SPECIAL ASSESSMENT UNIT WON'T HELP YOU.
INSPECTOR NIGHTINGALE HAS HIS OWN AGENDA.
I TOLD YOU THAT WE SHOULD DEAL WITH THIS OURSELVES.
HUSH.
CAN YOU HELP US?
NOT DIRECTLY. BUT WE CAN HELP YOU MANAGE THE SITUATION.
MANAGE?
WE CAN HELP YOU PUT PRESSURE ON INSPECTOR NIGHTINGALE.
AND WHAT DO YOU GET OUT OF THIS?
THAT'S OUR BUSINESS.
AND HOW DO WE GET TO THIS NIGHTINGALE?
THROUGH HIS APPRENTICE.
AND HOW DO WE GET TO *HIM*?
THE SAME WAY YOU GET TO ANYONE.
"YOU JUST NEED TO FIND THEIR WEAK SPOT.
AND GIVE IT A GOOD SQUEEZE."

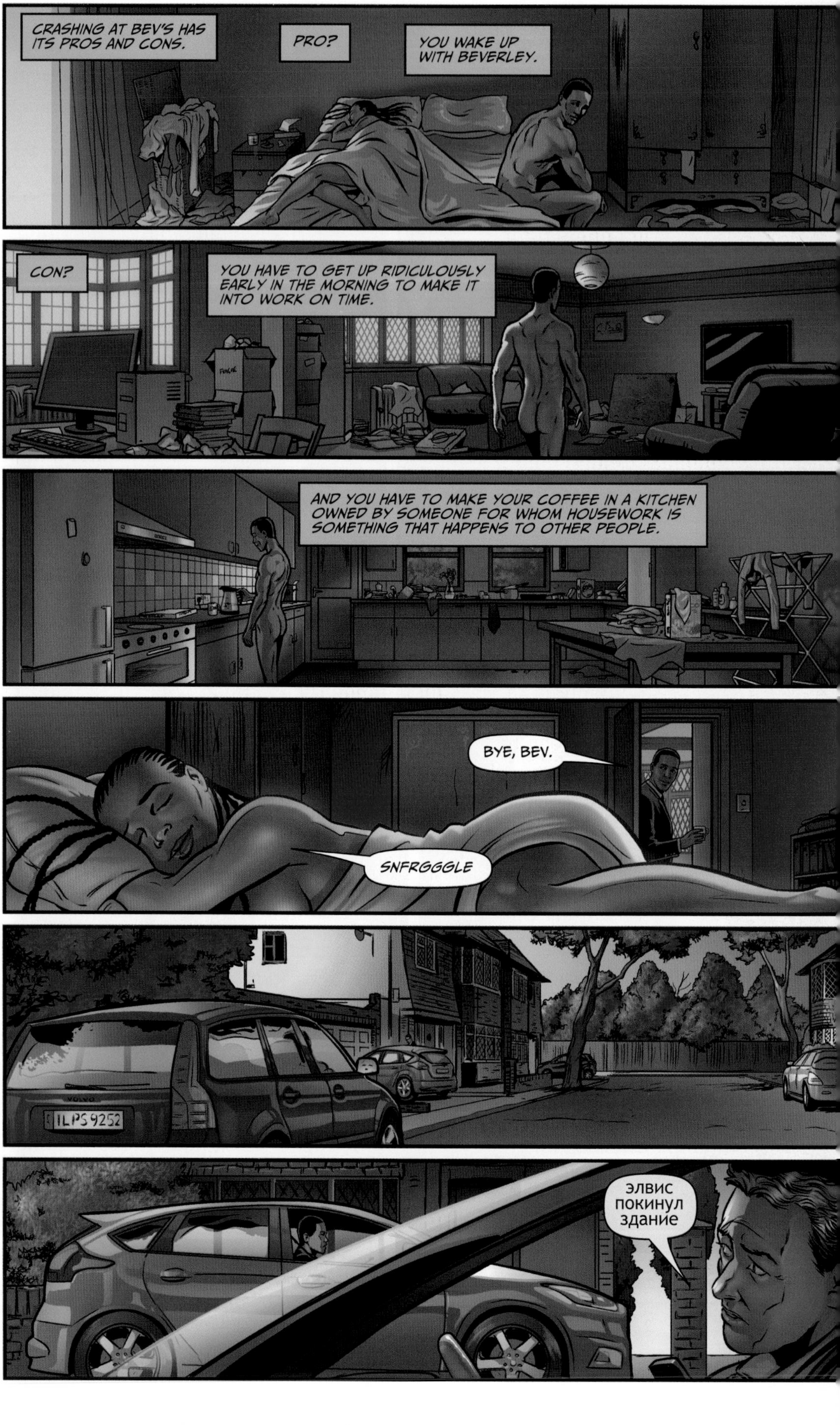
CRASHING AT BEV'S HAS ITS PROS AND CONS.
PRO?
YOU WAKE UP WITH BEVERLEY.
CON?
YOU HAVE TO GET UP RIDICULOUSLY EARLY IN THE MORNING TO MAKE IT INTO WORK ON TIME.
AND YOU HAVE TO MAKE YOUR COFFEE IN A KITCHEN OWNED BY SOMEONE FOR WHOM HOUSEWORK IS SOMETHING THAT HAPPENS TO OTHER PEOPLE.
BYE, BEV.
SNFRGGGLE
ILPS 9252
элвис покинул здание

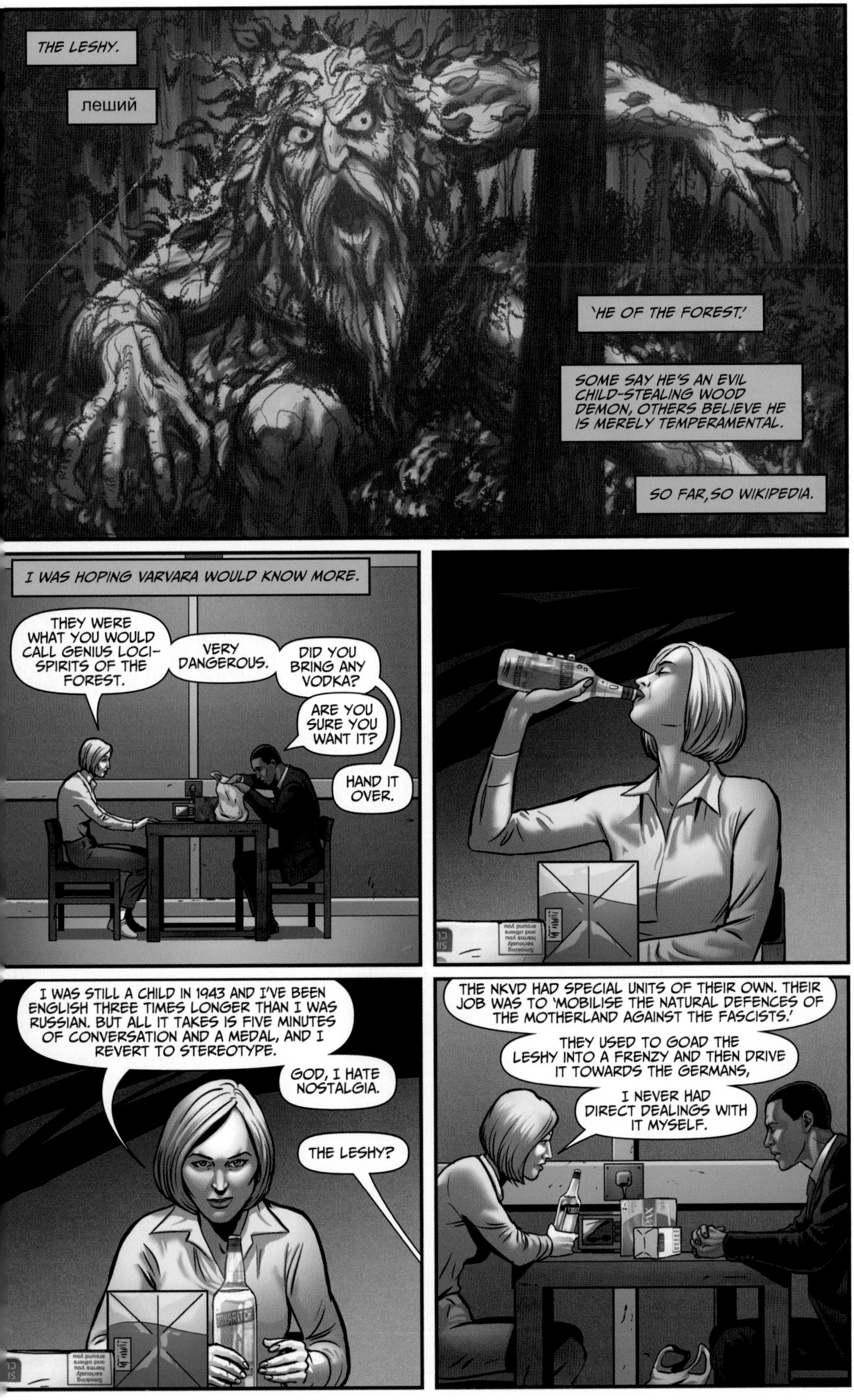
THE LESHY.
леший
'HE OF THE FOREST.'
SOME SAY HE'S AN EVIL CHILD-STEALING WOOD DEMON, OTHERS BELIEVE HE IS MERELY TEMPERAMENTAL.
SO FAR, SO WIKIPEDIA.
I WAS HOPING VARVARA WOULD KNOW MORE.
THEY WERE WHAT YOU WOULD CALL GENIUS LOCI- SPIRITS OF THE FOREST.
VERY DANGEROUS.
DID YOU BRING ANY VODKA?
ARE YOU SURE YOU WANT IT?
HAND IT OVER.
I WAS STILL A CHILD IN 1943 AND I'VE BEEN ENGLISH THREE TIMES LONGER THAN I WAS RUSSIAN. BUT ALL IT TAKES IS FIVE MINUTES OF CONVERSATION AND A MEDAL, AND I REVERT TO STEREOTYPE.
GOD, I HATE NOSTALGIA.
THE LESHY?
THE NKVD HAD SPECIAL UNITS OF THEIR OWN. THEIR JOB WAS TO 'MOBILISE THE NATURAL DEFENCES OF THE MOTHERLAND AGAINST THE FASCISTS.'
THEY USED TO GOAD THE LESHY INTO A FRENZY AND THEN DRIVE IT TOWARDS THE GERMANS,
I NEVER HAD DIRECT DEALINGS WITH IT MYSELF.

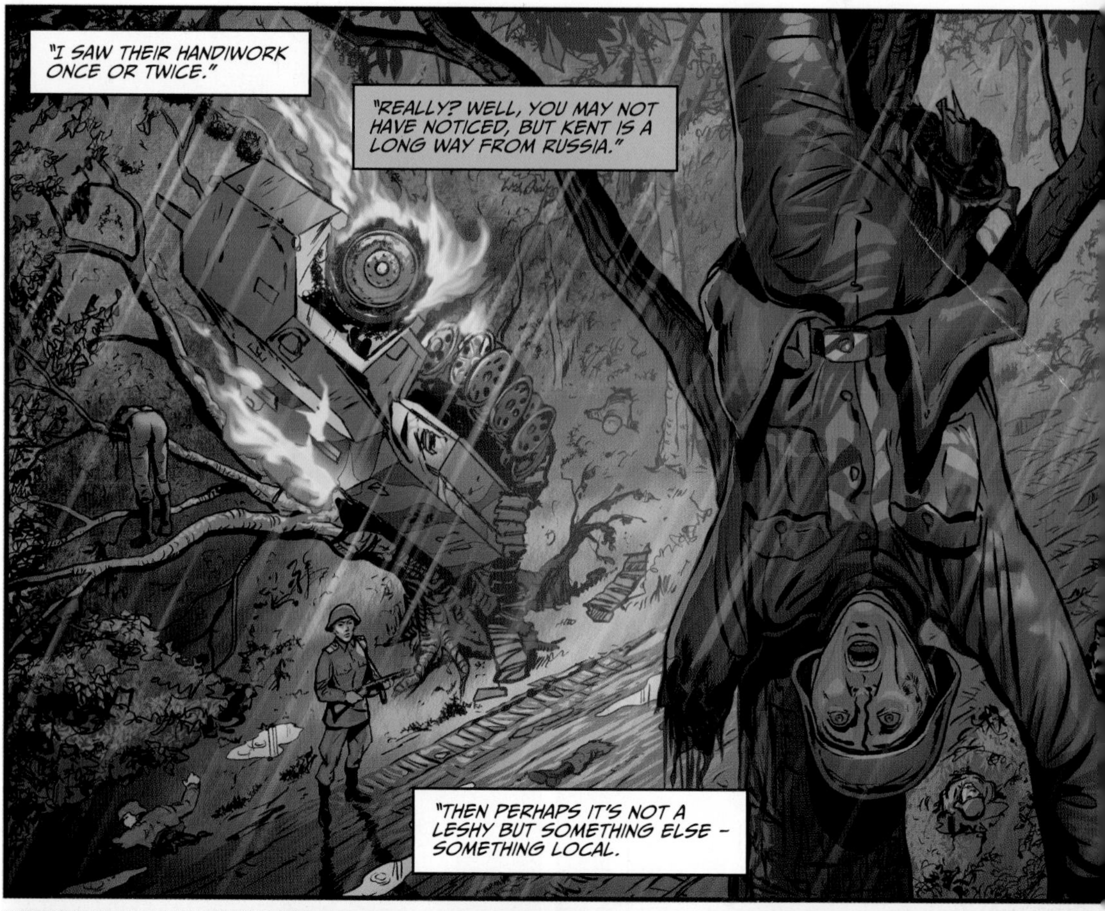
"I SAW THEIR HANDIWORK ONCE OR TWICE."
"REALLY? WELL, YOU MAY NOT HAVE NOTICED, BUT KENT IS A LONG WAY FROM RUSSIA."
"THEN PERHAPS IT'S NOT A LESHY BUT SOMETHING ELSE – SOMETHING LOCAL.

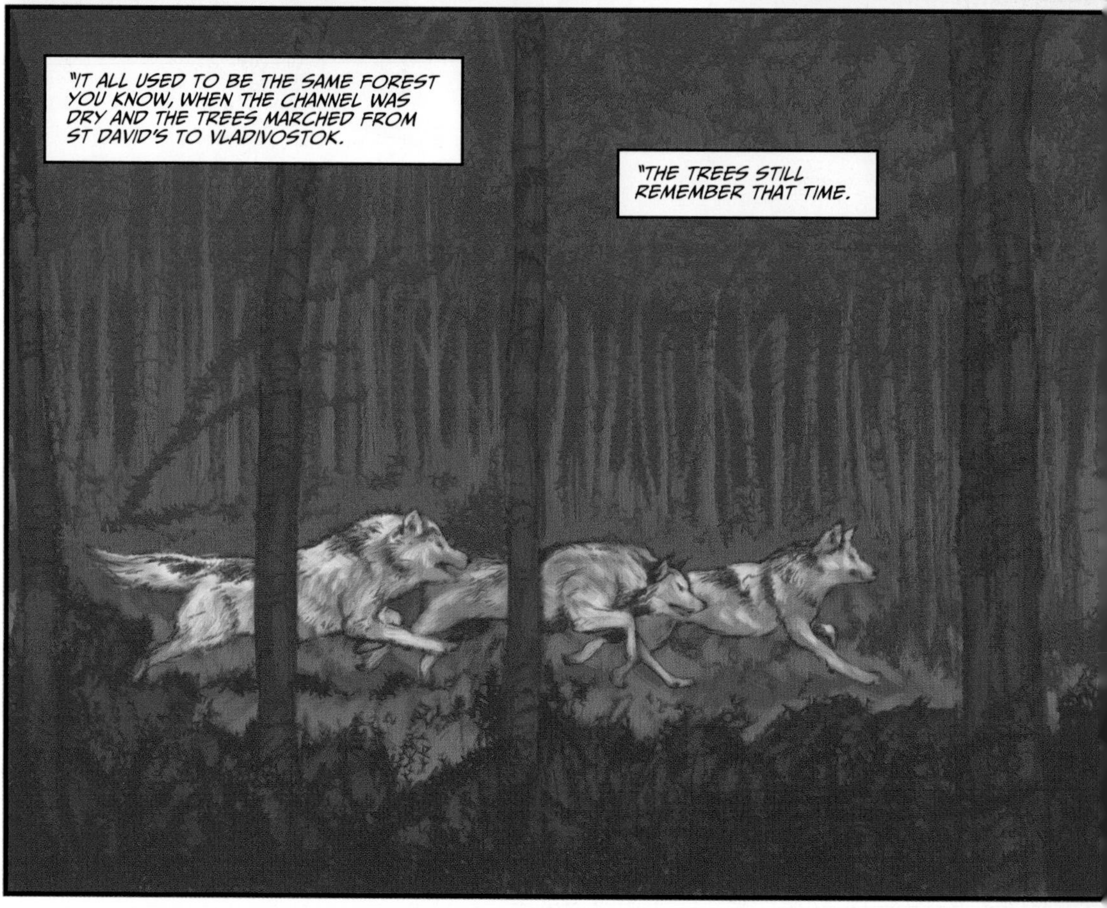
"IT ALL USED TO BE THE SAME FOREST YOU KNOW, WHEN THE CHANNEL WAS DRY AND THE TREES MARCHED FROM ST DAVID'S TO VLADIVOSTOK.
"THE TREES STILL REMEMBER THAT TIME.

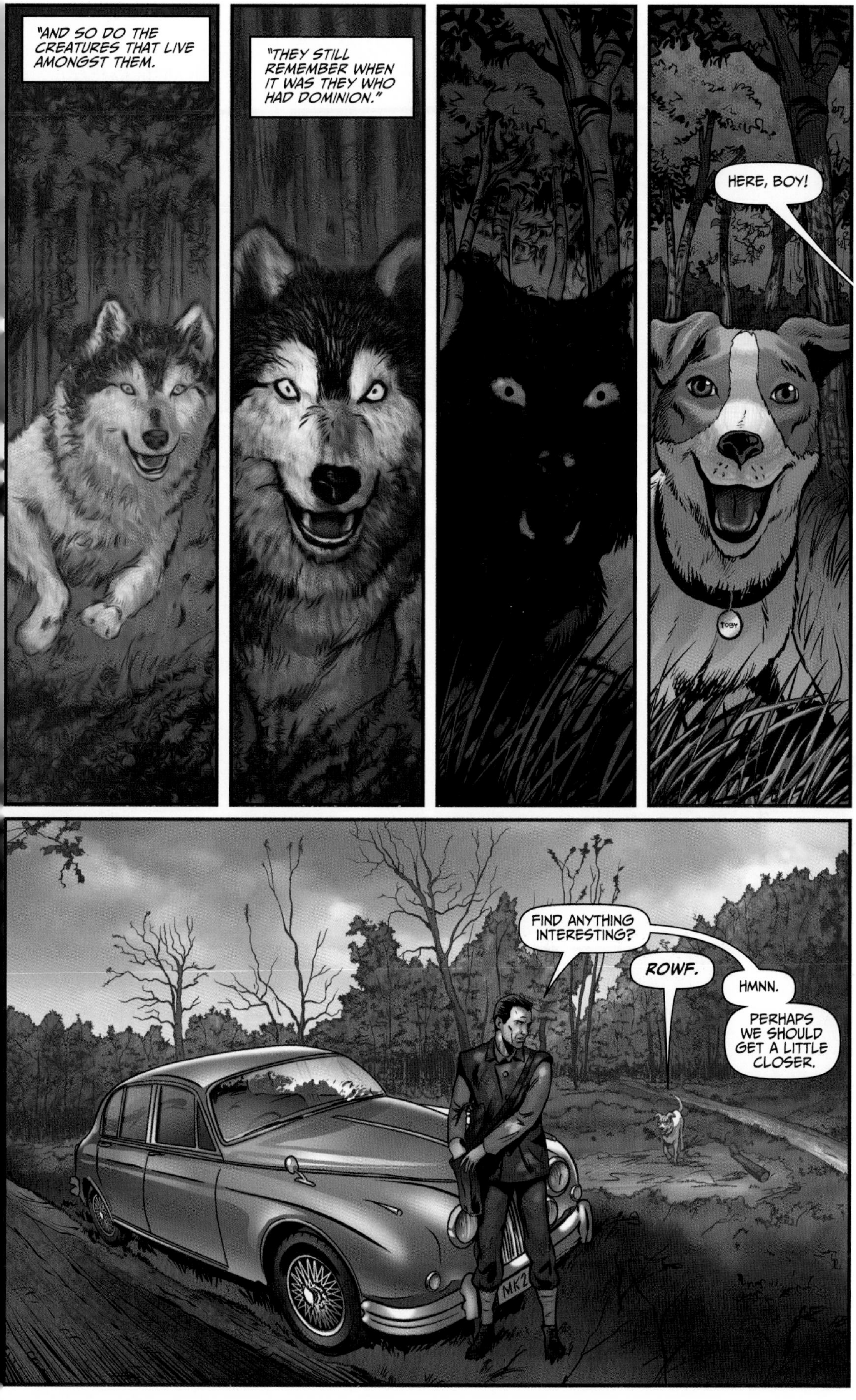
"AND SO DO THE CREATURES THAT LIVE AMONGST THEM.
"THEY STILL REMEMBER WHEN IT WAS THEY WHO HAD DOMINION."
HERE, BOY!
FIND ANYTHING INTERESTING?
ROWF.
HMNN.
PERHAPS WE SHOULD GET A LITTLE CLOSER.
MK2

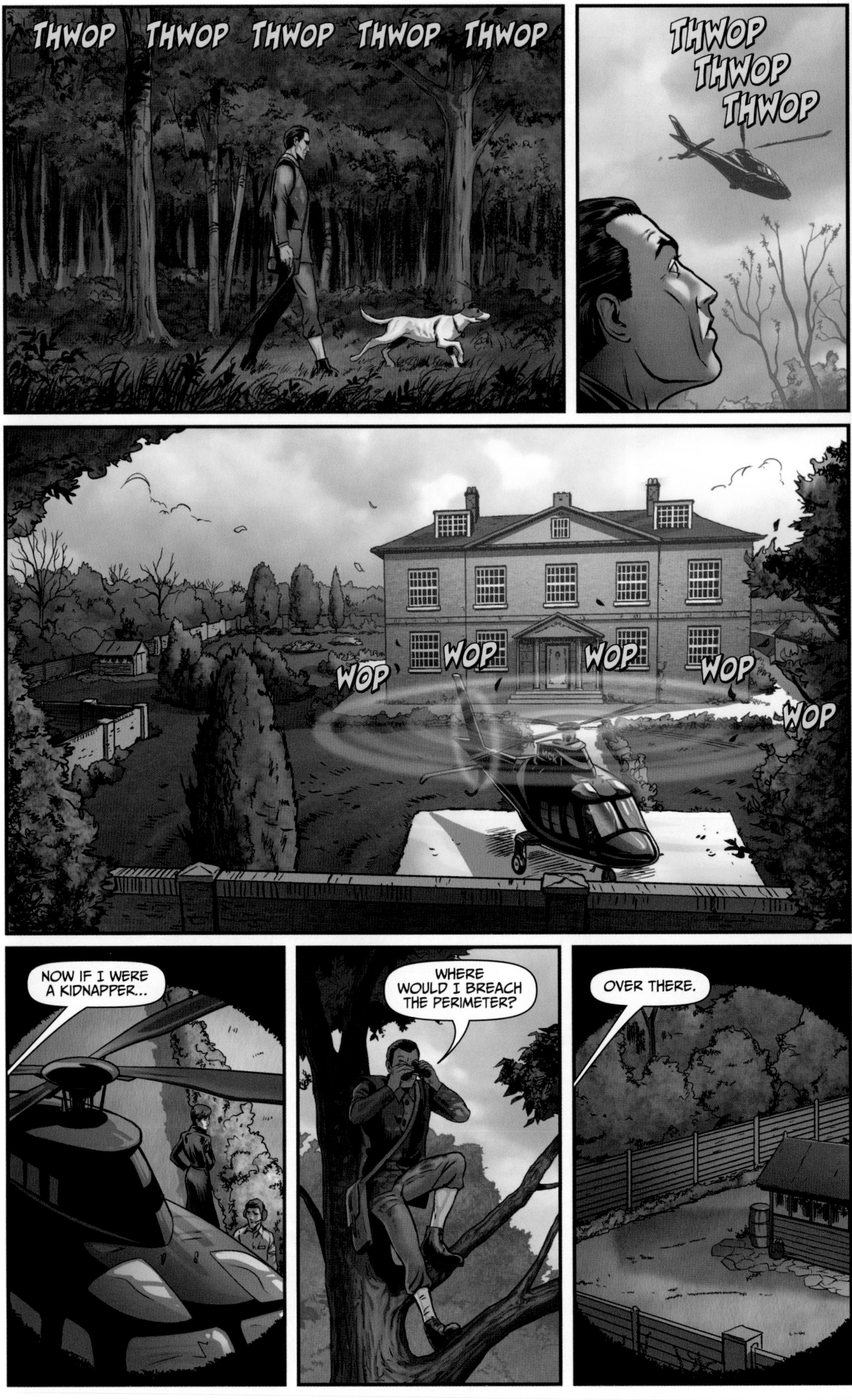
THWOP THWOP THWOP THWOP THWOP
THWOP
THWOP
THWOP
WOP
WOP
WOP
WOP
WOP
NOW IF I WERE A KIDNAPPER...
WHERE WOULD I BREACH THE PERIMETER?
OVER THERE.

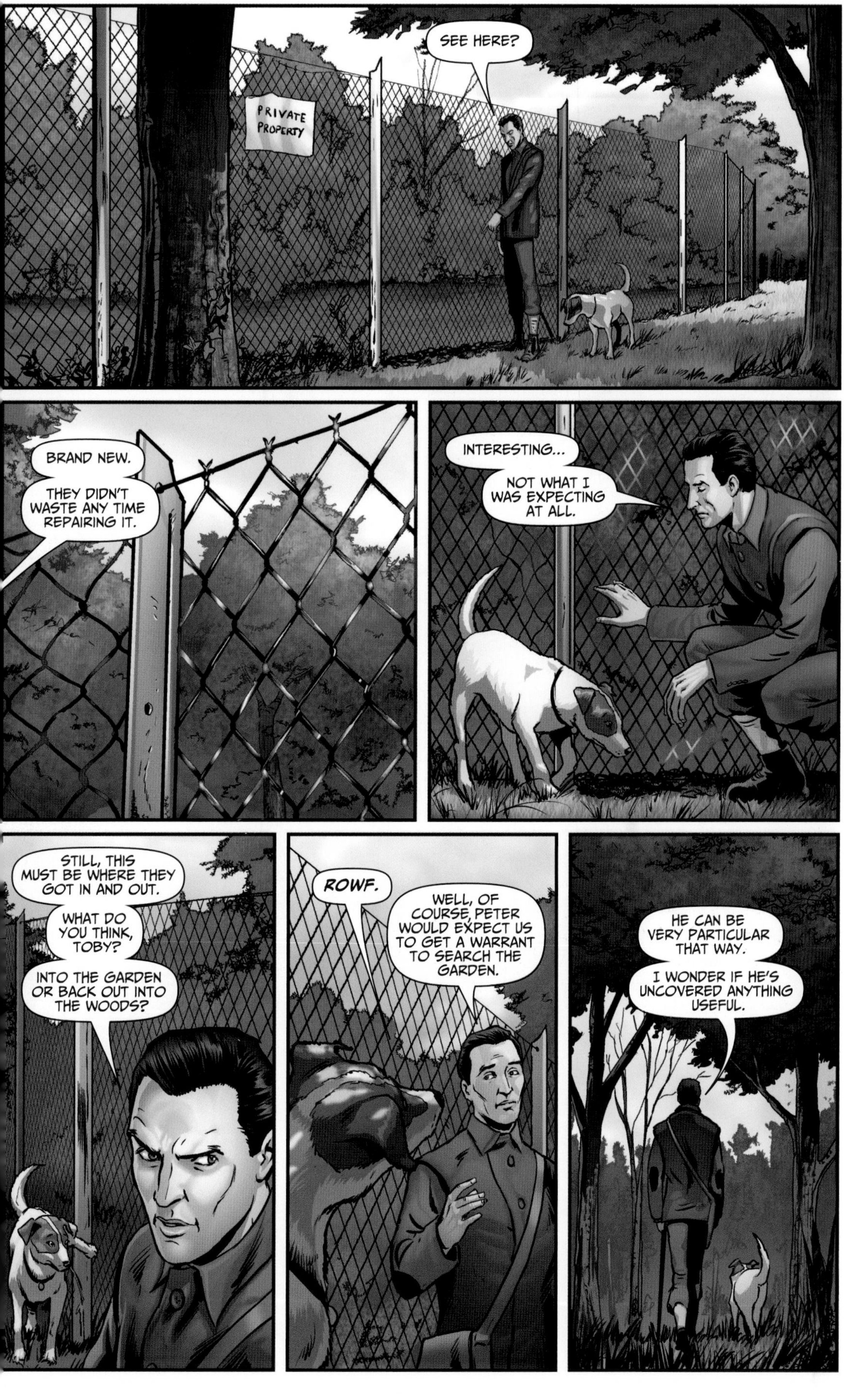
SEE HERE?
PRIVATE PROPERTY
BRAND NEW.
THEY DIDN'T WASTE ANY TIME REPAIRING IT.
INTERESTING...
NOT WHAT I WAS EXPECTING AT ALL.
STILL, THIS MUST BE WHERE THEY GOT IN AND OUT.
WHAT DO YOU THINK, TOBY?
INTO THE GARDEN OR BACK OUT INTO THE WOODS?
ROWF.
WELL, OF COURSE, PETER WOULD EXPECT US TO GET A WARRANT TO SEARCH THE GARDEN.
HE CAN BE VERY PARTICULAR THAT WAY.
I WONDER IF HE'S UNCOVERED ANYTHING USEFUL.

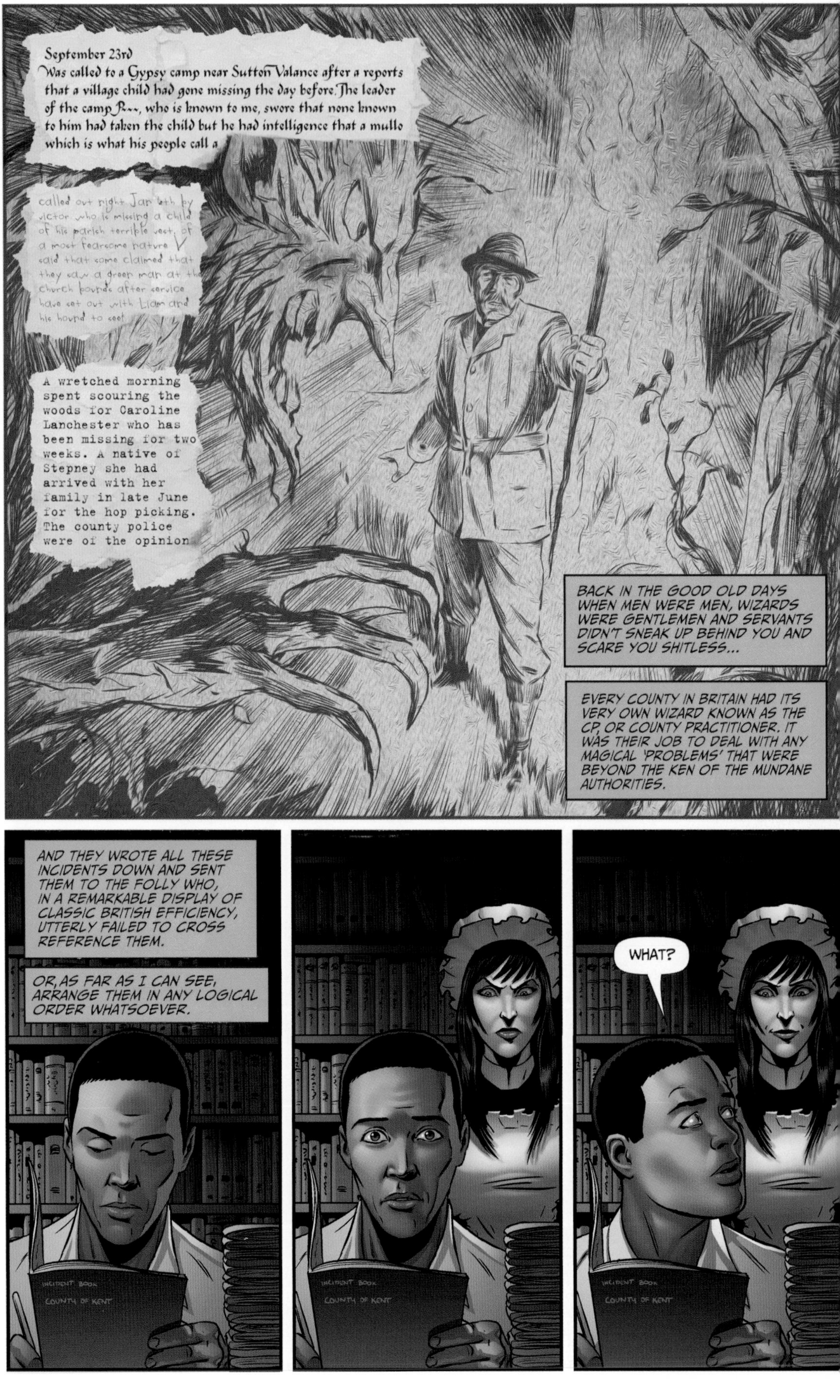

September 23rd
Was called to a Gypsy camp near Sutton Valance after a reports that a village child had gone missing the day before. The leader of the camp R~~, who is known to me, swore that none known to him had taken the child but he had intelligence that a mullo which is what his people call a
called out night Jan 6th by victor who is missing a child of his parish terrible vest. of a most fearsome nature V said that some claimed that they saw a green man at the church bounds after service have set out with Liam and his hound to seek
A wretched morning spent scouring the woods for Caroline Lanchester who has been missing for two weeks. A native of Stepney she had arrived with her family in late June for the hop picking. The county police were of the opinion
BACK IN THE GOOD OLD DAYS WHEN MEN WERE MEN, WIZARDS WERE GENTLEMEN AND SERVANTS DIDN'T SNEAK UP BEHIND YOU AND SCARE YOU SHITLESS...
EVERY COUNTY IN BRITAIN HAD ITS VERY OWN WIZARD KNOWN AS THE CP, OR COUNTY PRACTITIONER. IT WAS THEIR JOB TO DEAL WITH ANY MAGICAL 'PROBLEMS' THAT WERE BEYOND THE KEN OF THE MUNDANE AUTHORITIES.
AND THEY WROTE ALL THESE INCIDENTS DOWN AND SENT THEM TO THE FOLLY WHO, IN A REMARKABLE DISPLAY OF CLASSIC BRITISH EFFICIENCY, UTTERLY FAILED TO CROSS REFERENCE THEM.
OR, AS FAR AS I CAN SEE, ARRANGE THEM IN ANY LOGICAL ORDER WHATSOEVER.
INCIDENT BOOK
COUNTY OF KENT
WHAT?

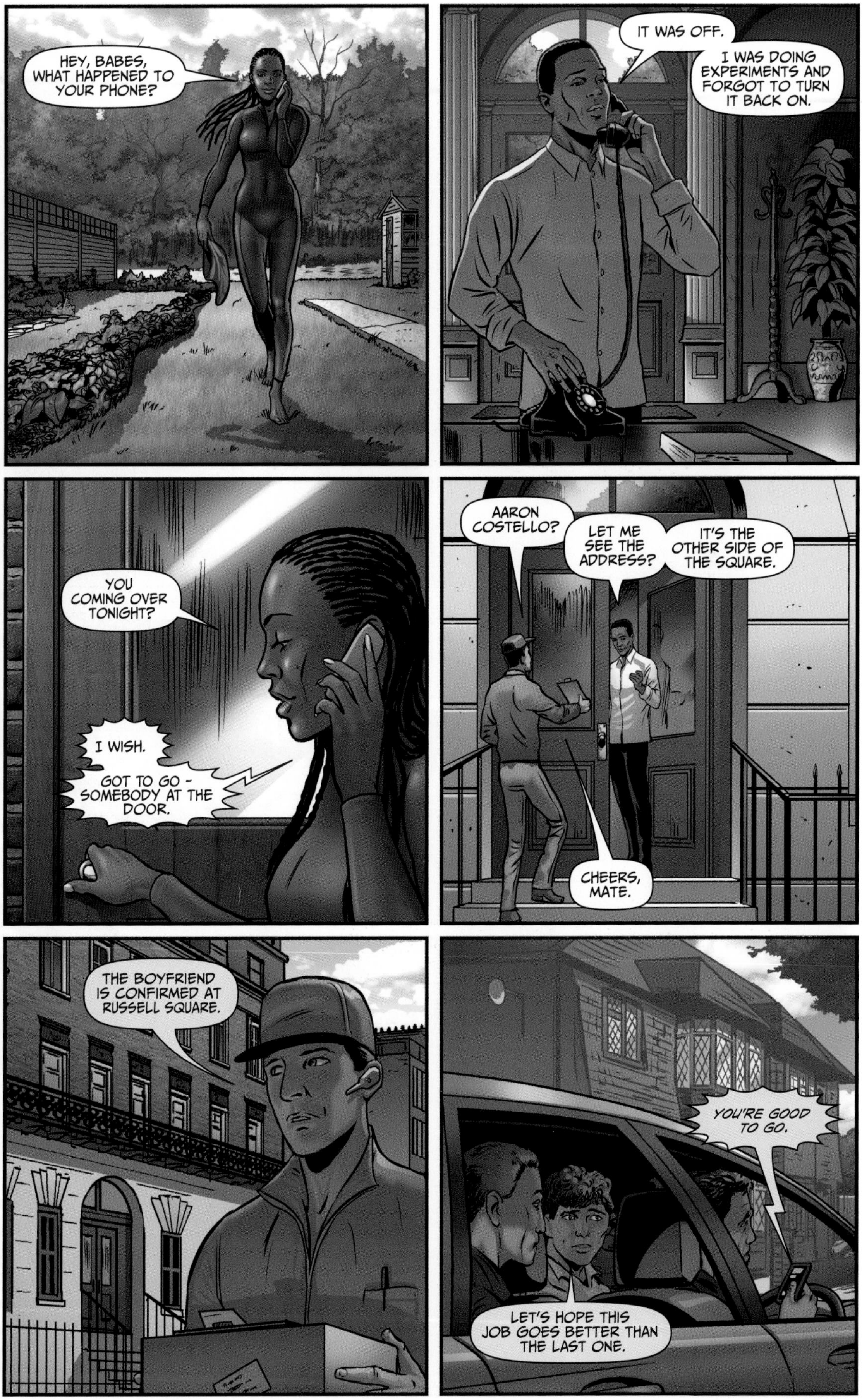
HEY, BABES, WHAT HAPPENED TO YOUR PHONE?
IT WAS OFF.
I WAS DOING EXPERIMENTS AND FORGOT TO TURN IT BACK ON.
YOU COMING OVER TONIGHT?
I WISH.
GOT TO GO - SOMEBODY AT THE DOOR.
AARON COSTELLO?
LET ME SEE THE ADDRESS?
IT'S THE OTHER SIDE OF THE SQUARE.
CHEERS, MATE.
THE BOYFRIEND IS CONFIRMED AT RUSSELL SQUARE.
YOU'RE GOOD TO GO.
LET'S HOPE THIS JOB GOES BETTER THAN THE LAST ONE.

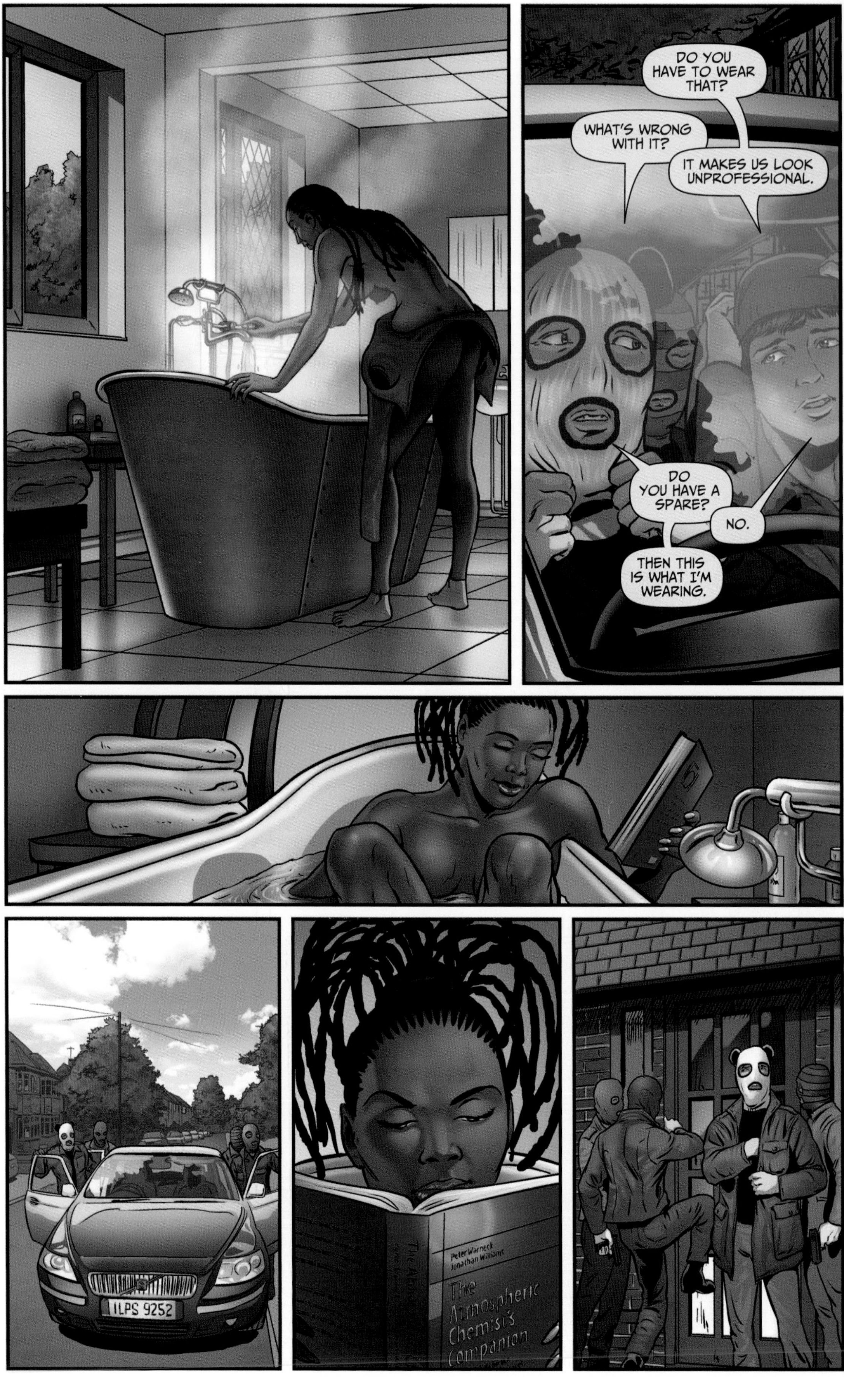
DO YOU HAVE TO WEAR THAT?
WHAT'S WRONG WITH IT?
IT MAKES US LOOK UNPROFESSIONAL.
DO YOU HAVE A SPARE?
NO.
THEN THIS IS WHAT I'M WEARING.
ILPS 9252
Peter Warneck
Jonathan Williams
The Atmospheric Chemist's Companion

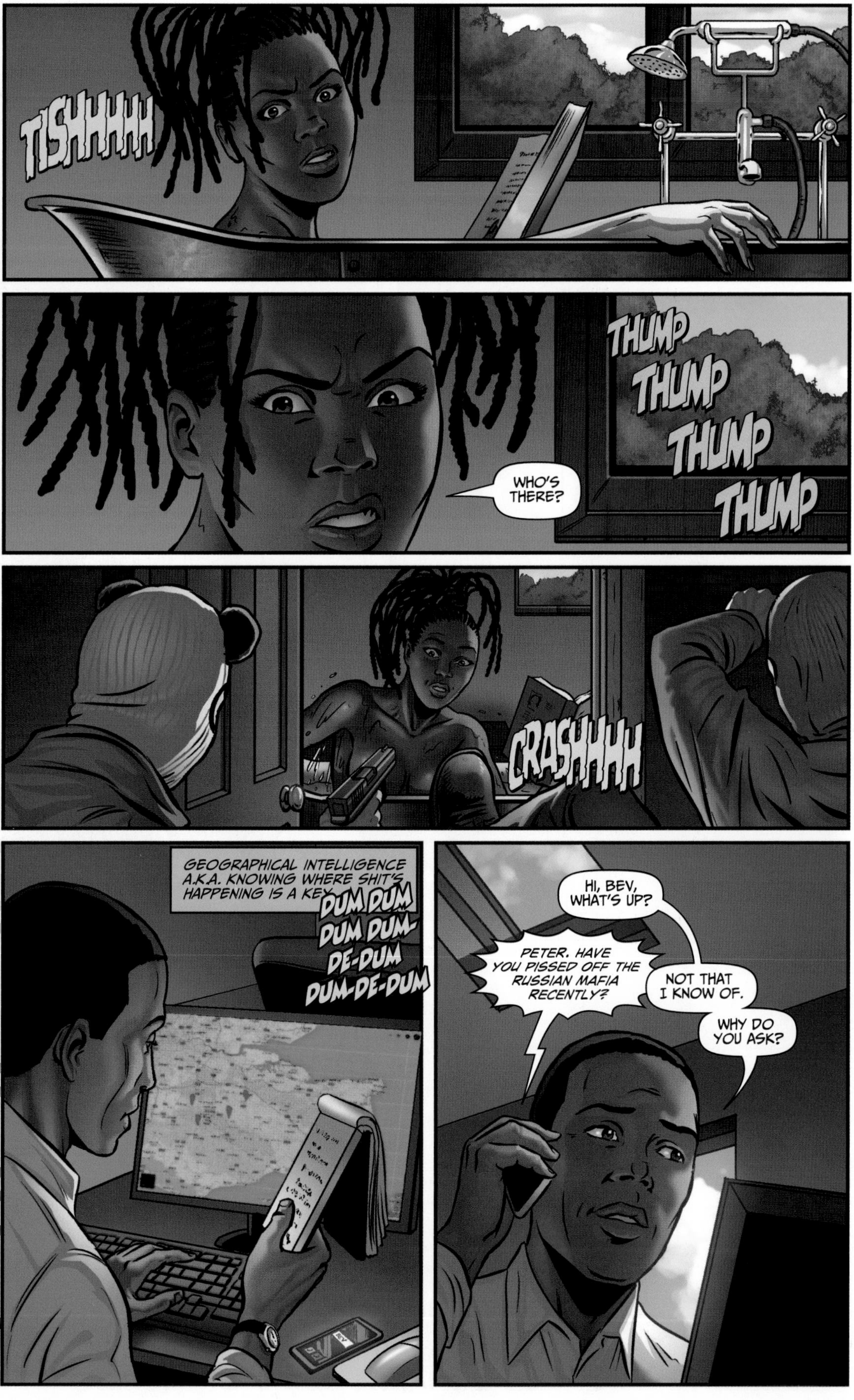
TISHHHH
THUMP
THUMP
THUMP
THUMP
WHO'S THERE?
CRASHHHH
GEOGRAPHICAL INTELLIGENCE A.K.A. KNOWING WHERE SHIT'S HAPPENING IS A KEY
DUM DUM DUM DUM-DE-DUM DUM-DE-DUM
HI, BEV, WHAT'S UP?
PETER. HAVE YOU PISSED OFF THE RUSSIAN MAFIA RECENTLY?
NOT THAT I KNOW OF.
WHY DO YOU ASK?

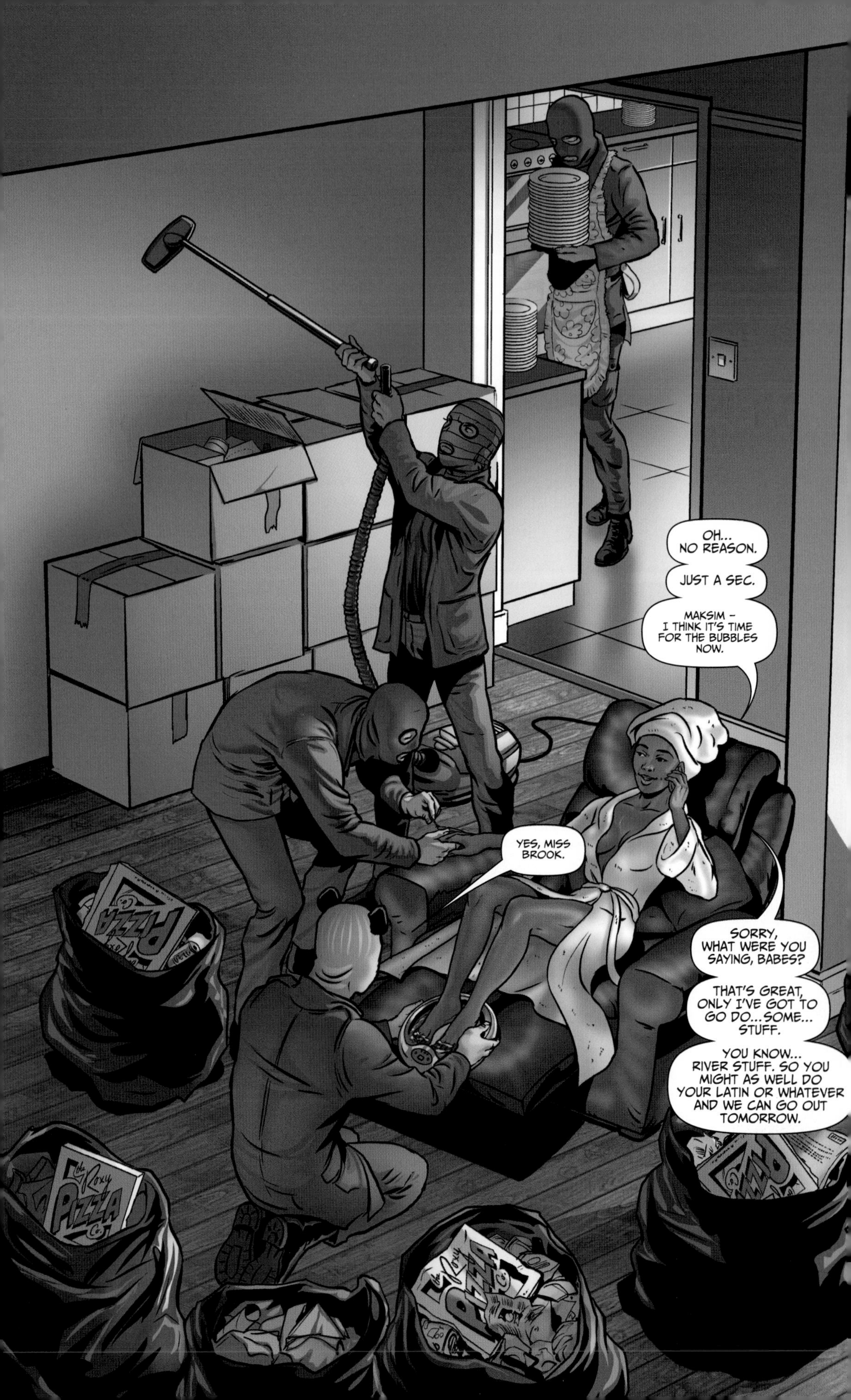
OH... NO REASON.
JUST A SEC.
MAKSIM – I THINK IT'S TIME FOR THE BUBBLES NOW.
YES, MISS BROOK.
SORRY, WHAT WERE YOU SAYING, BABES?
THAT'S GREAT, ONLY I'VE GOT TO GO DO...SOME... STUFF.
YOU KNOW... RIVER STUFF. SO YOU MIGHT AS WELL DO YOUR LATIN OR WHATEVER AND WE CAN GO OUT TOMORROW.
The Roxy PIZZA Co.

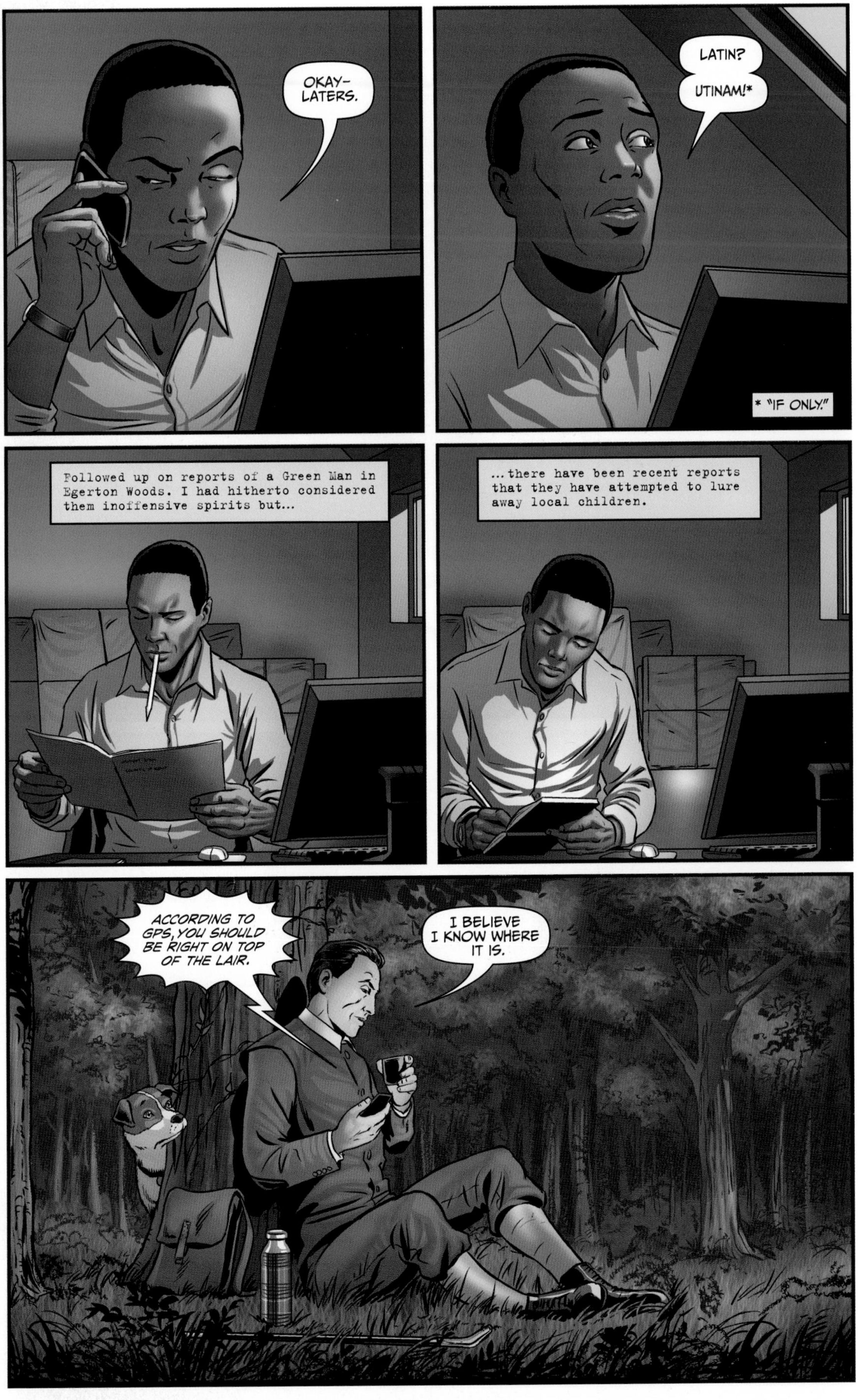
OKAY-
LATERS.
LATIN?
UTINAM!*
* "IF ONLY."
Followed up on reports of a Green Man in Egerton Woods. I had hitherto considered them inoffensive spirits but...
...there have been recent reports that they have attempted to lure away local children.
ACCORDING TO GPS, YOU SHOULD BE RIGHT ON TOP OF THE LAIR.
I BELIEVE I KNOW WHERE IT IS.

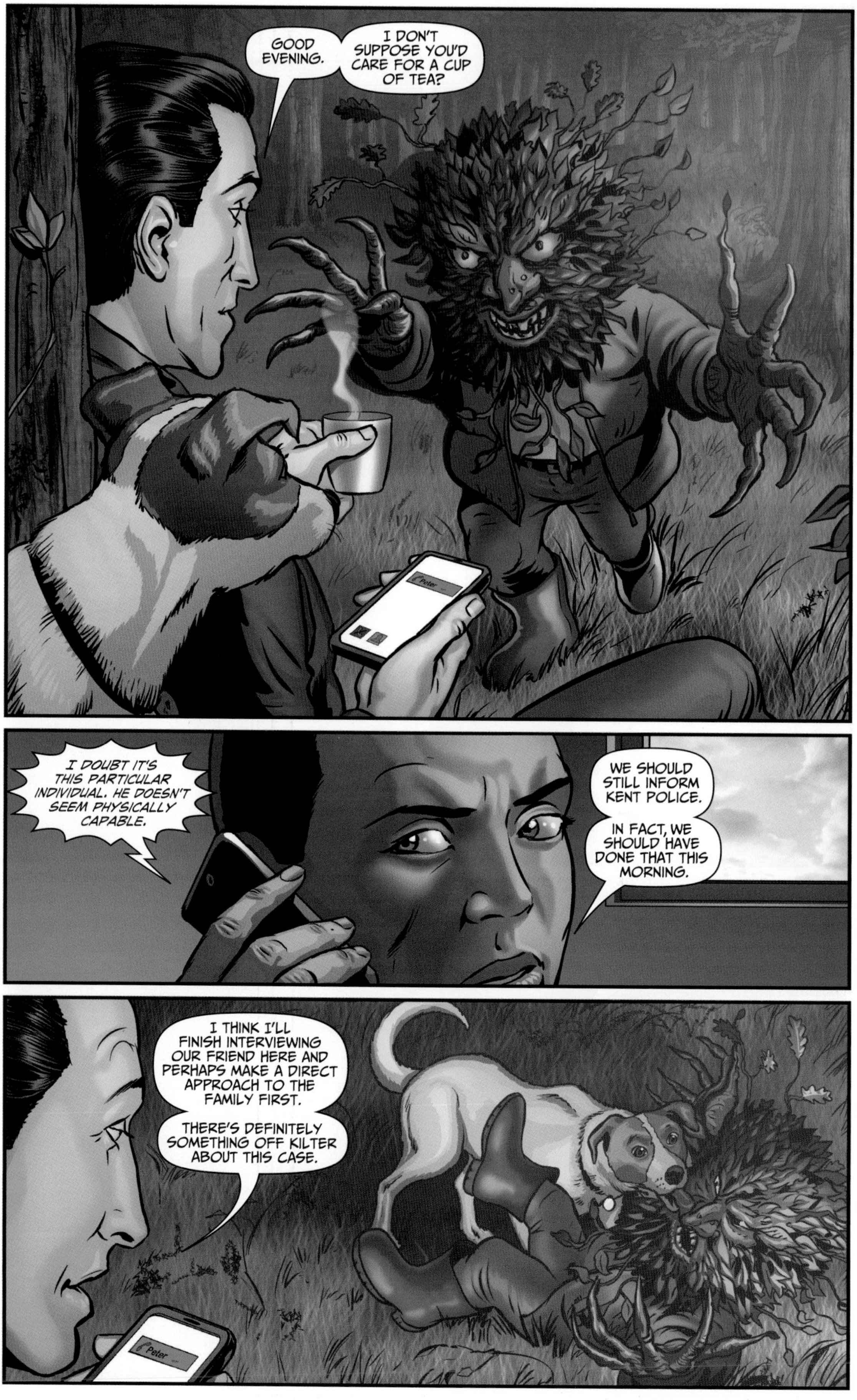
GOOD EVENING.
I DON'T SUPPOSE YOU'D CARE FOR A CUP OF TEA?
I DOUBT IT'S THIS PARTICULAR INDIVIDUAL. HE DOESN'T SEEM PHYSICALLY CAPABLE.
WE SHOULD STILL INFORM KENT POLICE.
IN FACT, WE SHOULD HAVE DONE THAT THIS MORNING.
I THINK I'LL FINISH INTERVIEWING OUR FRIEND HERE AND PERHAPS MAKE A DIRECT APPROACH TO THE FAMILY FIRST.
THERE'S DEFINITELY SOMETHING OFF KILTER ABOUT THIS CASE.

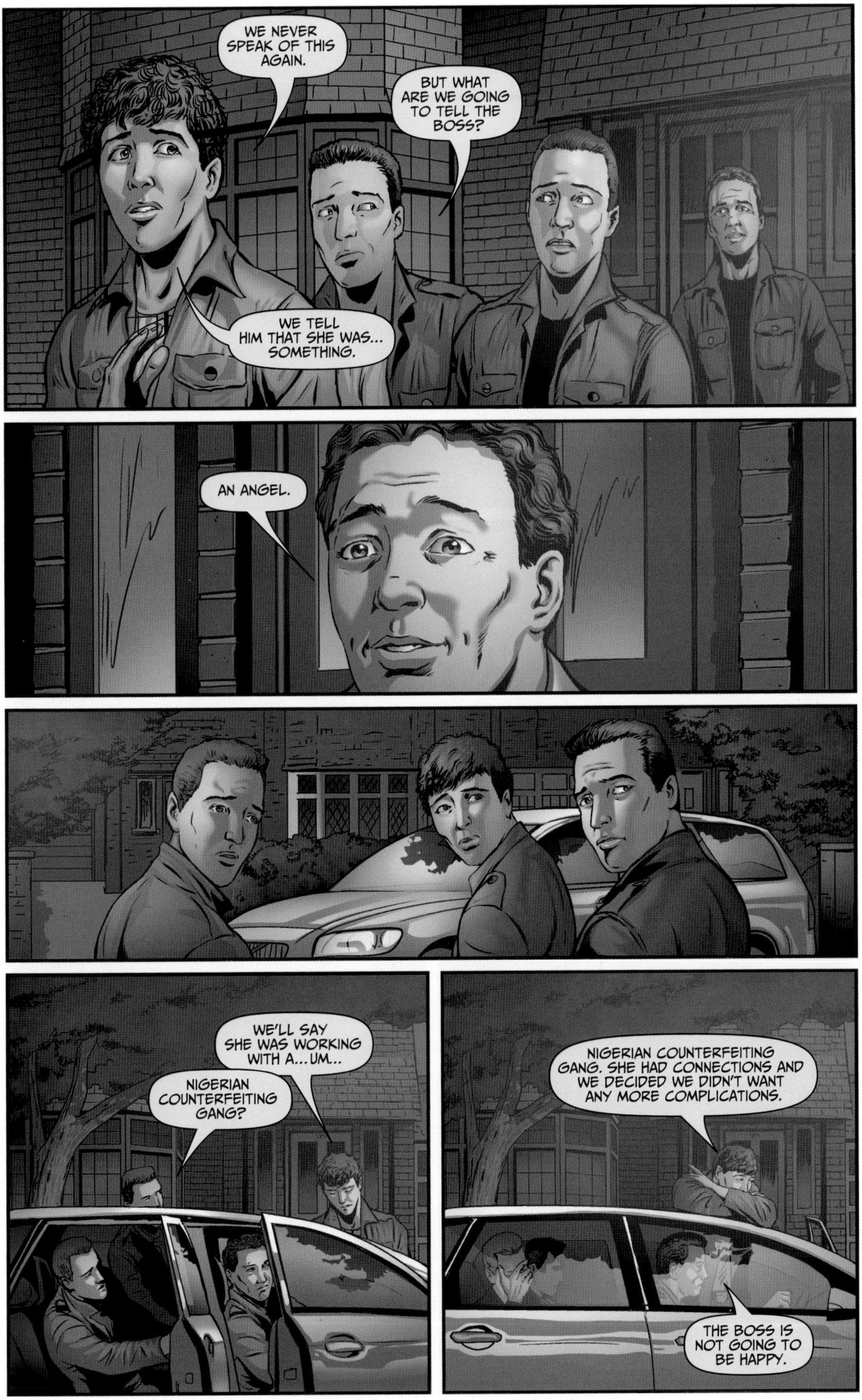
WE NEVER SPEAK OF THIS AGAIN.
BUT WHAT ARE WE GOING TO TELL THE BOSS?
WE TELL HIM THAT SHE WAS... SOMETHING.
AN ANGEL.
WE'LL SAY SHE WAS WORKING WITH A...UM...
NIGERIAN COUNTERFEITING GANG?
NIGERIAN COUNTERFEITING GANG. SHE HAD CONNECTIONS AND WE DECIDED WE DIDN'T WANT ANY MORE COMPLICATIONS.
THE BOSS IS NOT GOING TO BE HAPPY.

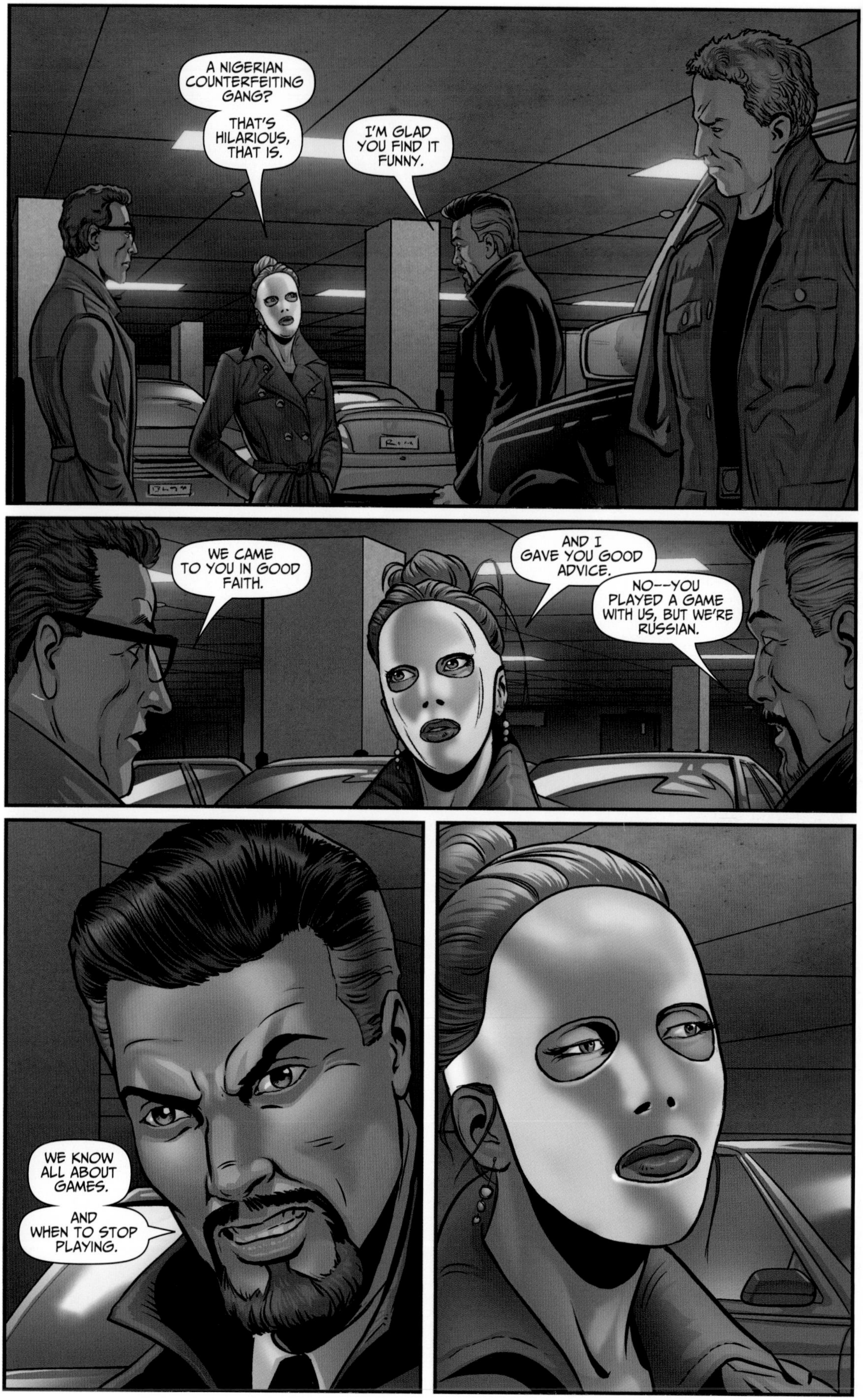

A NIGERIAN COUNTERFEITING GANG?
THAT'S HILARIOUS, THAT IS.
I'M GLAD YOU FIND IT FUNNY.
WE CAME TO YOU IN GOOD FAITH.
AND I GAVE YOU GOOD ADVICE.
NO--YOU PLAYED A GAME WITH US, BUT WE'RE RUSSIAN.
WE KNOW ALL ABOUT GAMES.
AND WHEN TO STOP PLAYING.

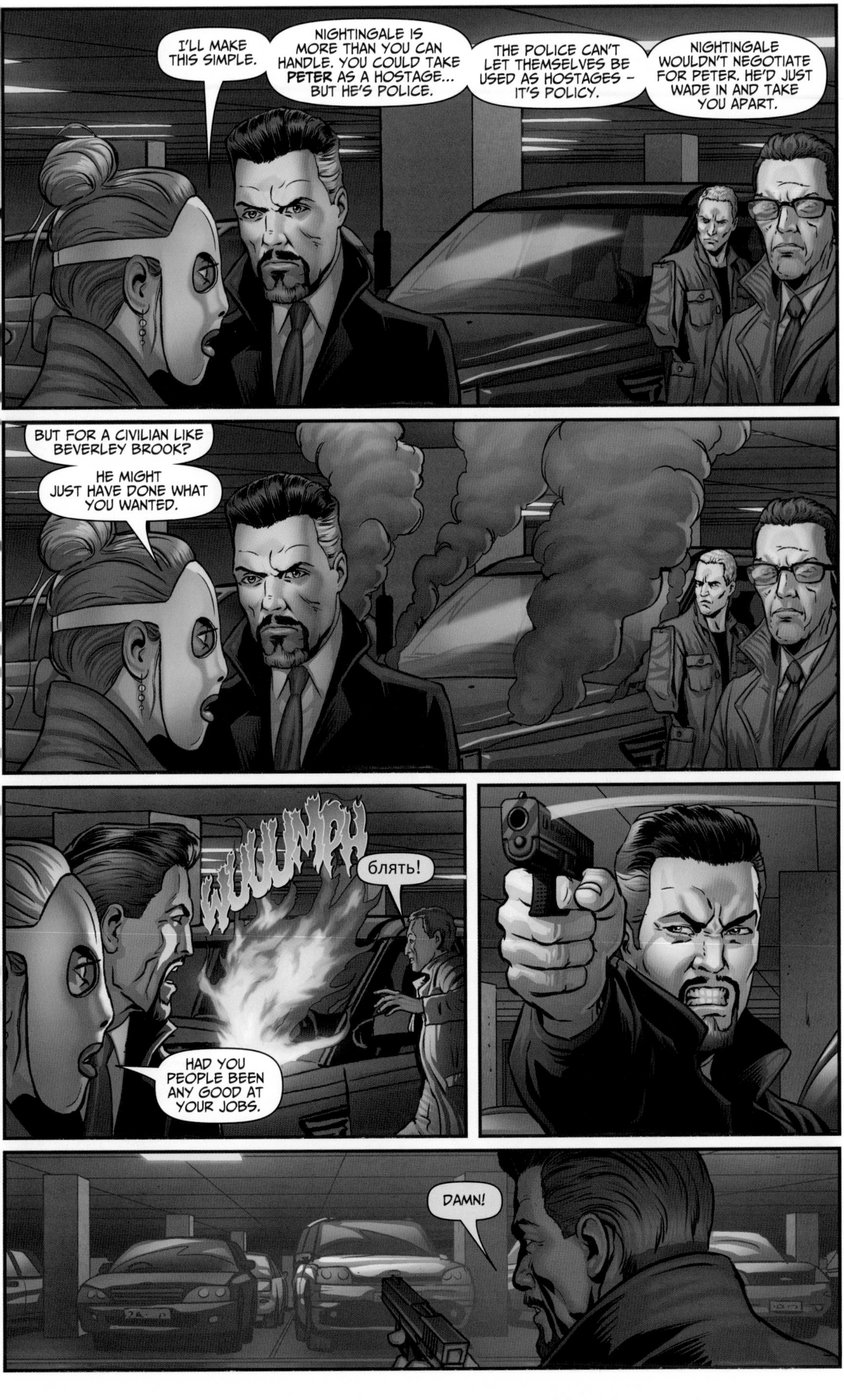
I'LL MAKE THIS SIMPLE.
NIGHTINGALE IS MORE THAN YOU CAN HANDLE. YOU COULD TAKE PETER AS A HOSTAGE... BUT HE'S POLICE.
THE POLICE CAN'T LET THEMSELVES BE USED AS HOSTAGES – IT'S POLICY.
NIGHTINGALE WOULDN'T NEGOTIATE FOR PETER. HE'D JUST WADE IN AND TAKE YOU APART.
BUT FOR A CIVILIAN LIKE BEVERLEY BROOK?
HE MIGHT JUST HAVE DONE WHAT YOU WANTED.
WUUMPH
блять!
HAD YOU PEOPLE BEEN ANY GOOD AT YOUR JOBS.
DAMN!

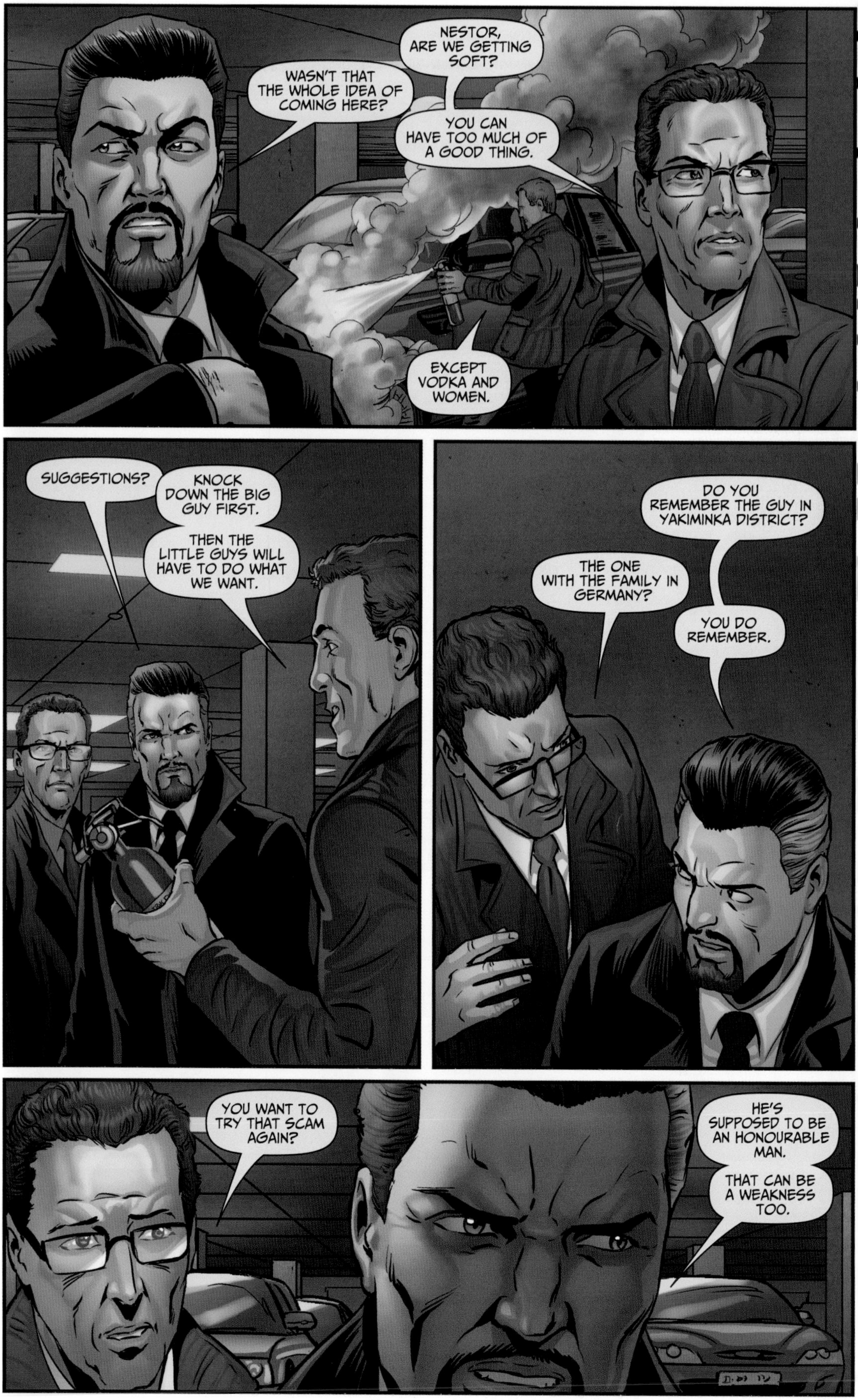
WASN'T THAT THE WHOLE IDEA OF COMING HERE?
NESTOR, ARE WE GETTING SOFT?
YOU CAN HAVE TOO MUCH OF A GOOD THING.
EXCEPT VODKA AND WOMEN.
SUGGESTIONS?
KNOCK DOWN THE BIG GUY FIRST.
THEN THE LITTLE GUYS WILL HAVE TO DO WHAT WE WANT.
DO YOU REMEMBER THE GUY IN YAKIMINKA DISTRICT?
THE ONE WITH THE FAMILY IN GERMANY?
YOU DO REMEMBER.
YOU WANT TO TRY THAT SCAM AGAIN?
HE'S SUPPOSED TO BE AN HONOURABLE MAN.
THAT CAN BE A WEAKNESS TOO.

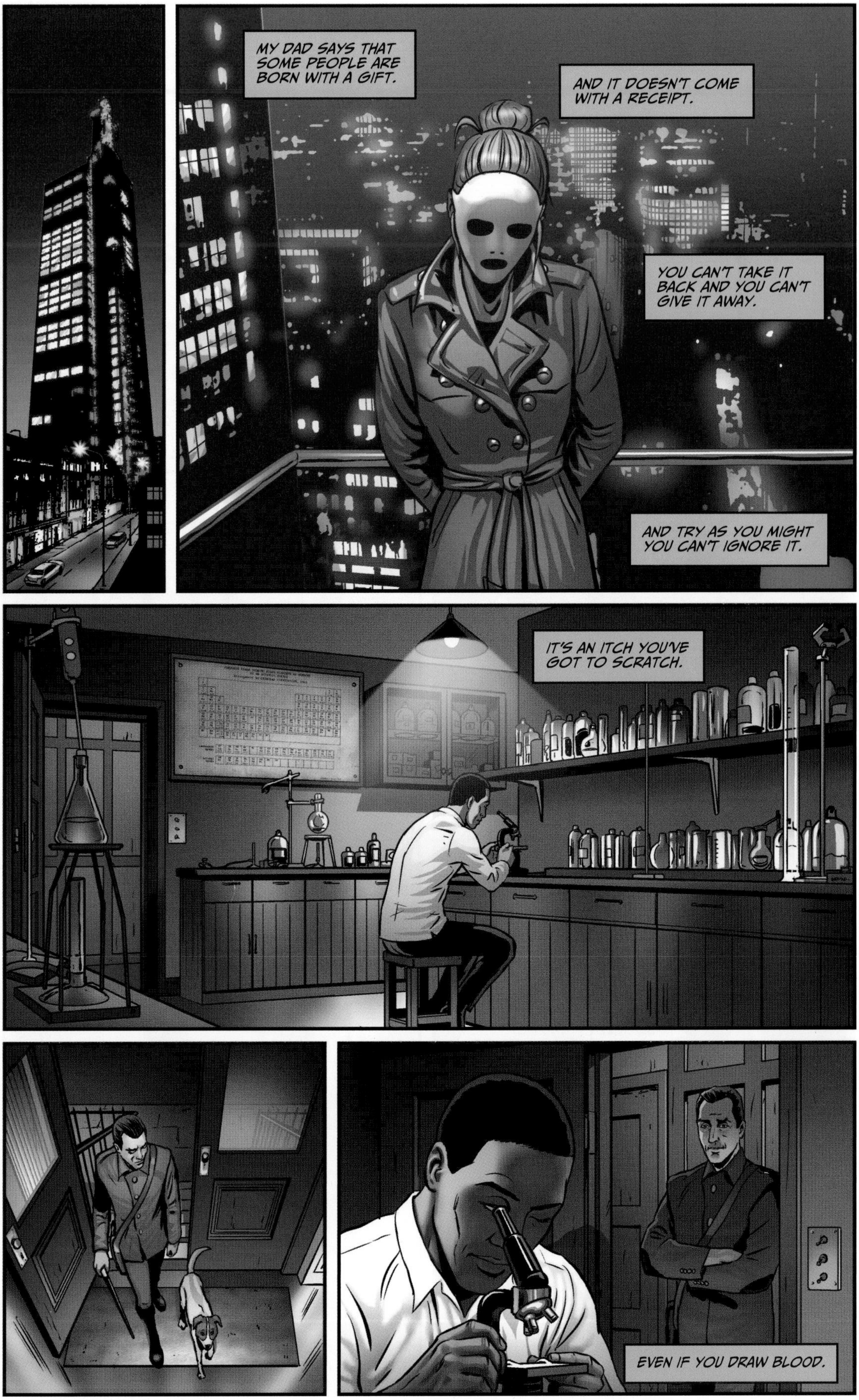
MY DAD SAYS THAT SOME PEOPLE ARE BORN WITH A GIFT.
AND IT DOESN'T COME WITH A RECEIPT.
YOU CAN'T TAKE IT BACK AND YOU CAN'T GIVE IT AWAY.
AND TRY AS YOU MIGHT YOU CAN'T IGNORE IT.
IT'S AN ITCH YOU'VE GOT TO SCRATCH.
EVEN IF YOU DRAW BLOOD.

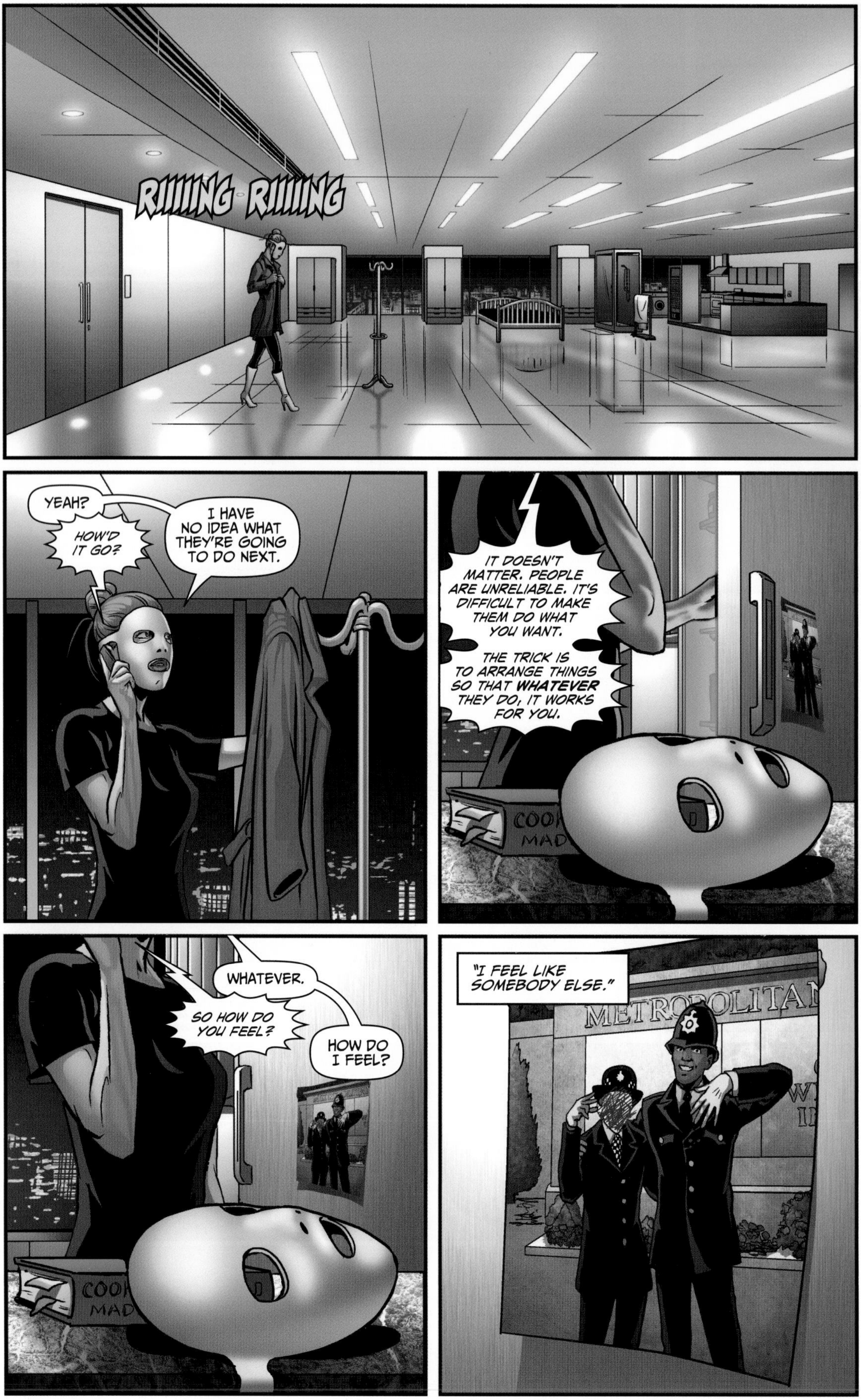

RIIIING RIIIING
YEAH?
HOW'D IT GO?
I HAVE NO IDEA WHAT THEY'RE GOING TO DO NEXT.
IT DOESN'T MATTER. PEOPLE ARE UNRELIABLE. IT'S DIFFICULT TO MAKE THEM DO WHAT YOU WANT.
THE TRICK IS TO ARRANGE THINGS SO THAT **WHATEVER** THEY DO, IT WORKS FOR YOU.
WHATEVER.
SO HOW DO YOU FEEL?
HOW DO I FEEL?
"I FEEL LIKE SOMEBODY ELSE."
METROPOLITAN

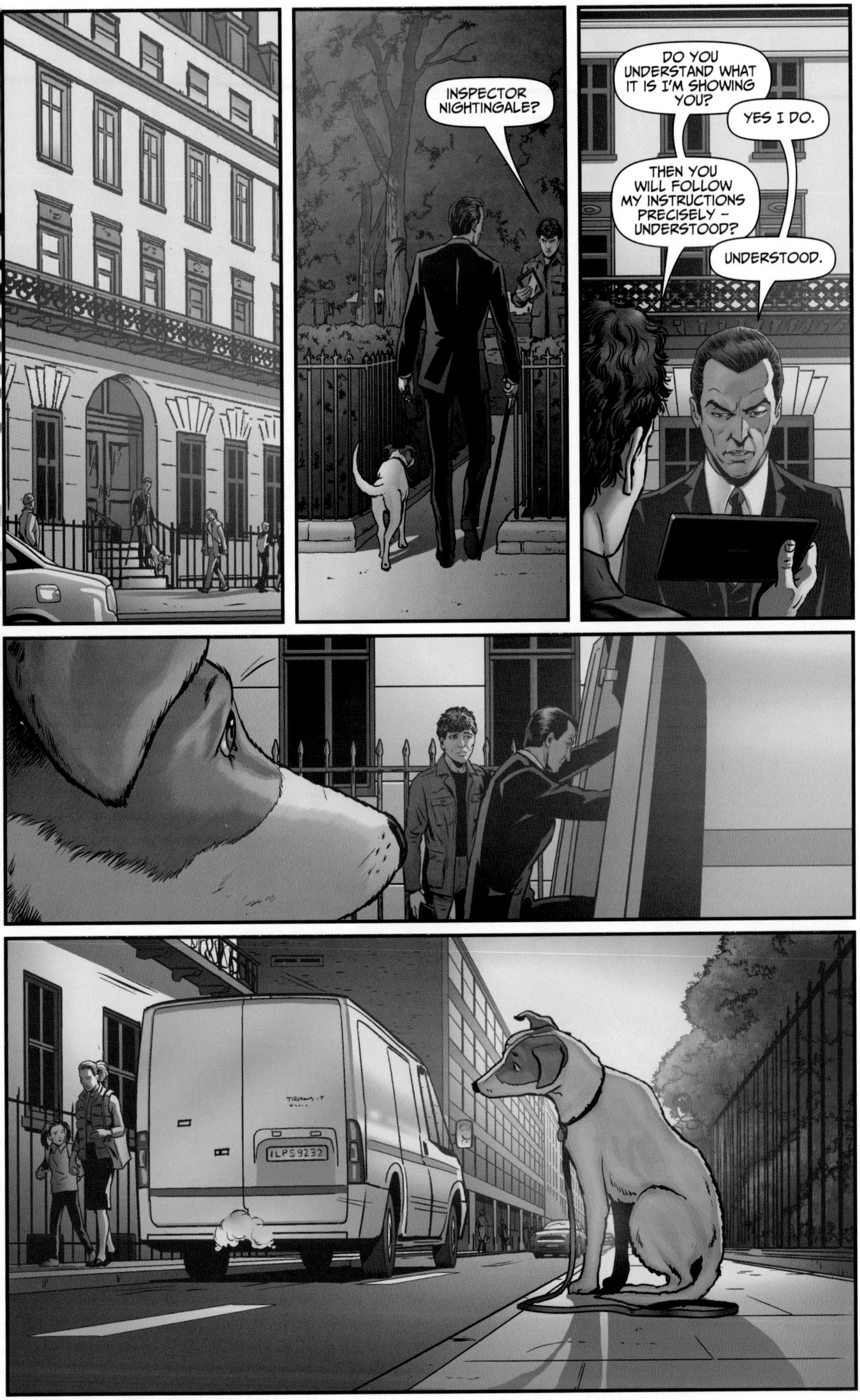
INSPECTOR NIGHTINGALE?
DO YOU UNDERSTAND WHAT IT IS I'M SHOWING YOU?
YES I DO.
THEN YOU WILL FOLLOW MY INSTRUCTIONS PRECISELY – UNDERSTOOD?
UNDERSTOOD.
ILPS9232

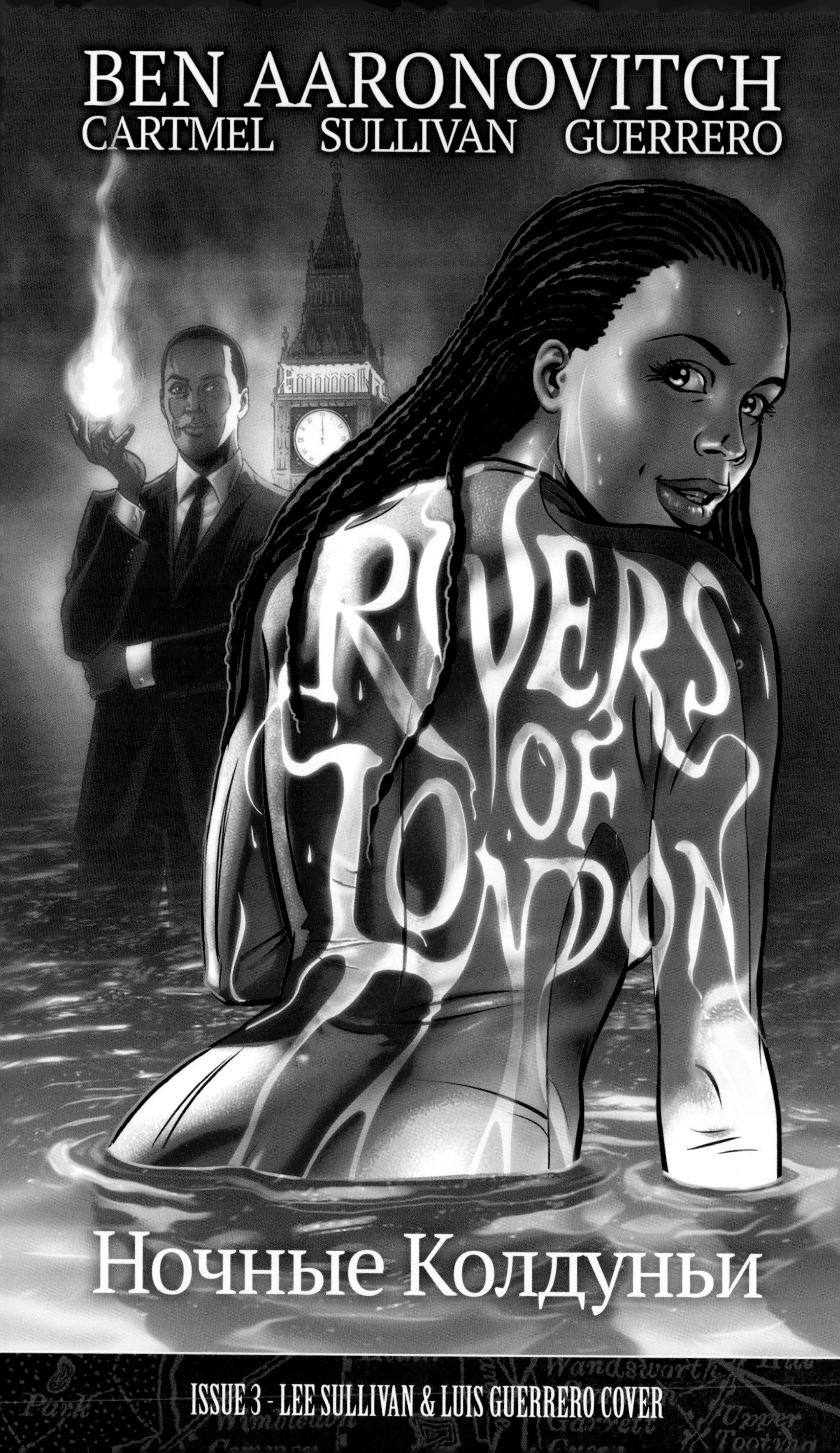
BEN AARONOVITCH
CARTMEL SULLIVAN GUERRERO
RIVERS OF LONDON
Ночные Колдуньи
ISSUE 3 - LEE SULLIVAN & LUIS GUERRERO COVER

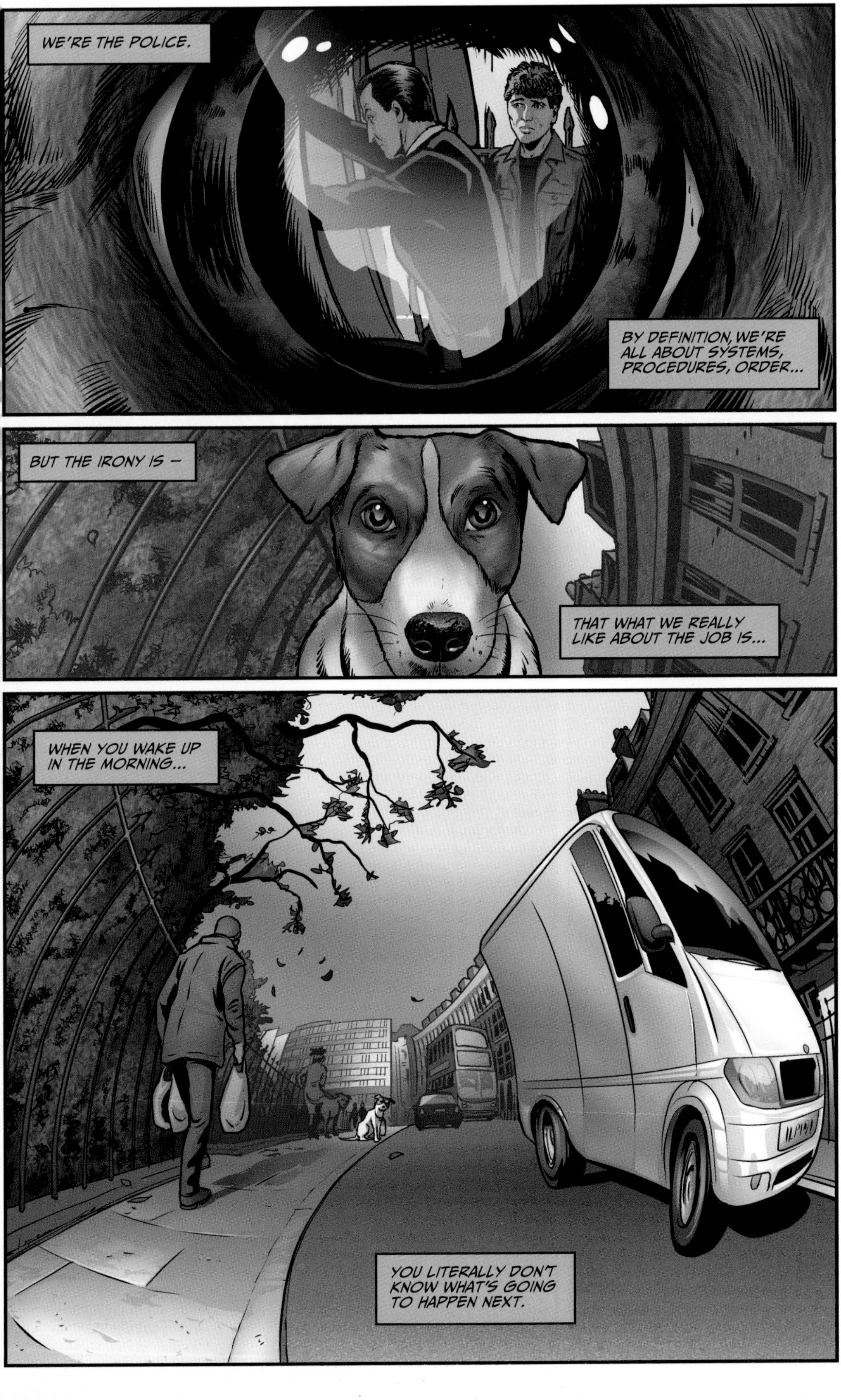
WE'RE THE POLICE.
BY DEFINITION, WE'RE ALL ABOUT SYSTEMS, PROCEDURES, ORDER...
BUT THE IRONY IS —
THAT WHAT WE REALLY LIKE ABOUT THE JOB IS...
WHEN YOU WAKE UP IN THE MORNING...
YOU LITERALLY DON'T KNOW WHAT'S GOING TO HAPPEN NEXT.

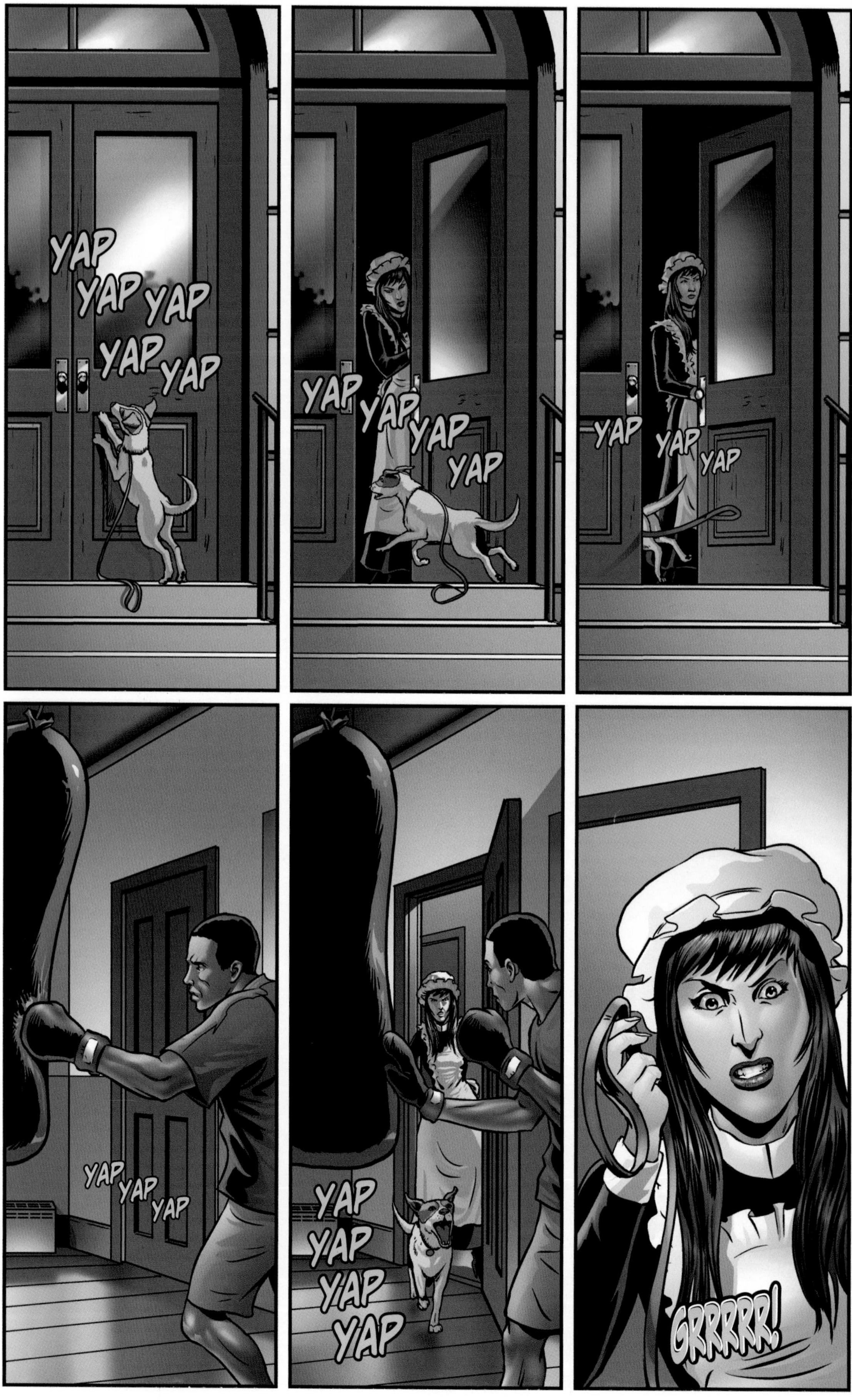
YAP
YAP YAP
YAP YAP
YAP
YAP
YAP
YAP
YAP
YAP
YAP
YAP YAP YAP
YAP
YAP
YAP
YAP
GRRRRR!

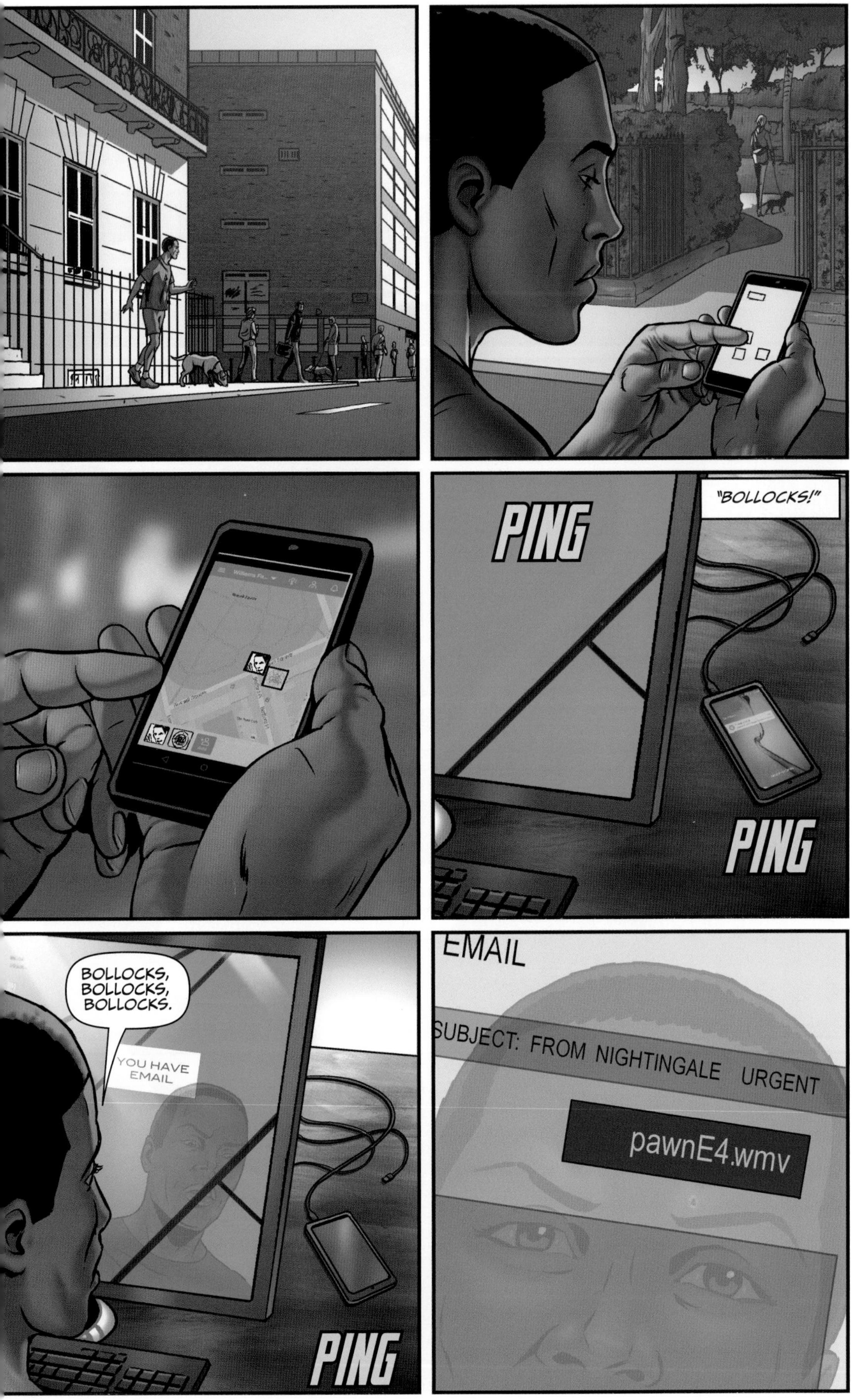
PING
"BOLLOCKS!"
PING
BOLLOCKS, BOLLOCKS, BOLLOCKS.
YOU HAVE EMAIL
PING
EMAIL
SUBJECT: FROM NIGHTINGALE URGENT
pawnE4.wmv

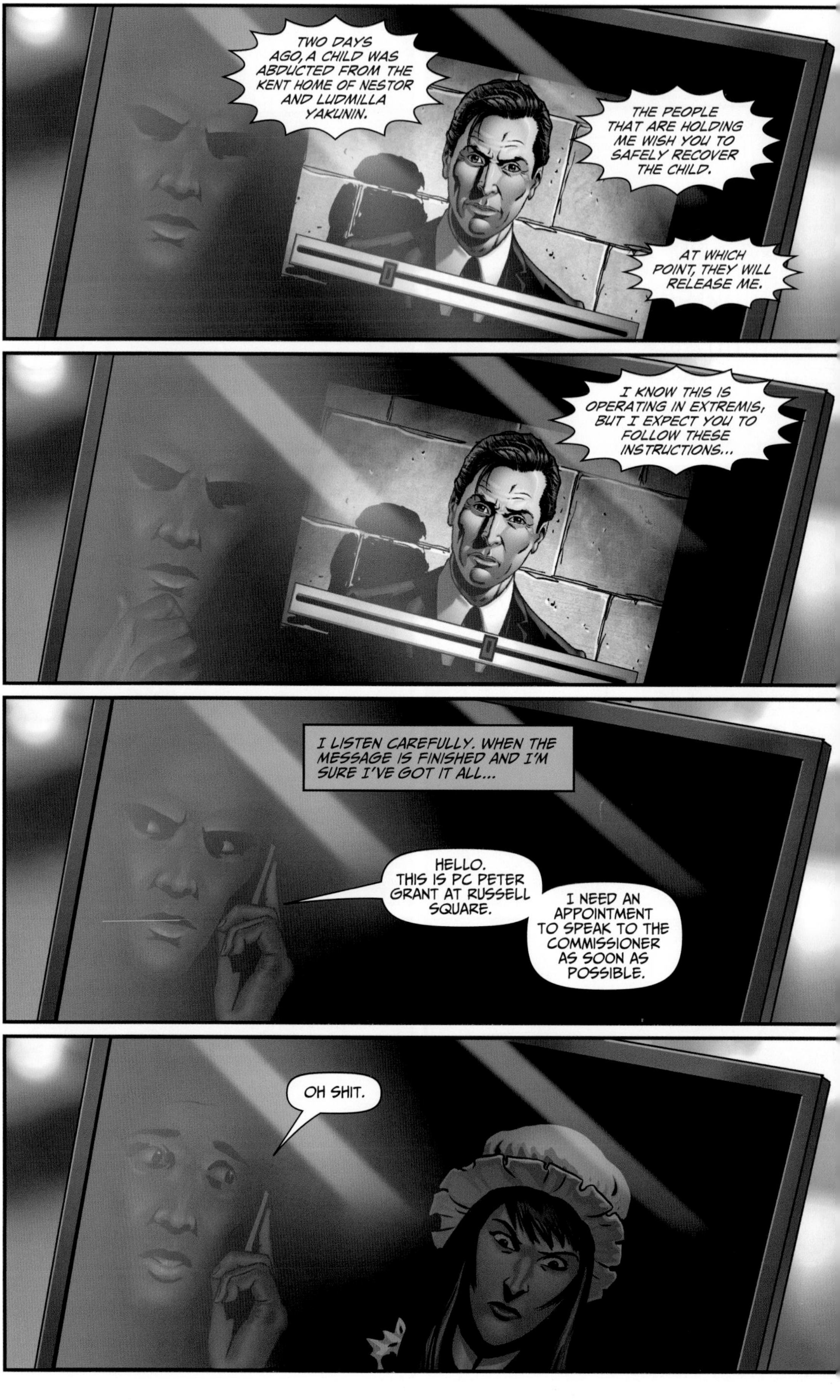
TWO DAYS AGO, A CHILD WAS ABDUCTED FROM THE KENT HOME OF NESTOR AND LUDMILLA YAKUNIN.
THE PEOPLE THAT ARE HOLDING ME WISH YOU TO SAFELY RECOVER THE CHILD.
AT WHICH POINT, THEY WILL RELEASE ME.
I KNOW THIS IS OPERATING IN EXTREMIS, BUT I EXPECT YOU TO FOLLOW THESE INSTRUCTIONS...
I LISTEN CAREFULLY. WHEN THE MESSAGE IS FINISHED AND I'M SURE I'VE GOT IT ALL...
HELLO. THIS IS PC PETER GRANT AT RUSSELL SQUARE.
I NEED AN APPOINTMENT TO SPEAK TO THE COMMISSIONER AS SOON AS POSSIBLE.
OH SHIT.

SHUNK

THUNK

TING

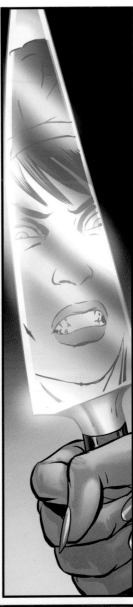

WHOA, WHOA, WHOA!

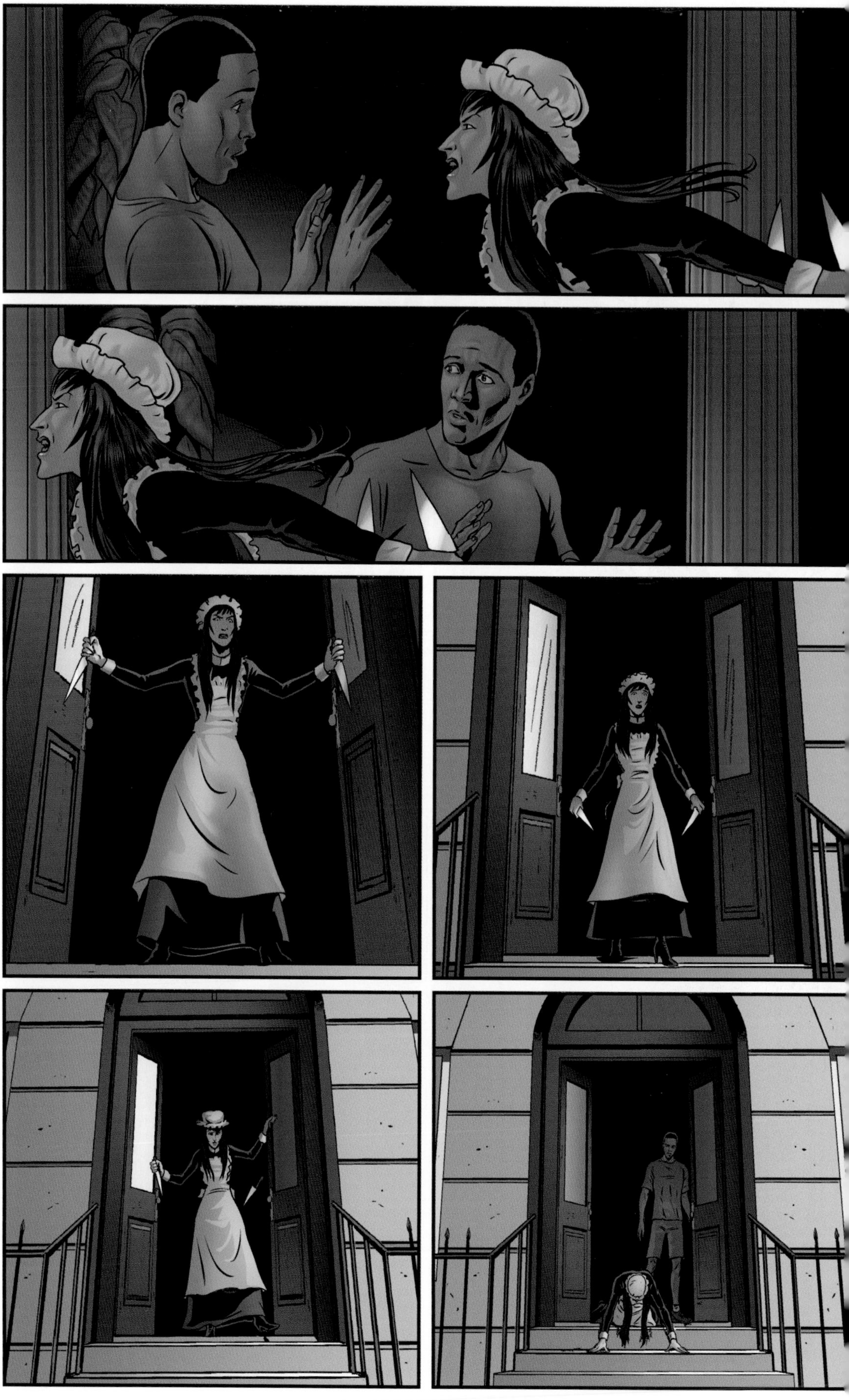

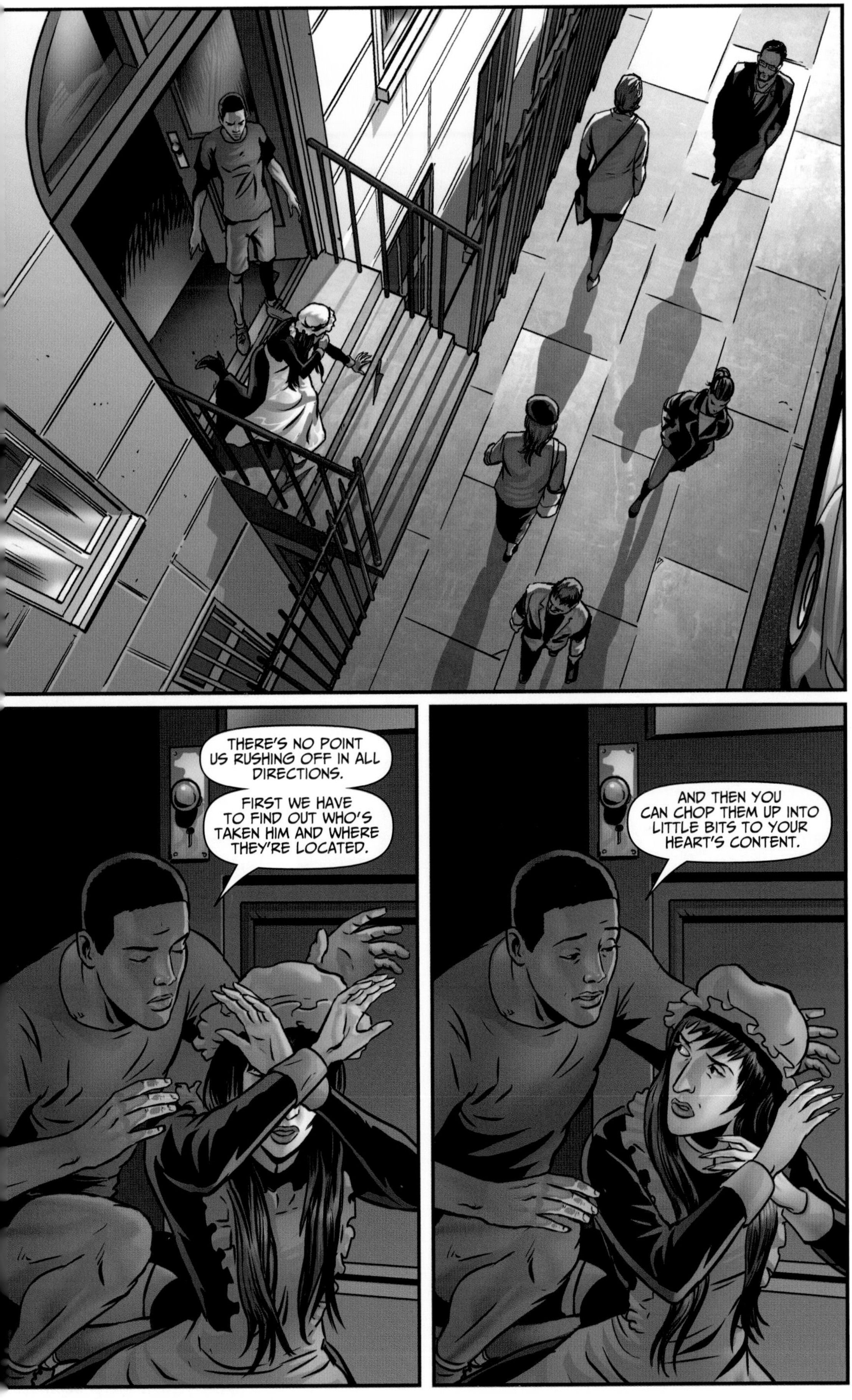
THERE'S NO POINT US RUSHING OFF IN ALL DIRECTIONS.
FIRST WE HAVE TO FIND OUT WHO'S TAKEN HIM AND WHERE THEY'RE LOCATED.
AND THEN YOU CAN CHOP THEM UP INTO LITTLE BITS TO YOUR HEART'S CONTENT.

"AH, YOU MUST BE THE NIGHTINGALE I'VE HEARD SO MUCH ABOUT!"

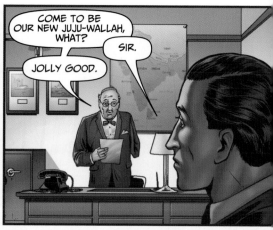

COME TO BE OUR NEW JUJU-WALLAH, WHAT?

SIR.

JOLLY GOOD.

"IF YOU FIND YOURSELF IN A SPOT OF BOTHER, WE HAVE A PLAIN-WORD CODE."

YOUR AVERAGE NATIVE JOHNNY NOT HAVING ENOUGH PROPER ENGLISH TO SPOT IT, YOU SEE.

I KNOW THIS SITUATION IS BOTH IRRITATING AND LESS THEN CHEERFUL, BUT I BELIEVE THEIR DEMANDS ARE REASONABLE.

THEY WANT YOU TO FIND THE LESHY AND RECOVER THE CHILD.

BUT IT IS VITAL THAT YOU DON'T CONTACT THE PRINCIPALS.

"DIFFICULT" MEANS "ATTEMPT AN IMMEDIATE RESOLUTION."

"IRRITATING" – "DEAL WITH THE UNDERLYING CAUSE."

"UNLUCKY" INDICATES A NATIVE THREAT, "VITAL" THE RUSSIANS AND "APROPOS" THE FRENCH.

I KNOW THIS IS OPERATING IN EXTREMIS, BUT I EXPECT YOU TO FOLLOW THESE INSTRUCTIONS.

"EXPECT" AND "INSTRUCTIONS" IN THE SAME SENTENCE...

USE WHATEVER MEANS ARE NECESSARY.

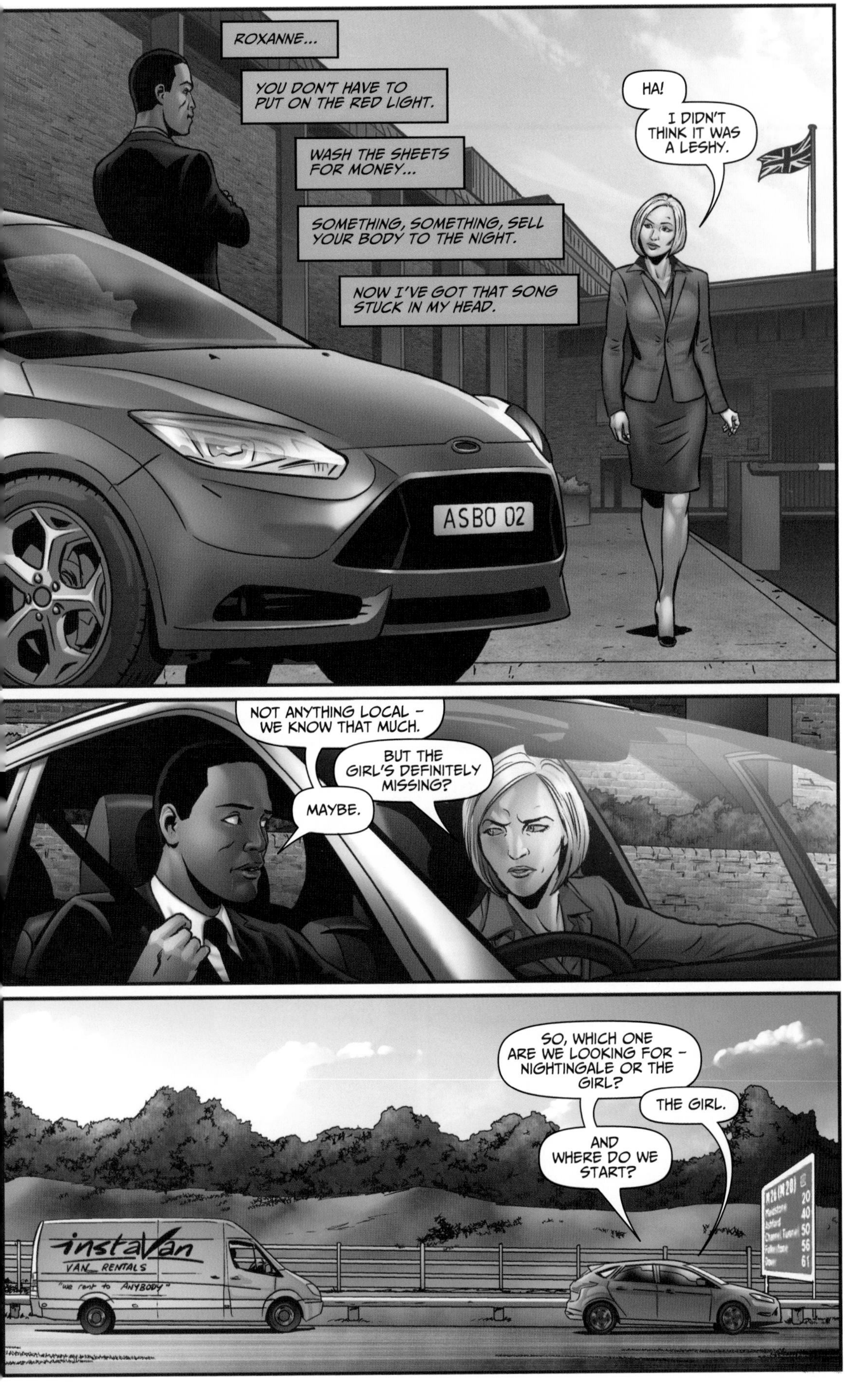
ROXANNE...
YOU DON'T HAVE TO PUT ON THE RED LIGHT.
WASH THE SHEETS FOR MONEY...
SOMETHING, SOMETHING, SELL YOUR BODY TO THE NIGHT.
NOW I'VE GOT THAT SONG STUCK IN MY HEAD.
HA!
I DIDN'T THINK IT WAS A LESHY.
ASBO 02
NOT ANYTHING LOCAL – WE KNOW THAT MUCH.
BUT THE GIRL'S DEFINITELY MISSING?
MAYBE.
SO, WHICH ONE ARE WE LOOKING FOR – NIGHTINGALE OR THE GIRL?
THE GIRL.
AND WHERE DO WE START?
instaVan
VAN RENTALS
"we rent to ANYBODY"

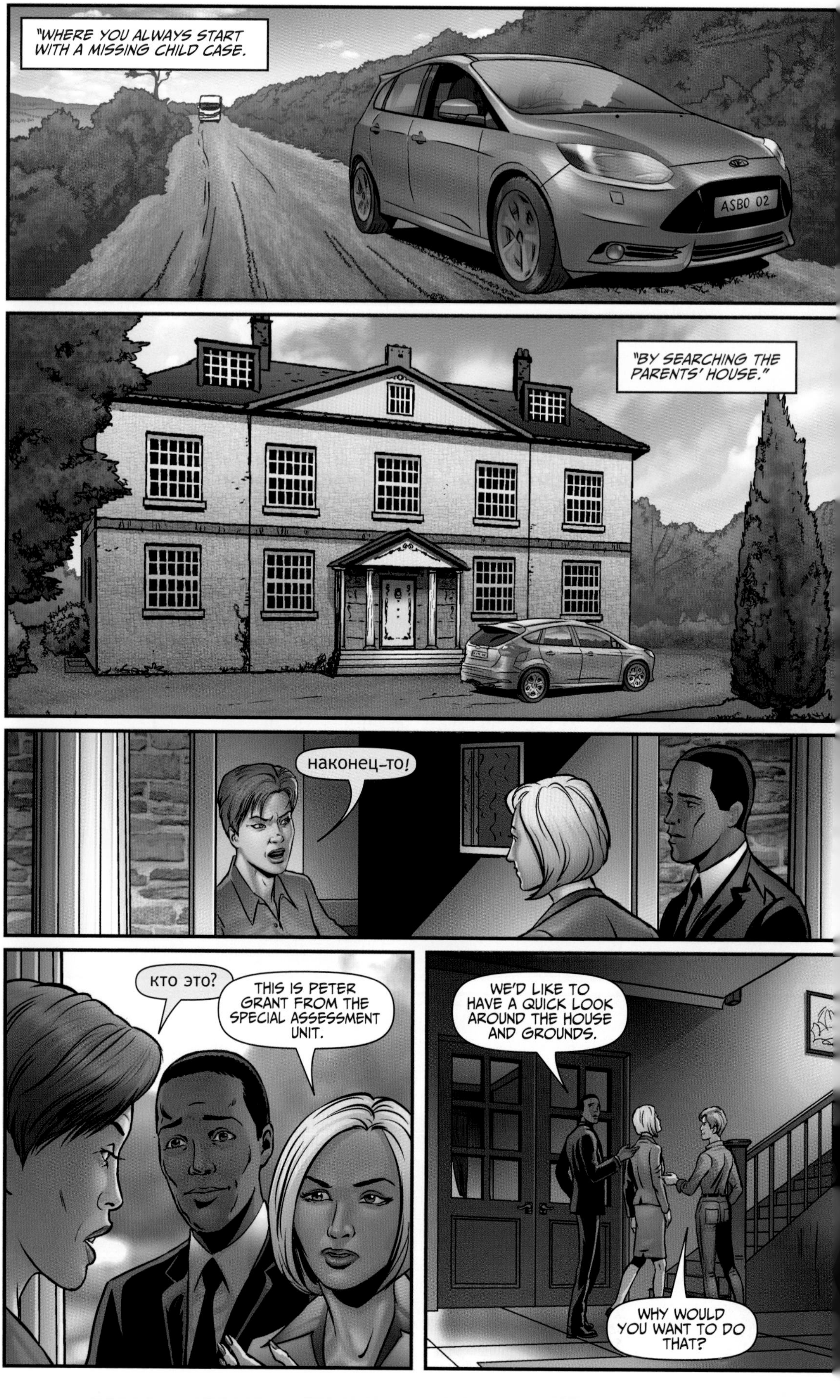
"WHERE YOU ALWAYS START WITH A MISSING CHILD CASE.
ASBO 02
"BY SEARCHING THE PARENTS' HOUSE."
наконец-то!
кто это?
THIS IS PETER GRANT FROM THE SPECIAL ASSESSMENT UNIT.
WE'D LIKE TO HAVE A QUICK LOOK AROUND THE HOUSE AND GROUNDS.
WHY WOULD YOU WANT TO DO THAT?

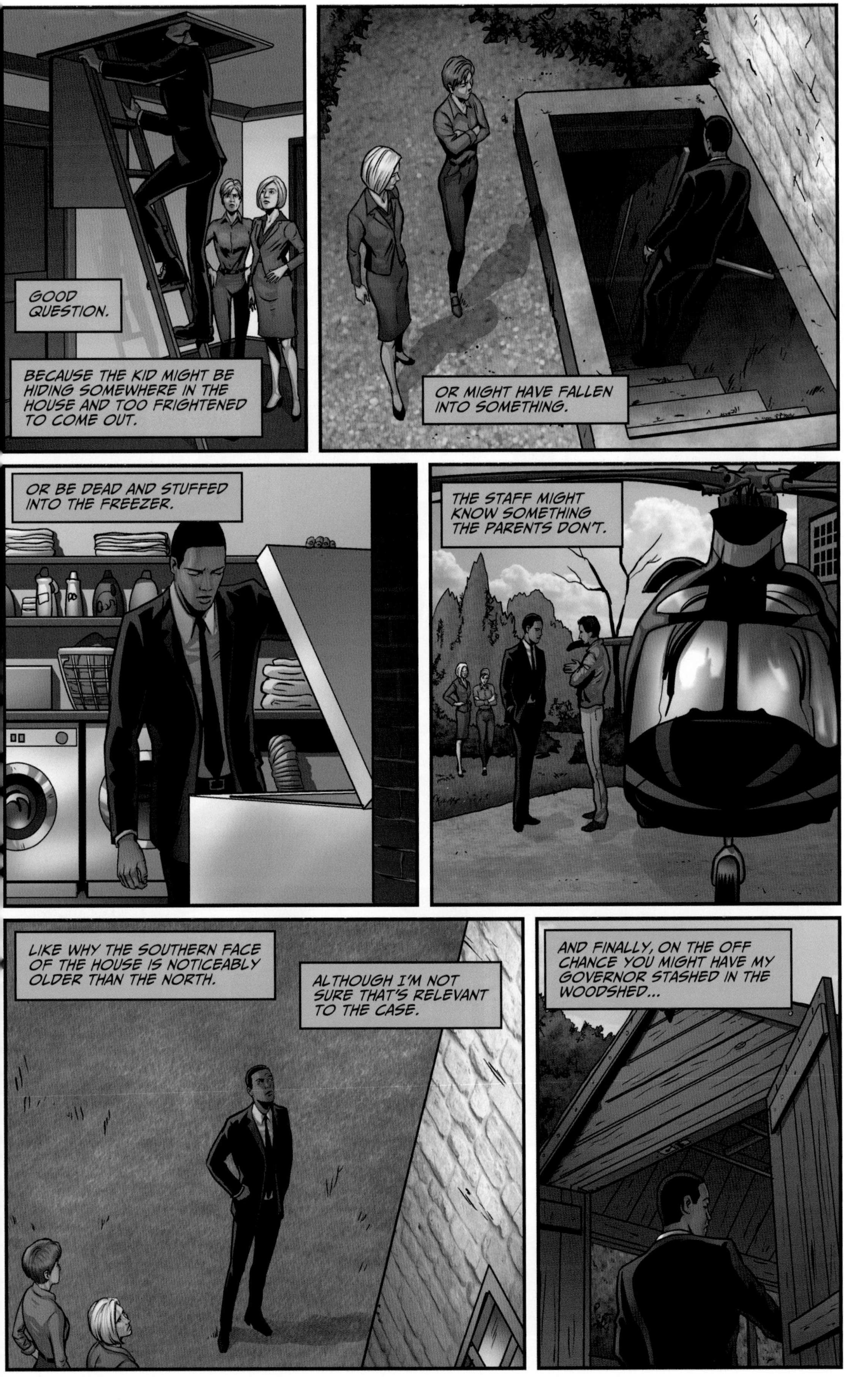
GOOD QUESTION.
BECAUSE THE KID MIGHT BE HIDING SOMEWHERE IN THE HOUSE AND TOO FRIGHTENED TO COME OUT.
OR MIGHT HAVE FALLEN INTO SOMETHING.
OR BE DEAD AND STUFFED INTO THE FREEZER.
THE STAFF MIGHT KNOW SOMETHING THE PARENTS DON'T.
LIKE WHY THE SOUTHERN FACE OF THE HOUSE IS NOTICEABLY OLDER THAN THE NORTH.
ALTHOUGH I'M NOT SURE THAT'S RELEVANT TO THE CASE.
AND FINALLY, ON THE OFF CHANCE YOU MIGHT HAVE MY GOVERNOR STASHED IN THE WOODSHED...

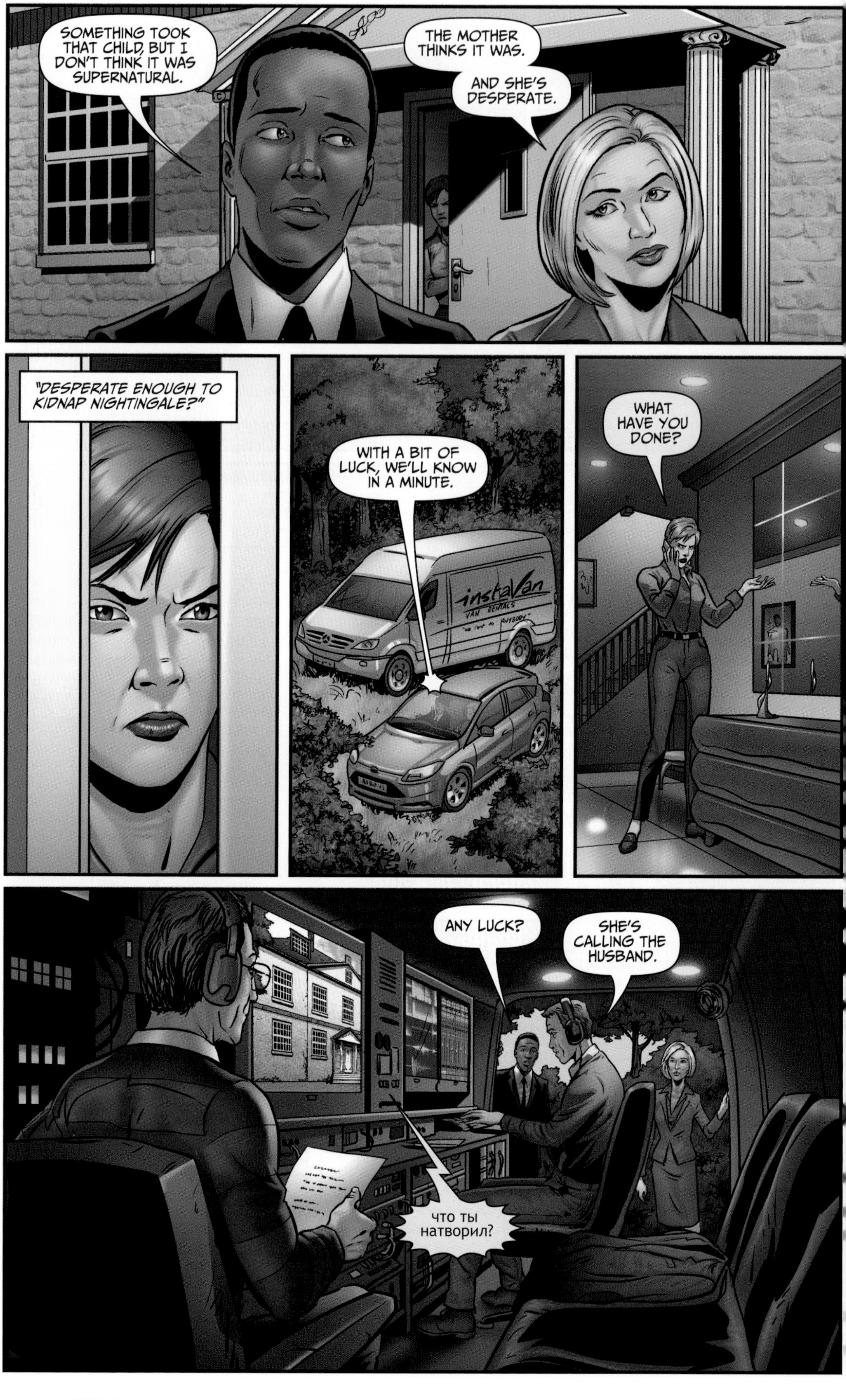
SOMETHING TOOK THAT CHILD, BUT I DON'T THINK IT WAS SUPERNATURAL.
THE MOTHER THINKS IT WAS.
AND SHE'S DESPERATE.
"DESPERATE ENOUGH TO KIDNAP NIGHTINGALE?"
WITH A BIT OF LUCK, WE'LL KNOW IN A MINUTE.
instaVan
VAN RENTALS
WHAT HAVE YOU DONE?
ANY LUCK?
SHE'S CALLING THE HUSBAND.
что ты натворил?

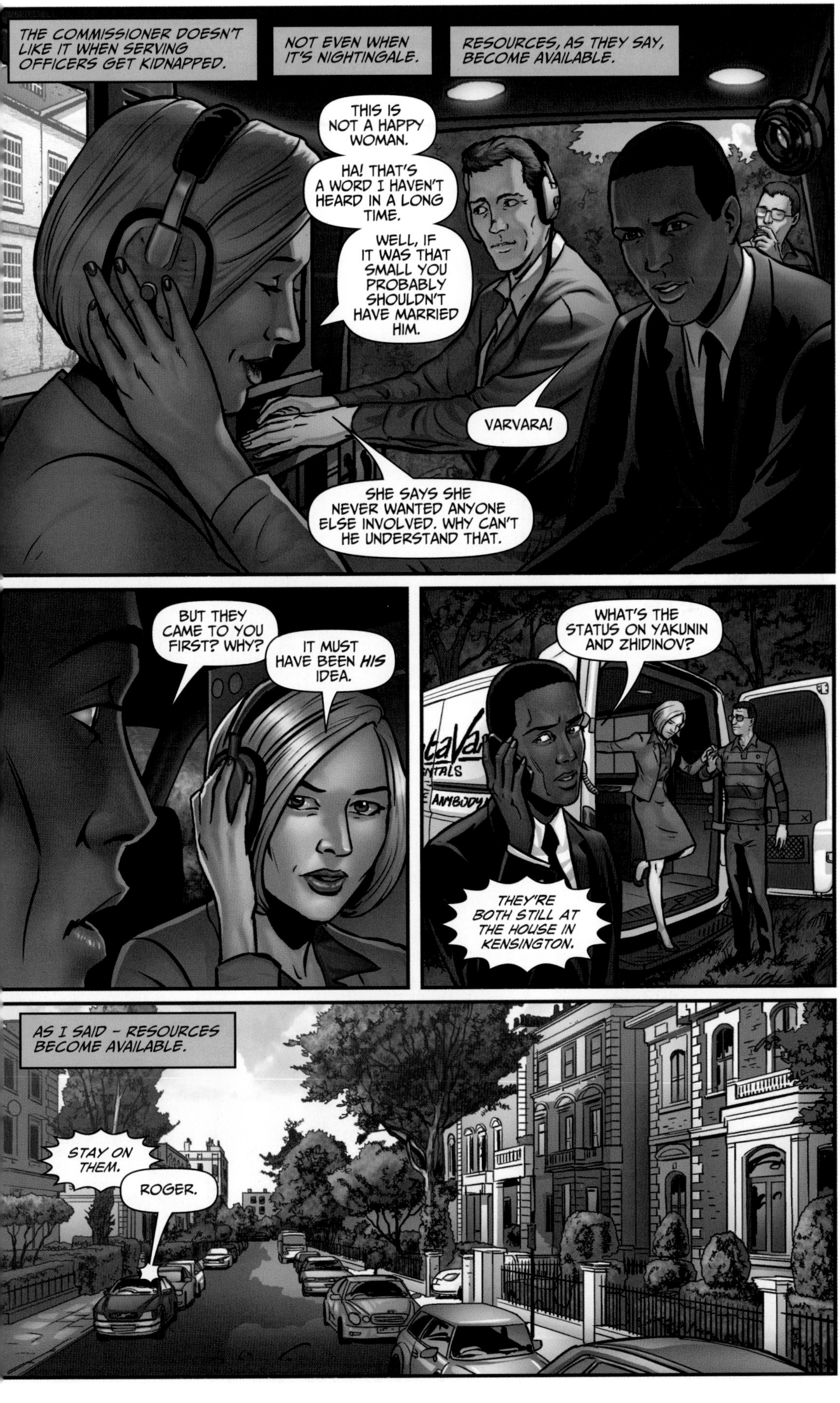
THE COMMISSIONER DOESN'T LIKE IT WHEN SERVING OFFICERS GET KIDNAPPED.
NOT EVEN WHEN IT'S NIGHTINGALE.
RESOURCES, AS THEY SAY, BECOME AVAILABLE.
THIS IS NOT A HAPPY WOMAN.
HA! THAT'S A WORD I HAVEN'T HEARD IN A LONG TIME.
WELL, IF IT WAS THAT SMALL YOU PROBABLY SHOULDN'T HAVE MARRIED HIM.
VARVARA!
SHE SAYS SHE NEVER WANTED ANYONE ELSE INVOLVED. WHY CAN'T HE UNDERSTAND THAT.
BUT THEY CAME TO YOU FIRST? WHY?
IT MUST HAVE BEEN HIS IDEA.
WHAT'S THE STATUS ON YAKUNIN AND ZHIDINOV?
THEY'RE BOTH STILL AT THE HOUSE IN KENSINGTON.
AS I SAID - RESOURCES BECOME AVAILABLE.
STAY ON THEM.
ROGER.

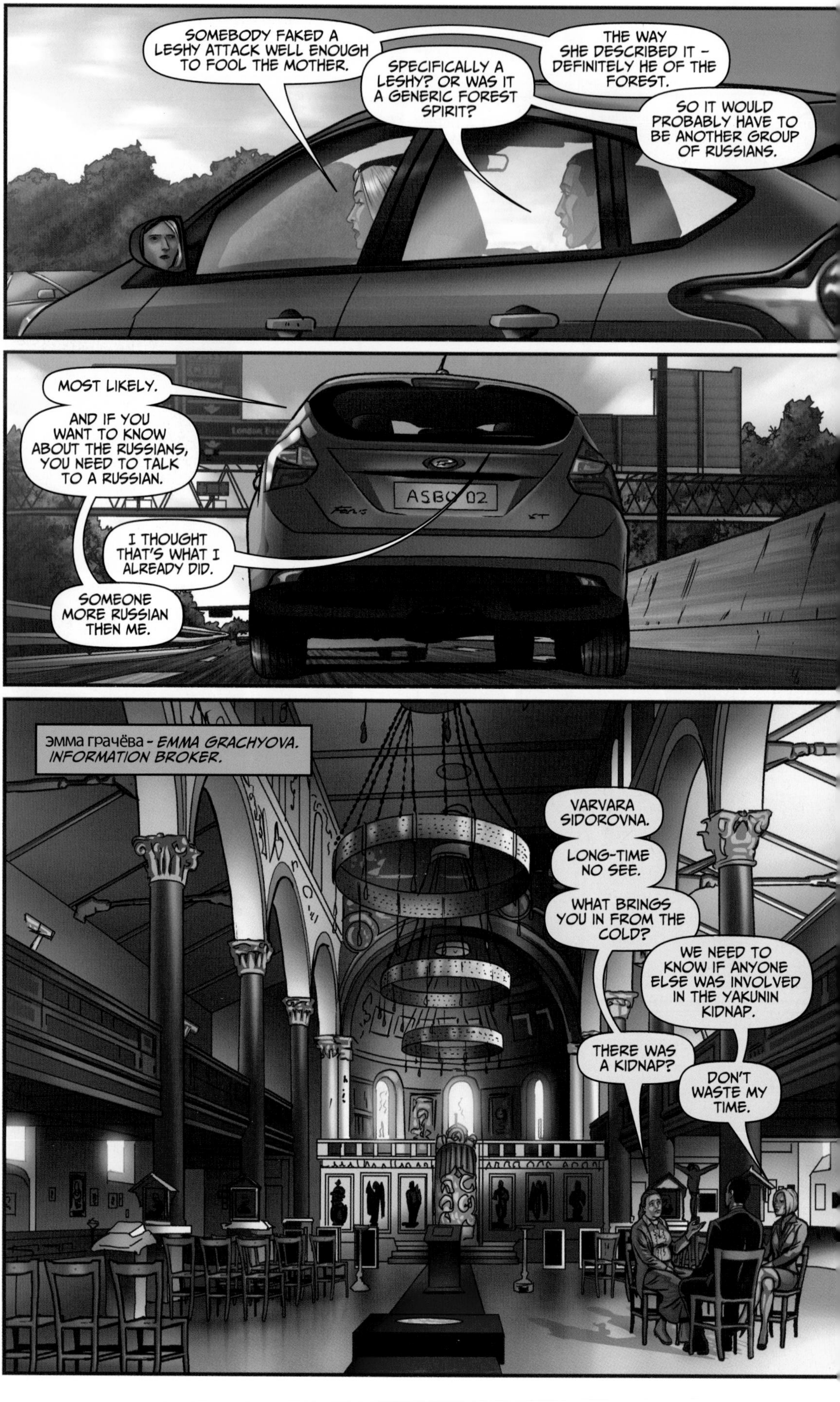
SOMEBODY FAKED A LESHY ATTACK WELL ENOUGH TO FOOL THE MOTHER.
SPECIFICALLY A LESHY? OR WAS IT A GENERIC FOREST SPIRIT?
THE WAY SHE DESCRIBED IT – DEFINITELY HE OF THE FOREST.
SO IT WOULD PROBABLY HAVE TO BE ANOTHER GROUP OF RUSSIANS.
MOST LIKELY.
AND IF YOU WANT TO KNOW ABOUT THE RUSSIANS, YOU NEED TO TALK TO A RUSSIAN.
ASBO 02
I THOUGHT THAT'S WHAT I ALREADY DID.
SOMEONE MORE RUSSIAN THEN ME.
эмма грачёва – *EMMA GRACHYOVA. INFORMATION BROKER.*
VARVARA SIDOROVNA.
LONG-TIME NO SEE.
WHAT BRINGS YOU IN FROM THE COLD?
WE NEED TO KNOW IF ANYONE ELSE WAS INVOLVED IN THE YAKUNIN KIDNAP.
THERE WAS A KIDNAP?
DON'T WASTE MY TIME.

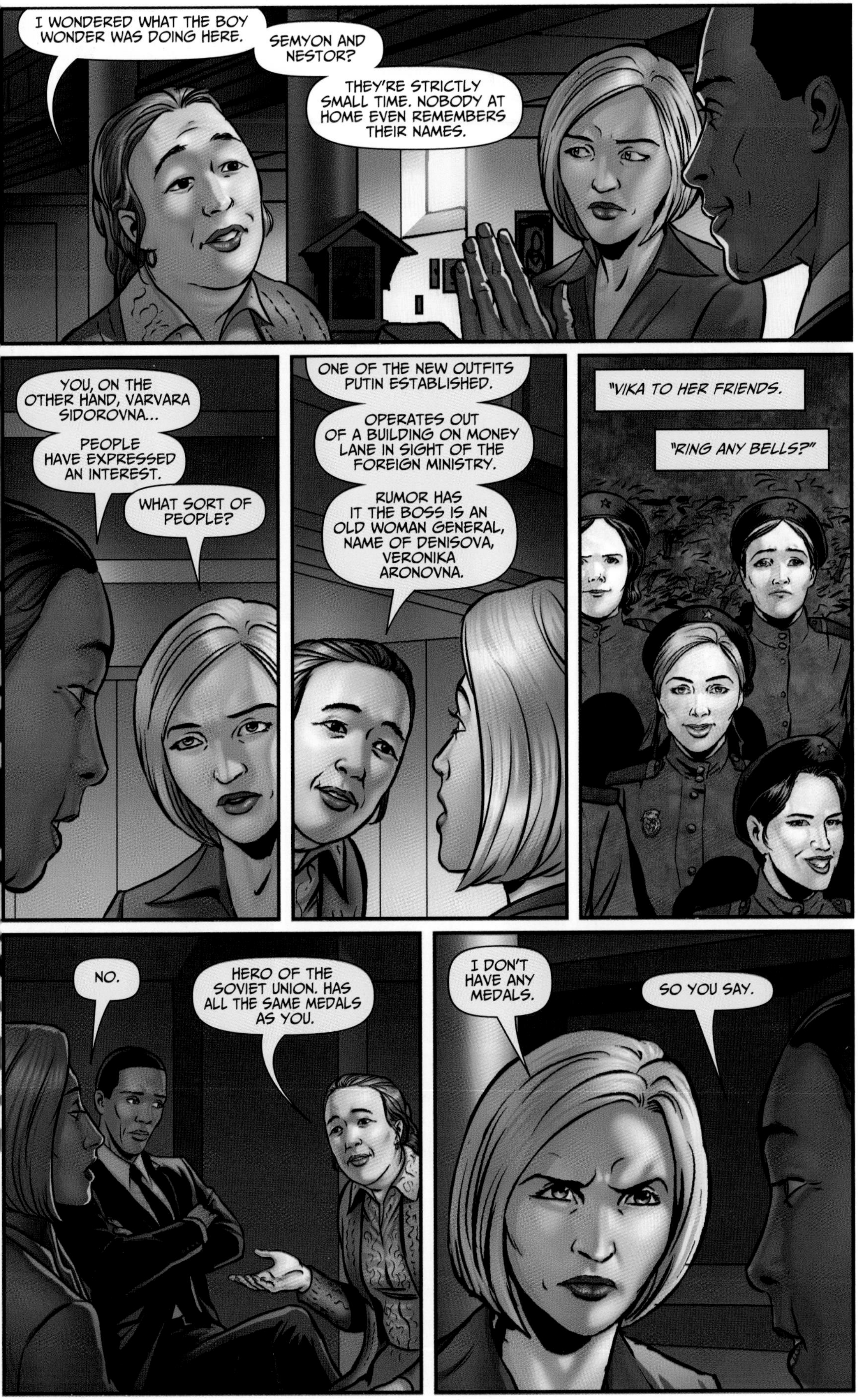
I WONDERED WHAT THE BOY WONDER WAS DOING HERE.
SEMYON AND NESTOR?
THEY'RE STRICTLY SMALL TIME. NOBODY AT HOME EVEN REMEMBERS THEIR NAMES.
YOU, ON THE OTHER HAND, VARVARA SIDOROVNA...
PEOPLE HAVE EXPRESSED AN INTEREST.
WHAT SORT OF PEOPLE?
ONE OF THE NEW OUTFITS PUTIN ESTABLISHED.
OPERATES OUT OF A BUILDING ON MONEY LANE IN SIGHT OF THE FOREIGN MINISTRY.
RUMOR HAS IT THE BOSS IS AN OLD WOMAN GENERAL, NAME OF DENISOVA, VERONIKA ARONOVNA.
"VIKA TO HER FRIENDS.
"RING ANY BELLS?"
NO.
HERO OF THE SOVIET UNION. HAS ALL THE SAME MEDALS AS YOU.
I DON'T HAVE ANY MEDALS.
SO YOU SAY.

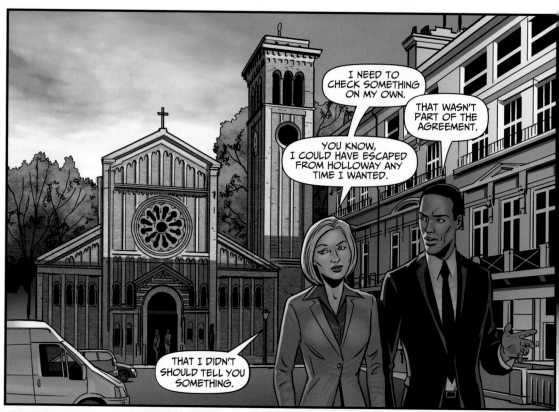

I NEED TO CHECK SOMETHING ON MY OWN.

THAT WASN'T PART OF THE AGREEMENT.

YOU KNOW, I COULD HAVE ESCAPED FROM HOLLOWAY ANY TIME I WANTED.

THAT I DIDN'T SHOULD TELL YOU SOMETHING.

THAT WE STILL HAVE SOMETHING YOU WANT.

DON'T WORRY. I'LL MEET YOU AT THE FOLLY NICE AND EARLY.

I CAN'T GO BACK TO THE FOLLY. THEY'LL BE WATCHING IT.

"YOU'RE LEAVING IT UNGUARDED?"

"AREN'T YOU WORRIED SOMEBODY MIGHT TRY TO BREAK IN?"

"GOD, I HOPE NOT."

"THE MESS WOULD BE HORRIBLE."

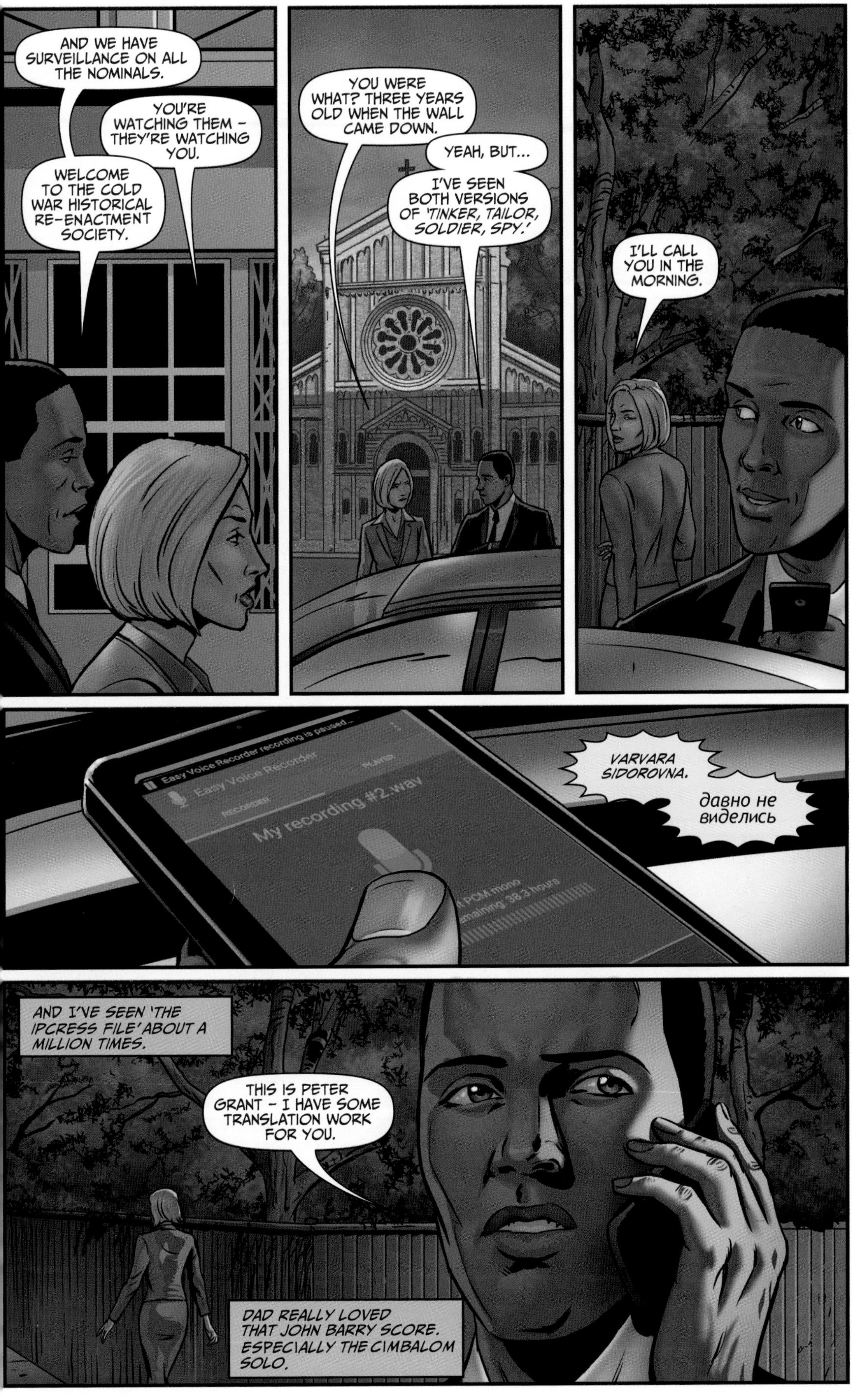
AND WE HAVE SURVEILLANCE ON ALL THE NOMINALS.
YOU'RE WATCHING THEM – THEY'RE WATCHING YOU.
WELCOME TO THE COLD WAR HISTORICAL RE-ENACTMENT SOCIETY.
YOU WERE WHAT? THREE YEARS OLD WHEN THE WALL CAME DOWN.
YEAH, BUT...
I'VE SEEN BOTH VERSIONS OF 'TINKER, TAILOR, SOLDIER, SPY.'
I'LL CALL YOU IN THE MORNING.
Easy Voice Recorder recording is paused...
Easy Voice Recorder
RECORDER
PLAYER
My recording #2.wav
VARVARA SIDOROVNA.
давно не виделись
AND I'VE SEEN 'THE IPCRESS FILE' ABOUT A MILLION TIMES.
THIS IS PETER GRANT – I HAVE SOME TRANSLATION WORK FOR YOU.
DAD REALLY LOVED THAT JOHN BARRY SCORE. ESPECIALLY THE CIMBALOM SOLO.

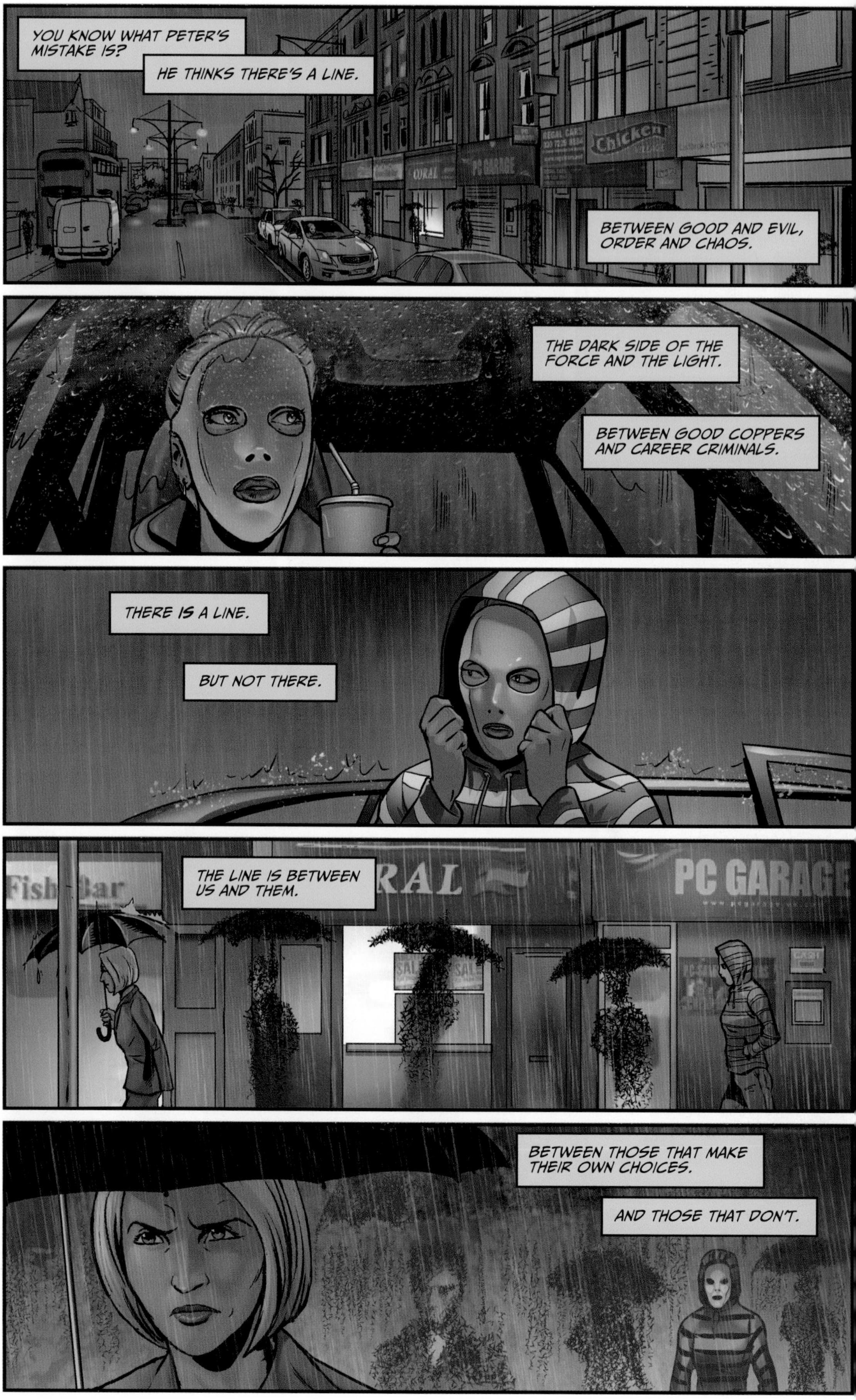
YOU KNOW WHAT PETER'S MISTAKE IS?
HE THINKS THERE'S A LINE.
PC GARAGE
BETWEEN GOOD AND EVIL, ORDER AND CHAOS.
THE DARK SIDE OF THE FORCE AND THE LIGHT.
BETWEEN GOOD COPPERS AND CAREER CRIMINALS.
THERE IS A LINE.
BUT NOT THERE.
Fish Bar
THE LINE IS BETWEEN US AND THEM.
PC GARAGE
BETWEEN THOSE THAT MAKE THEIR OWN CHOICES.
AND THOSE THAT DON'T.

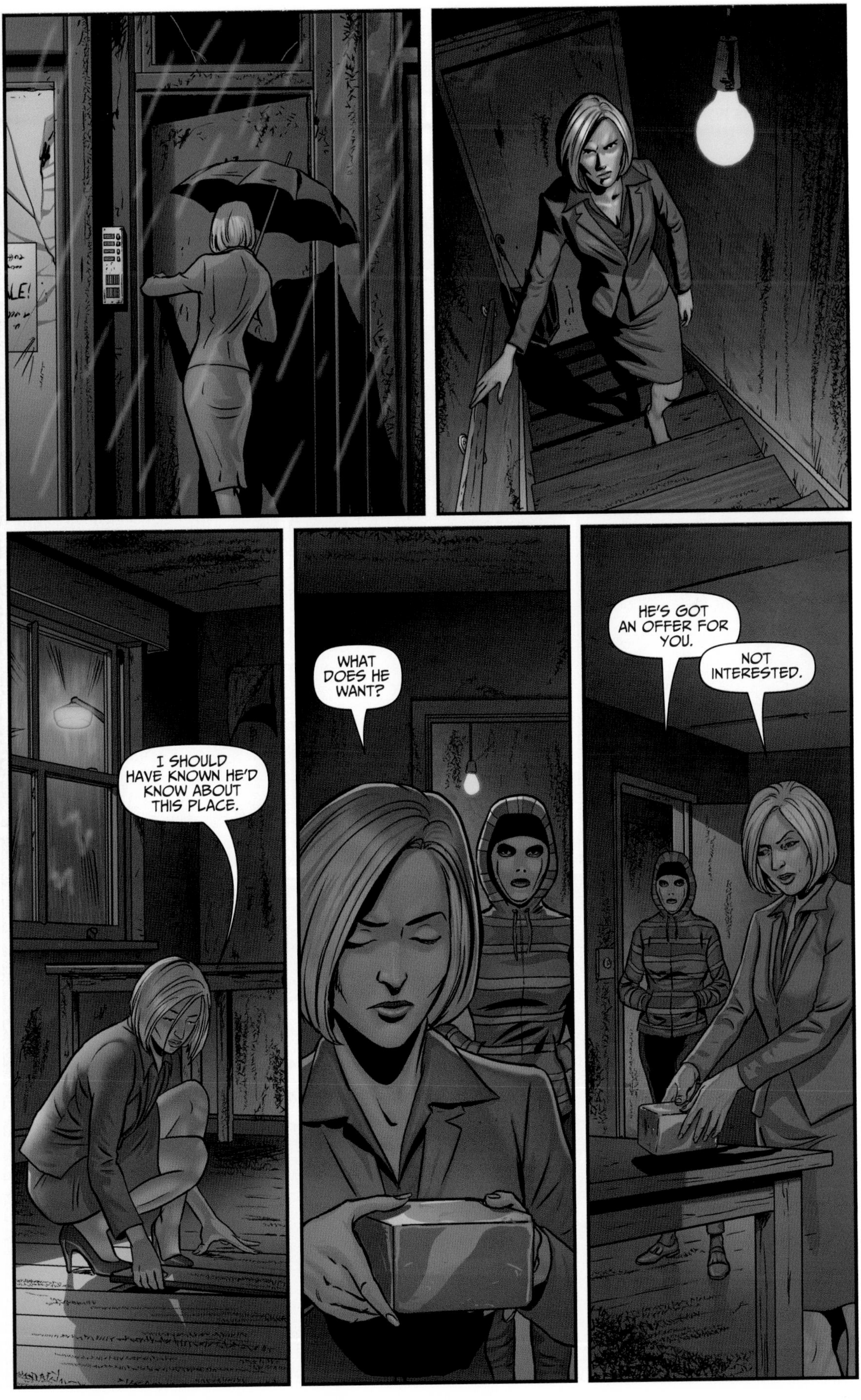
I SHOULD HAVE KNOWN HE'D KNOW ABOUT THIS PLACE.
WHAT DOES HE WANT?
HE'S GOT AN OFFER FOR YOU.
NOT INTERESTED.

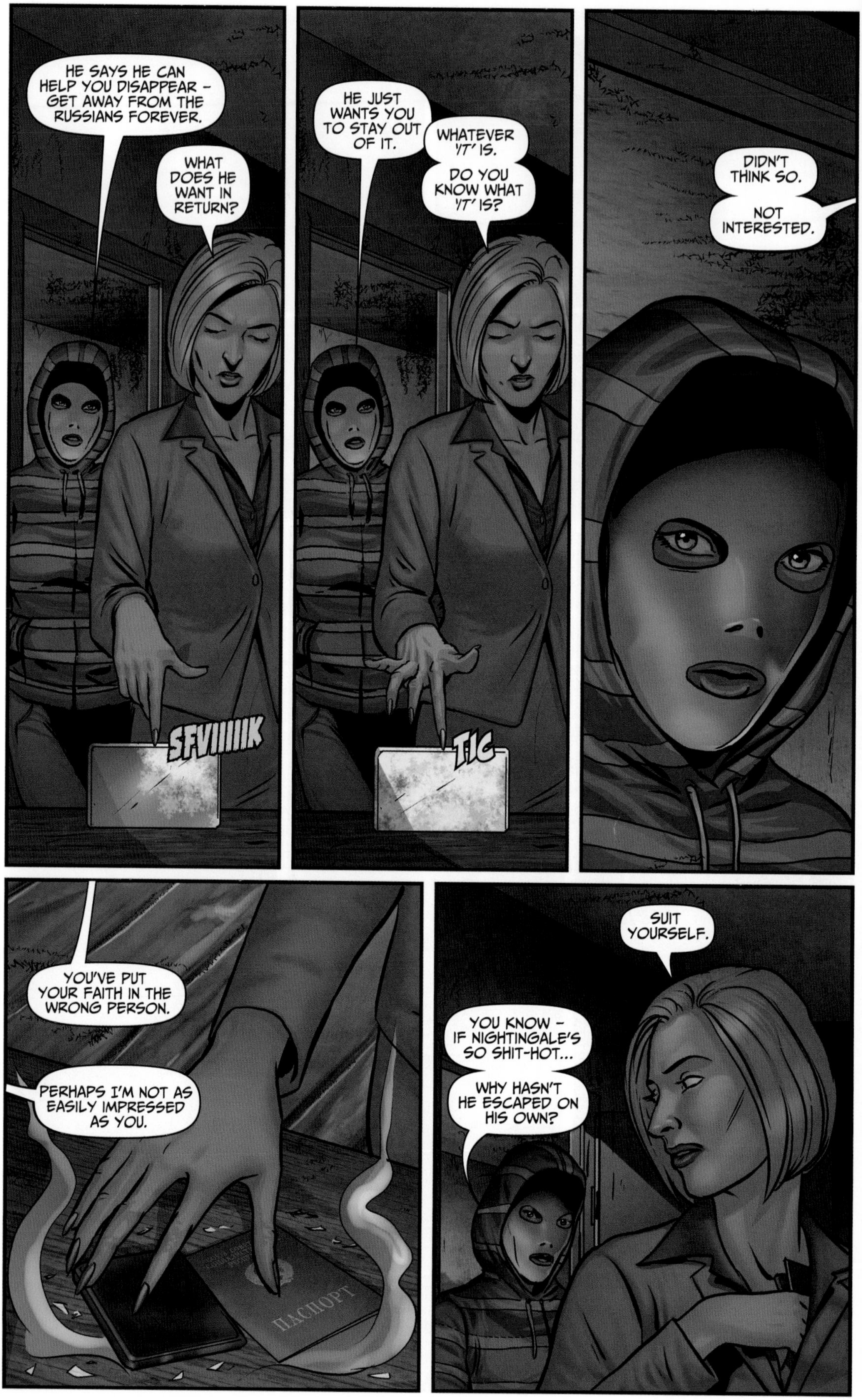
HE SAYS HE CAN HELP YOU DISAPPEAR - GET AWAY FROM THE RUSSIANS FOREVER.
WHAT DOES HE WANT IN RETURN?
SFVIIIIIK
HE JUST WANTS YOU TO STAY OUT OF IT.
WHATEVER 'IT' IS.
DO YOU KNOW WHAT 'IT' IS?
TIC
DIDN'T THINK SO.
NOT INTERESTED.
YOU'VE PUT YOUR FAITH IN THE WRONG PERSON.
PERHAPS I'M NOT AS EASILY IMPRESSED AS YOU.
ПАСПОРТ
SUIT YOURSELF.
YOU KNOW - IF NIGHTINGALE'S SO SHIT-HOT...
WHY HASN'T HE ESCAPED ON HIS OWN?

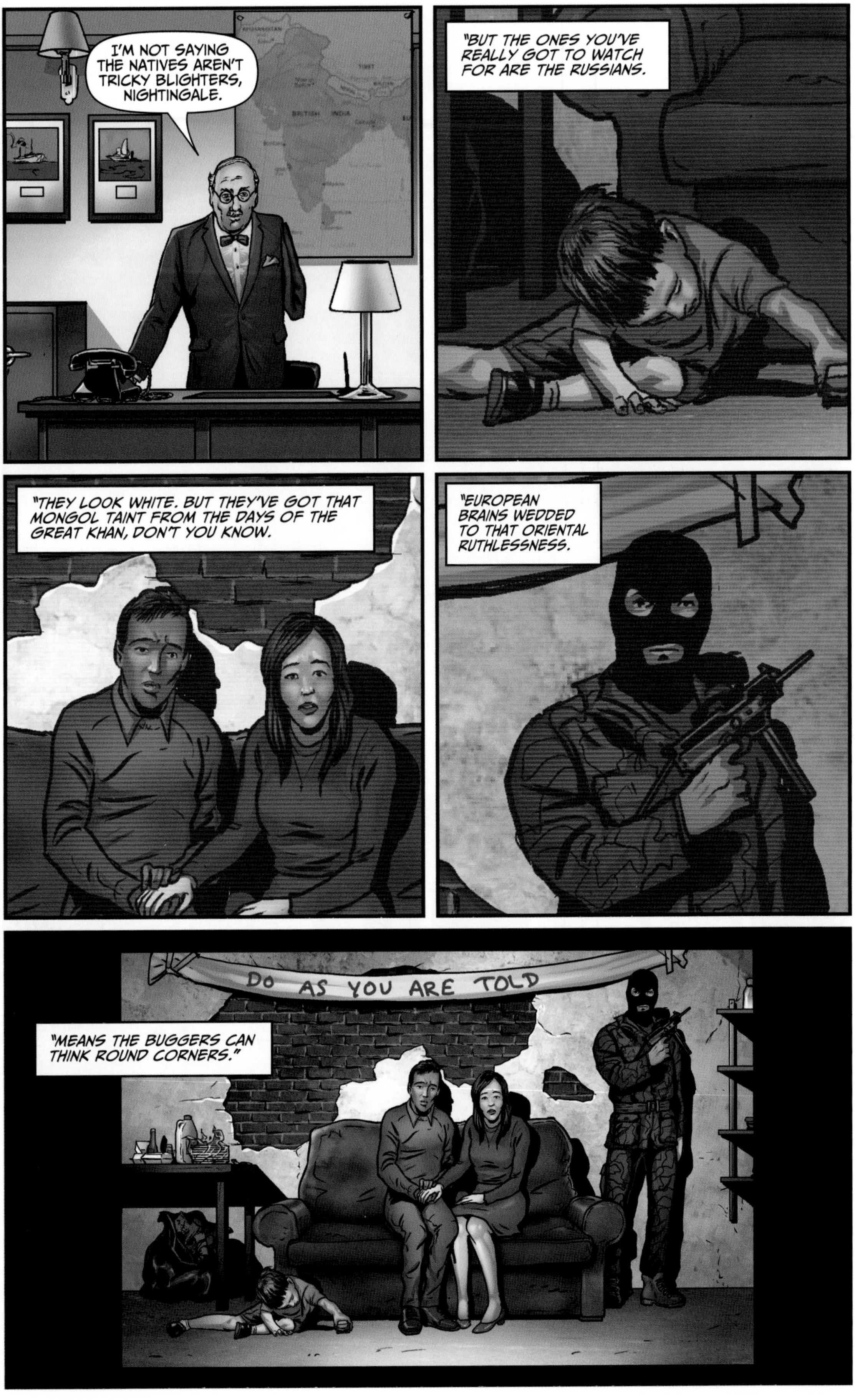
I'M NOT SAYING THE NATIVES AREN'T TRICKY BLIGHTERS, NIGHTINGALE.
"BUT THE ONES YOU'VE REALLY GOT TO WATCH FOR ARE THE RUSSIANS.
"THEY LOOK WHITE. BUT THEY'VE GOT THAT MONGOL TAINT FROM THE DAYS OF THE GREAT KHAN, DON'T YOU KNOW.
"EUROPEAN BRAINS WEDDED TO THAT ORIENTAL RUTHLESSNESS.
DO AS YOU ARE TOLD
"MEANS THE BUGGERS CAN THINK ROUND CORNERS."

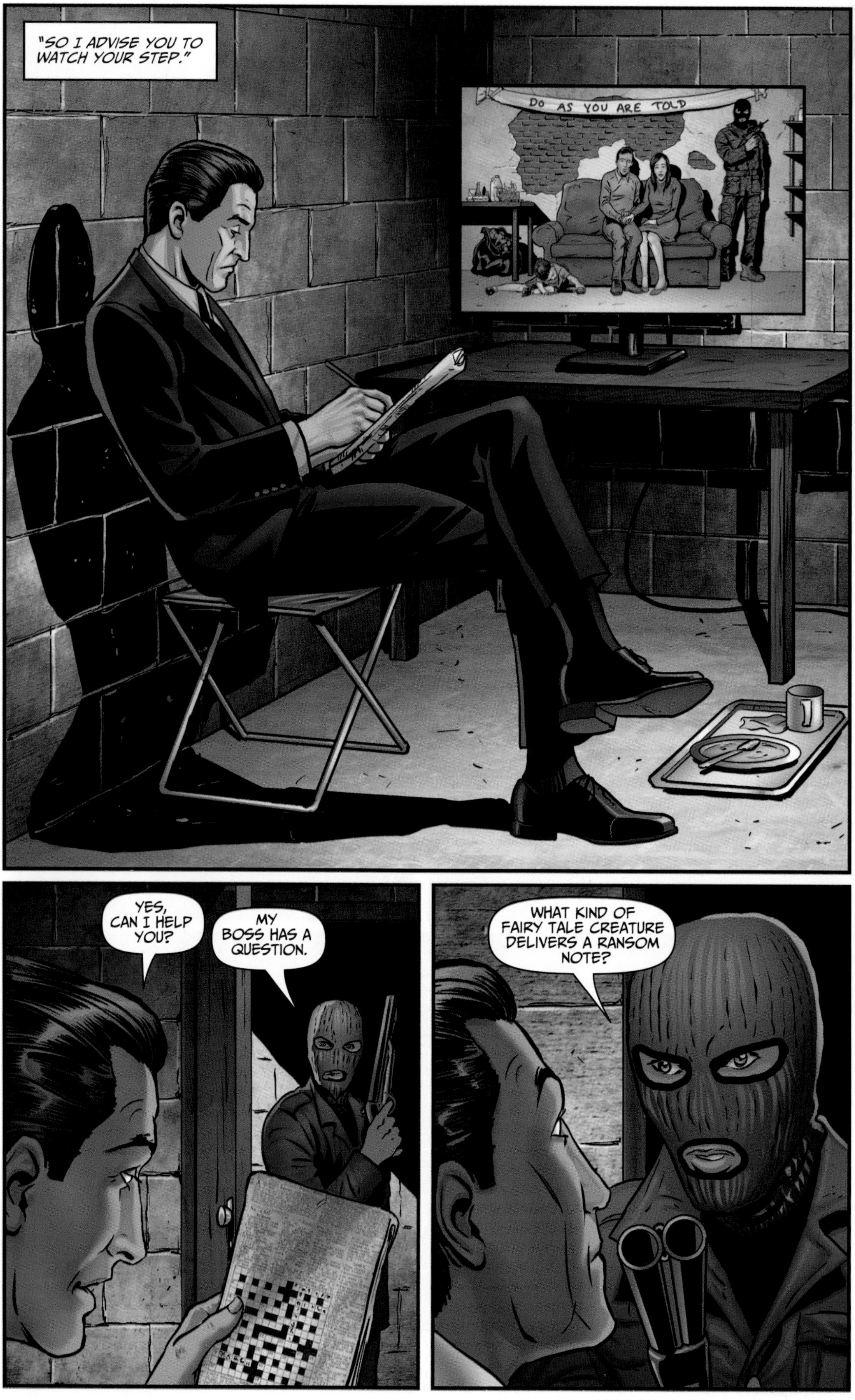
"SO I ADVISE YOU TO WATCH YOUR STEP."
DO AS YOU ARE TOLD
YES, CAN I HELP YOU?
MY BOSS HAS A QUESTION.
WHAT KIND OF FAIRY TALE CREATURE DELIVERS A RANSOM NOTE?

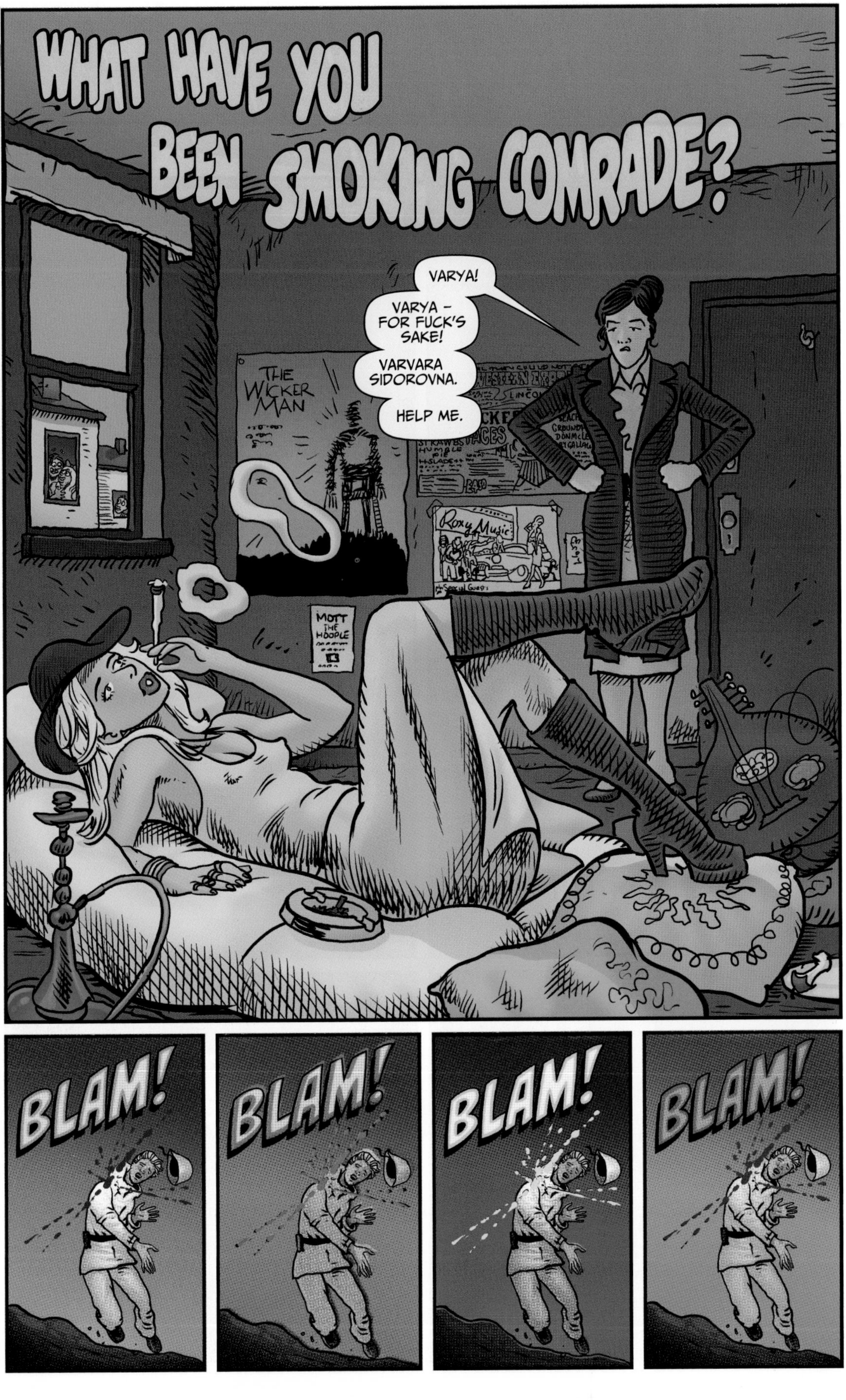
WHAT HAVE YOU BEEN SMOKING COMRADE?
VARYA!
VARYA – FOR FUCK'S SAKE!
VARVARA SIDOROVNA.
HELP ME.
THE WICKER MAN
Roxy Music
MOTT THE HOOPLE
BLAM!
BLAM!
BLAM!
BLAM!

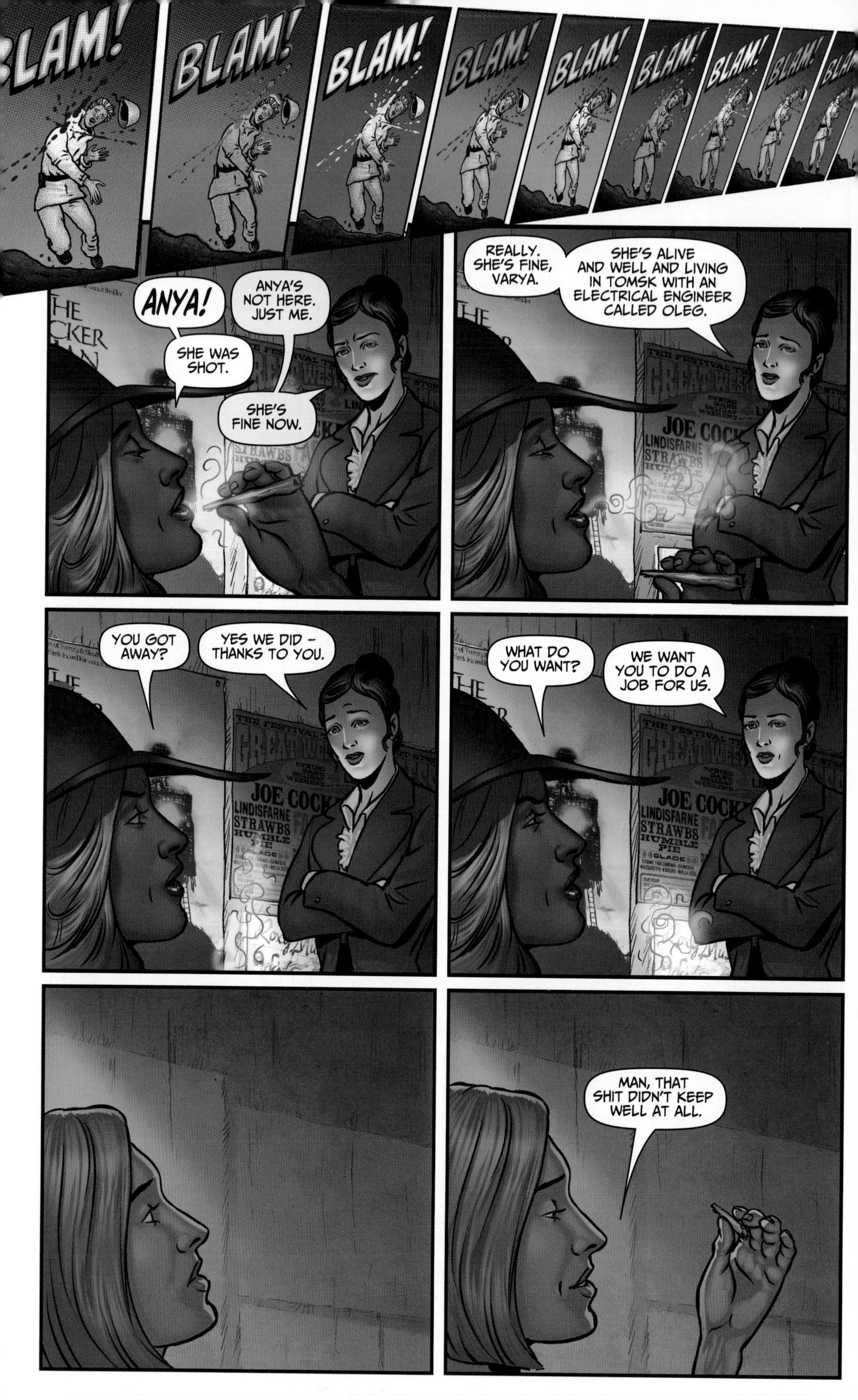
BLAM!
BLAM!
BLAM!
BLAM!
BLAM!
BLAM!
BLAM!
BLAM!
ANYA!
SHE WAS SHOT.
ANYA'S NOT HERE. JUST ME.
SHE'S FINE NOW.
REALLY. SHE'S FINE, VARYA.
SHE'S ALIVE AND WELL AND LIVING IN TOMSK WITH AN ELECTRICAL ENGINEER CALLED OLEG.
YOU GOT AWAY?
YES WE DID - THANKS TO YOU.
WHAT DO YOU WANT?
WE WANT YOU TO DO A JOB FOR US.
MAN, THAT SHIT DIDN'T KEEP WELL AT ALL.

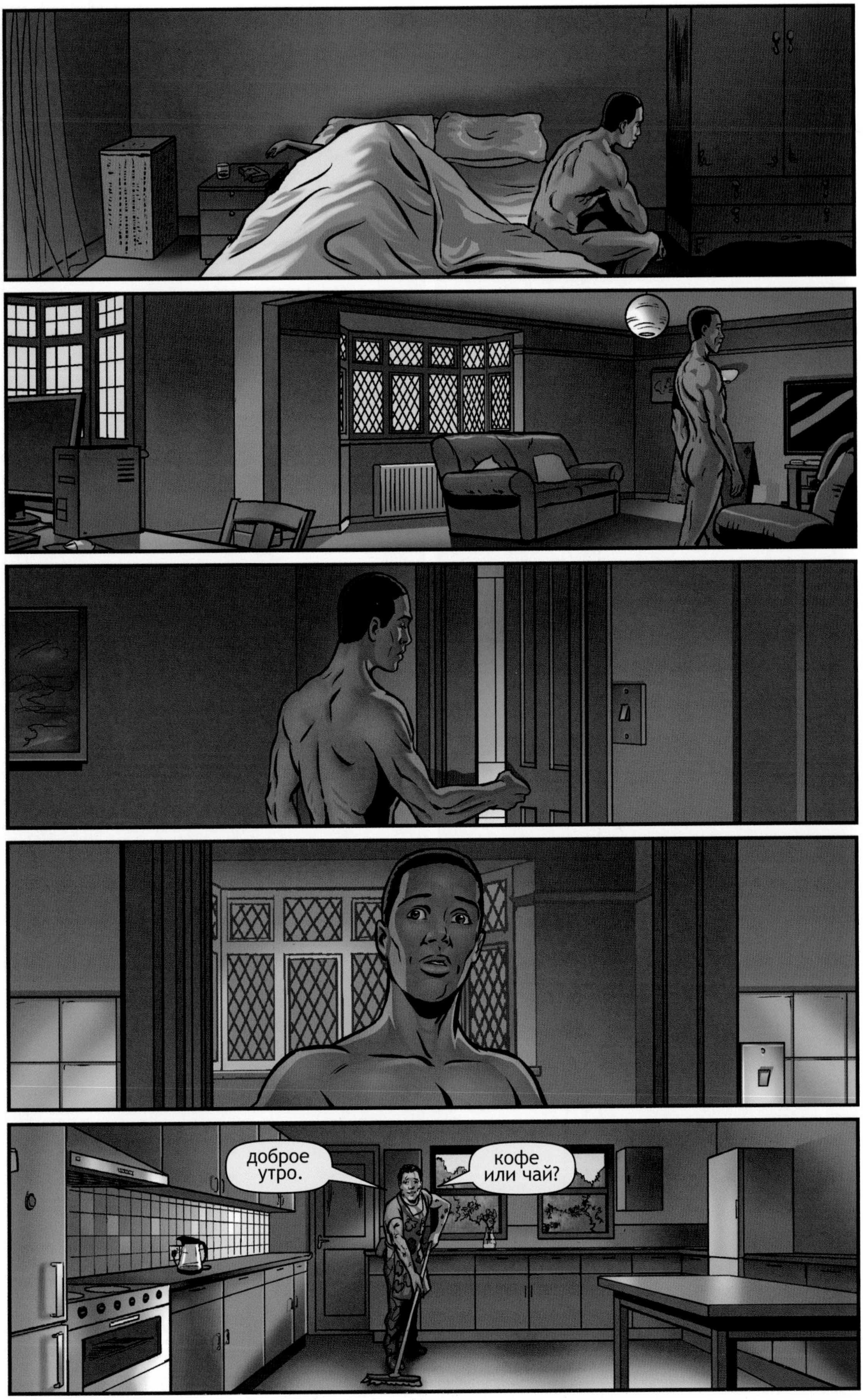
доброе утро.
кофе или чай?

BEV?
HMNNN?
WHY IS THERE A RUSSIAN GANGSTER IN YOUR KITCHEN?
I CAN EXPLAIN.
WHAT?
YOU HAD THEM ALL HERE – UNDER CONTROL?
AND YOU DIDN'T THINK TO TELL ME?
ALL SHALL LOVE ME AND DESPAIR
AND WHAT WOULD YOU HAVE DONE?
UM...
YEAH?
I'D AT LEAST HAVE COME ROUND AND ASKED THEM SOME QUESTIONS.

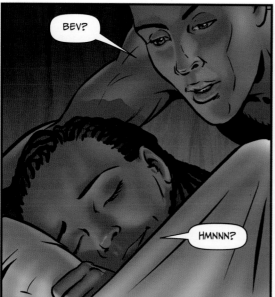

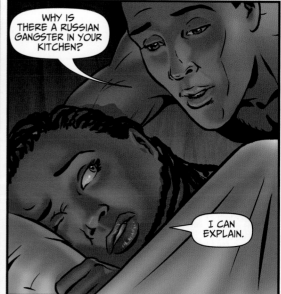

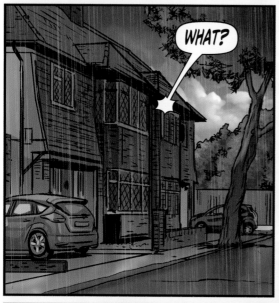

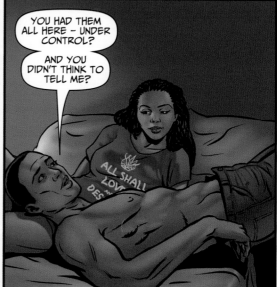

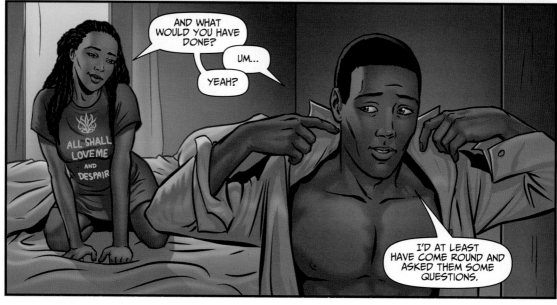

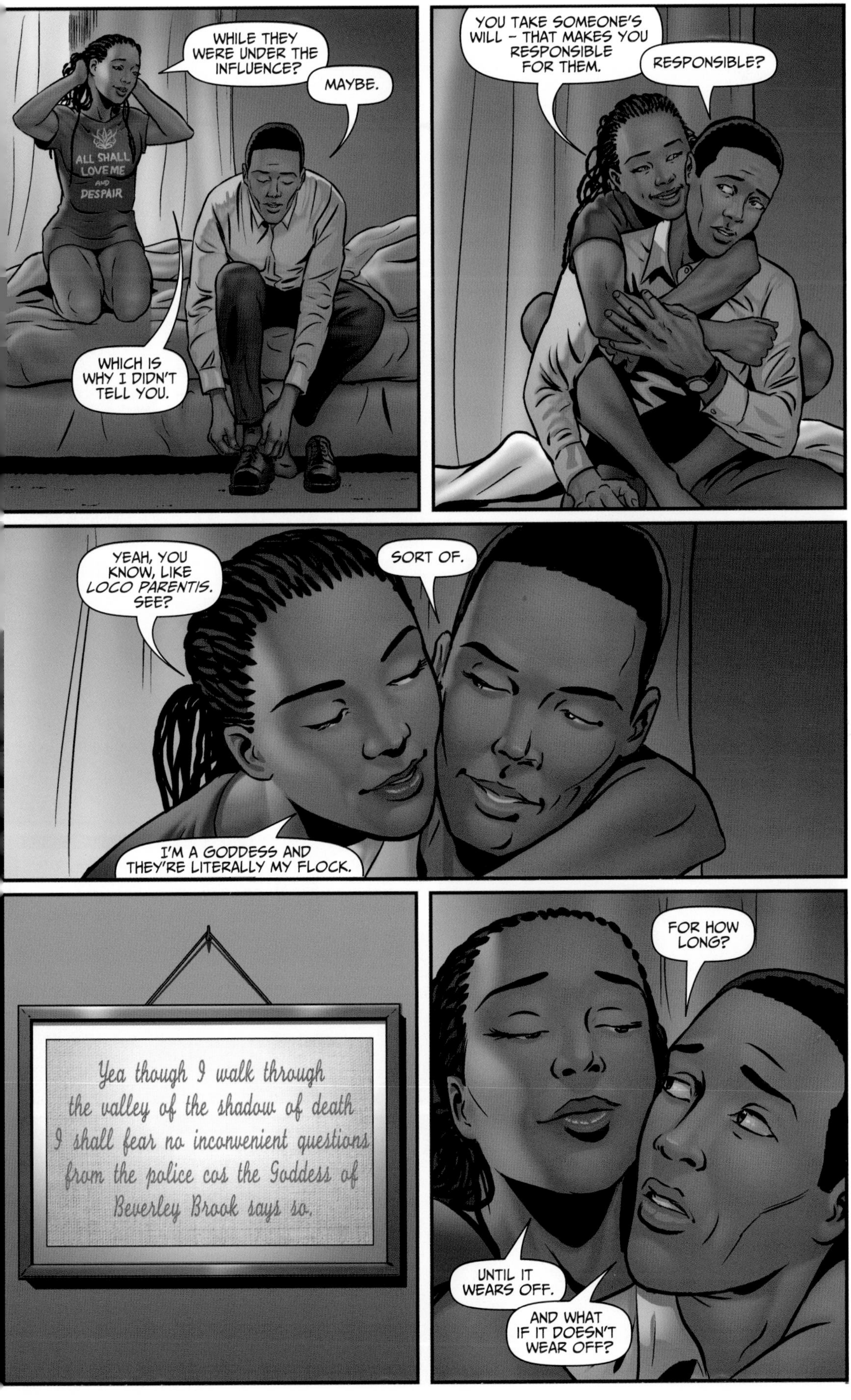
WHILE THEY WERE UNDER THE INFLUENCE?
ALL SHALL LOVE ME AND DESPAIR
MAYBE.
WHICH IS WHY I DIDN'T TELL YOU.
YOU TAKE SOMEONE'S WILL – THAT MAKES YOU RESPONSIBLE FOR THEM.
RESPONSIBLE?
YEAH, YOU KNOW, LIKE LOCO PARENTIS. SEE?
SORT OF.
I'M A GODDESS AND THEY'RE LITERALLY MY FLOCK.
Yea though I walk through the valley of the shadow of death I shall fear no inconvenient questions from the police cos the Goddess of Beverley Brook says so.
FOR HOW LONG?
UNTIL IT WEARS OFF.
AND WHAT IF IT DOESN'T WEAR OFF?

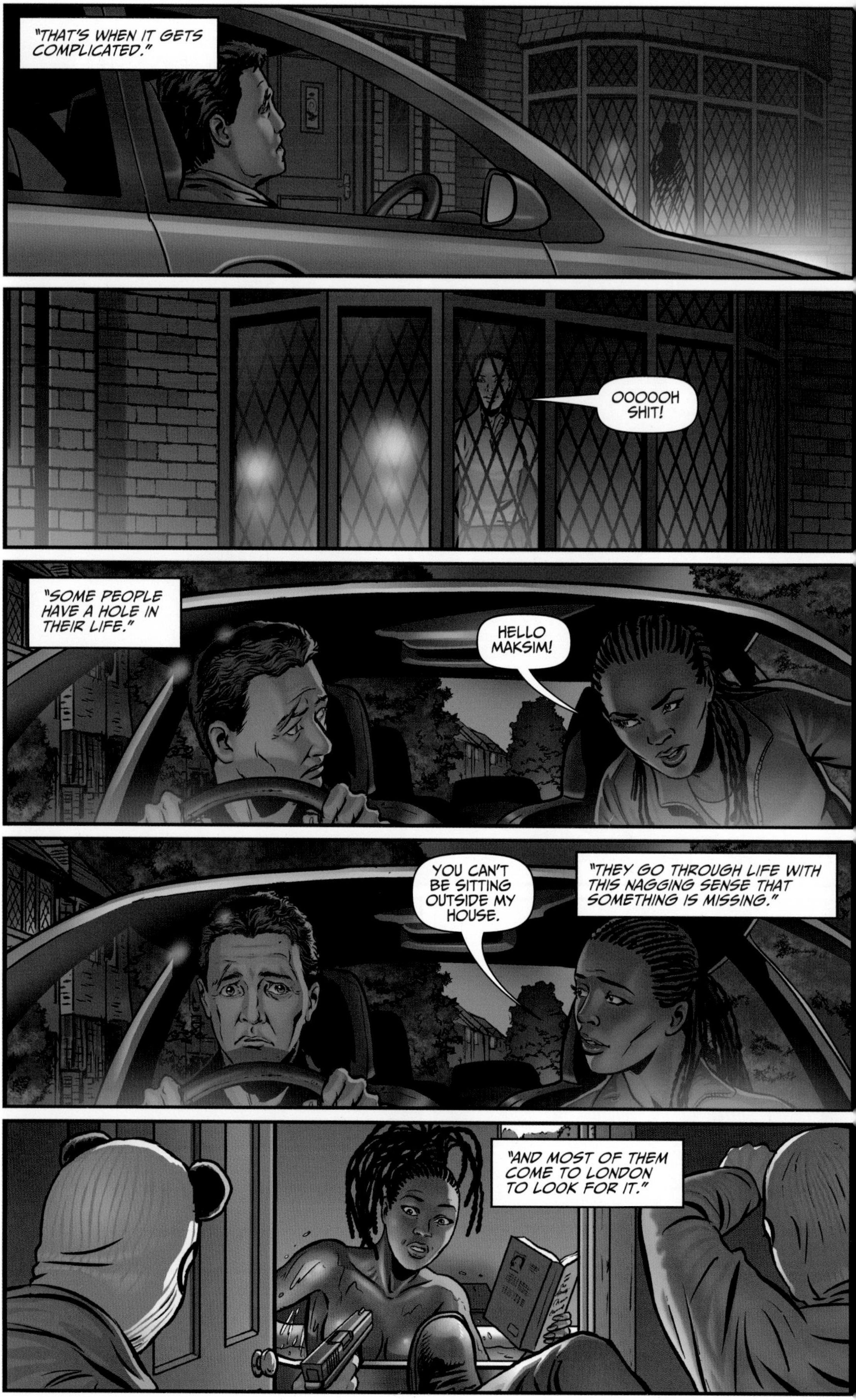
"THAT'S WHEN IT GETS COMPLICATED."
OOOOOH SHIT!
"SOME PEOPLE HAVE A HOLE IN THEIR LIFE."
HELLO MAKSIM!
YOU CAN'T BE SITTING OUTSIDE MY HOUSE.
"THEY GO THROUGH LIFE WITH THIS NAGGING SENSE THAT SOMETHING IS MISSING."
"AND MOST OF THEM COME TO LONDON TO LOOK FOR IT."

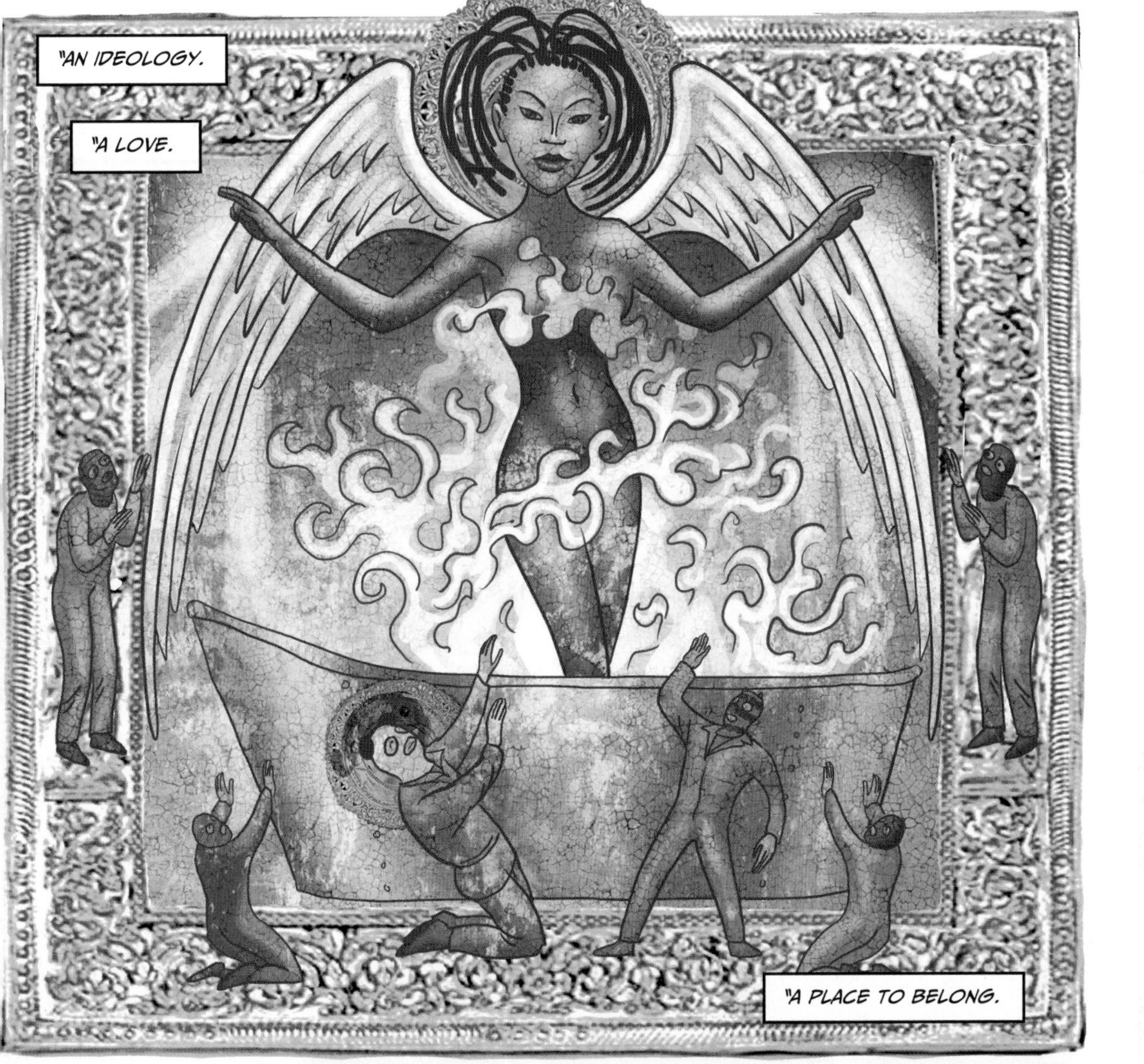
"AN IDEOLOGY.
"A LOVE.
"A PLACE TO BELONG.

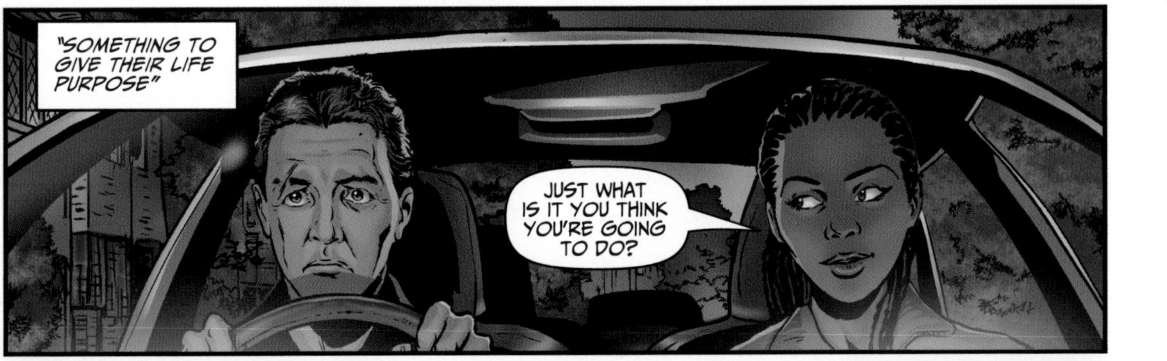
"SOMETHING TO GIVE THEIR LIFE PURPOSE"
JUST WHAT IS IT YOU THINK YOU'RE GOING TO DO?

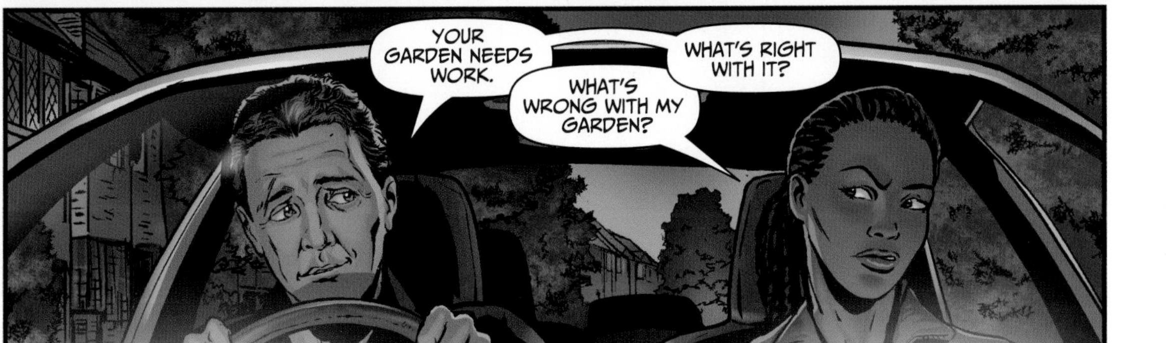
YOUR GARDEN NEEDS WORK.
WHAT'S WRONG WITH MY GARDEN?
WHAT'S RIGHT WITH IT?

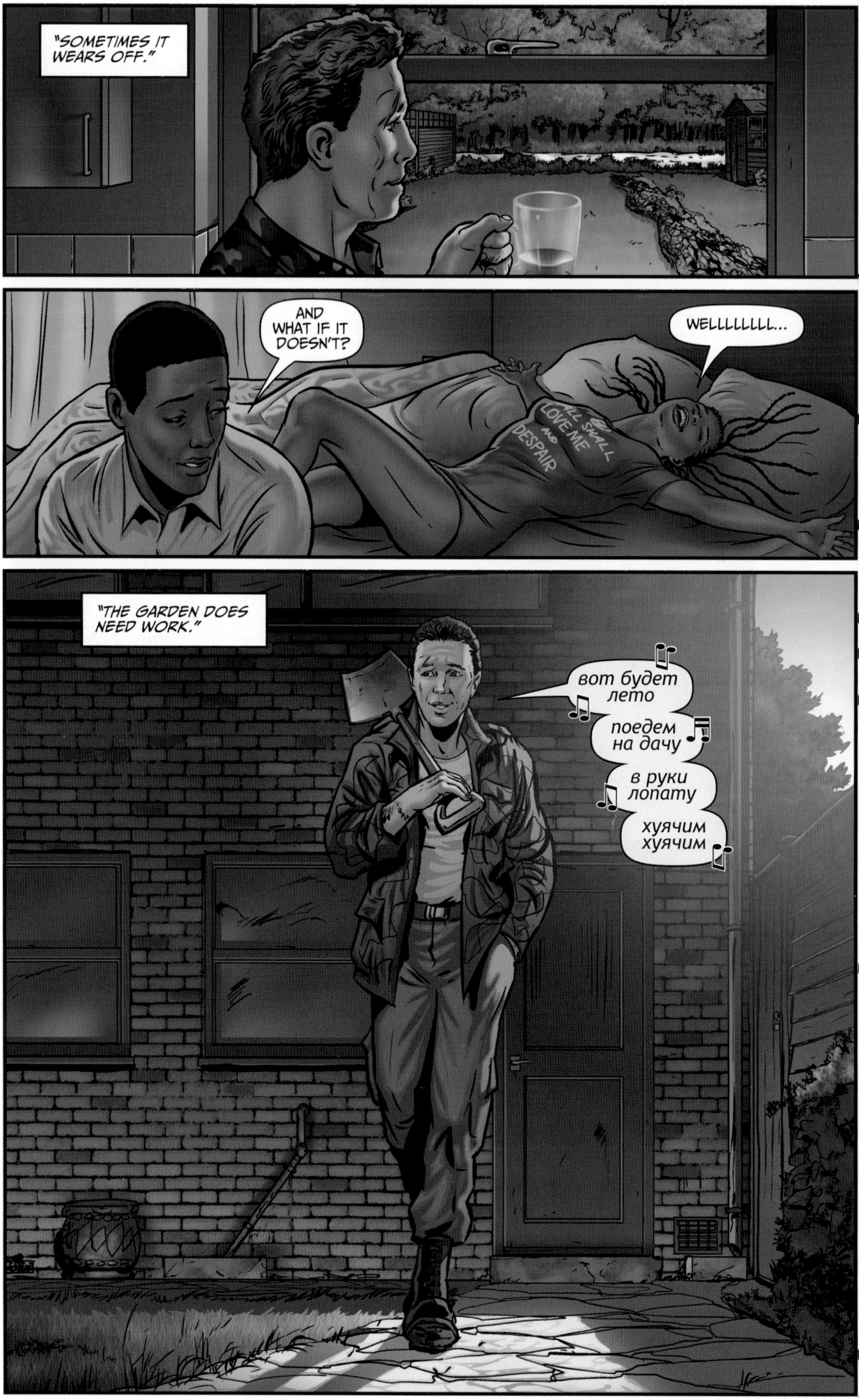
"SOMETIMES IT WEARS OFF."
AND WHAT IF IT DOESN'T?
WELLLLLLLLL...
ALL SHALL LOVE ME AND DESPAIR
"THE GARDEN DOES NEED WORK."
вот будет лето
поедем на дачу
в руки лопату
хуячим хуячим

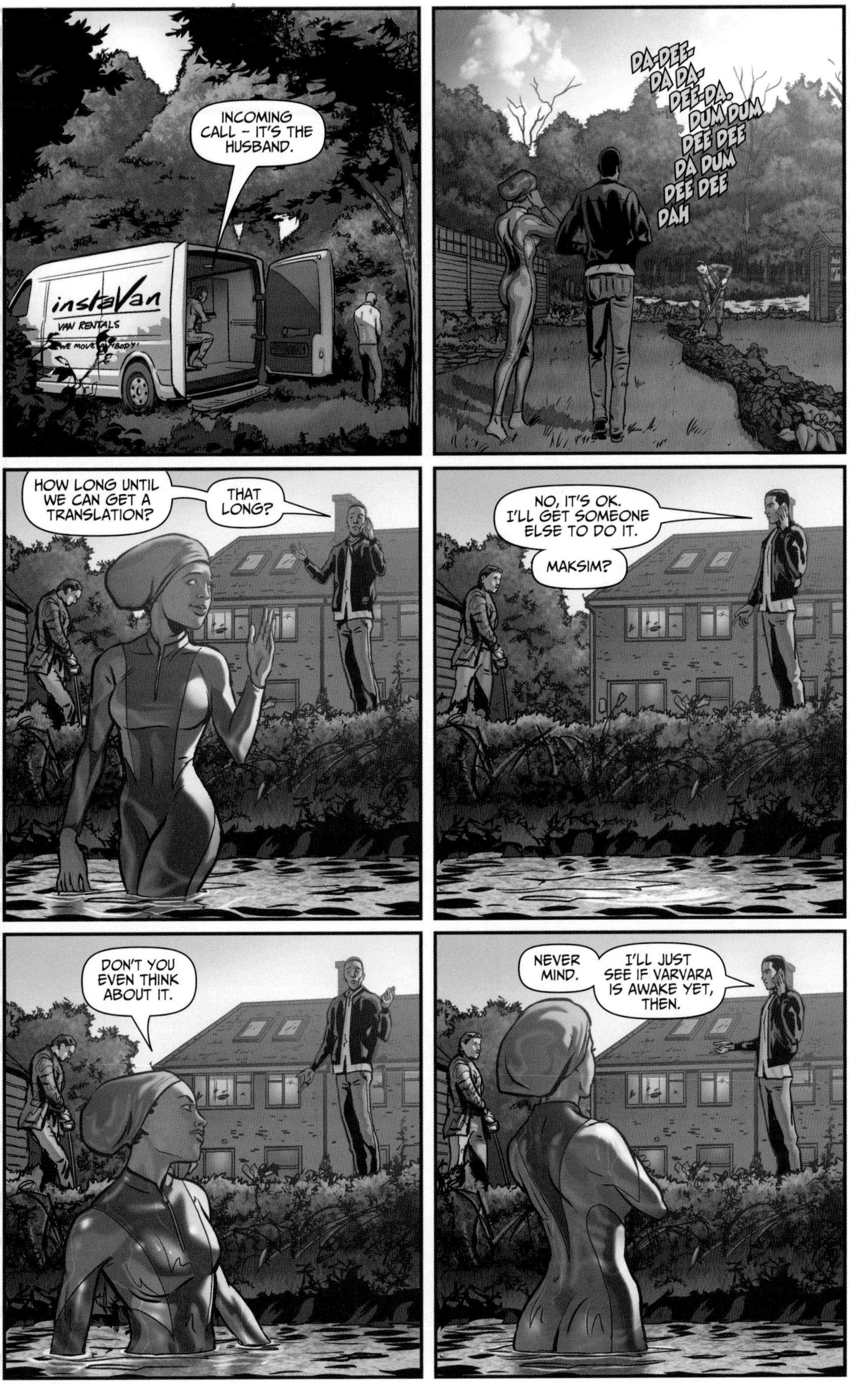
INCOMING CALL – IT'S THE HUSBAND.
instaVan
VAN RENTALS
DA-DEE-DA DA-DEE-DA. DUM DUM DEE DEE DA DUM DEE DEE DAH
HOW LONG UNTIL WE CAN GET A TRANSLATION?
THAT LONG?
NO, IT'S OK. I'LL GET SOMEONE ELSE TO DO IT.
MAKSIM?
DON'T YOU EVEN THINK ABOUT IT.
NEVER MIND.
I'LL JUST SEE IF VARVARA IS AWAKE YET, THEN.

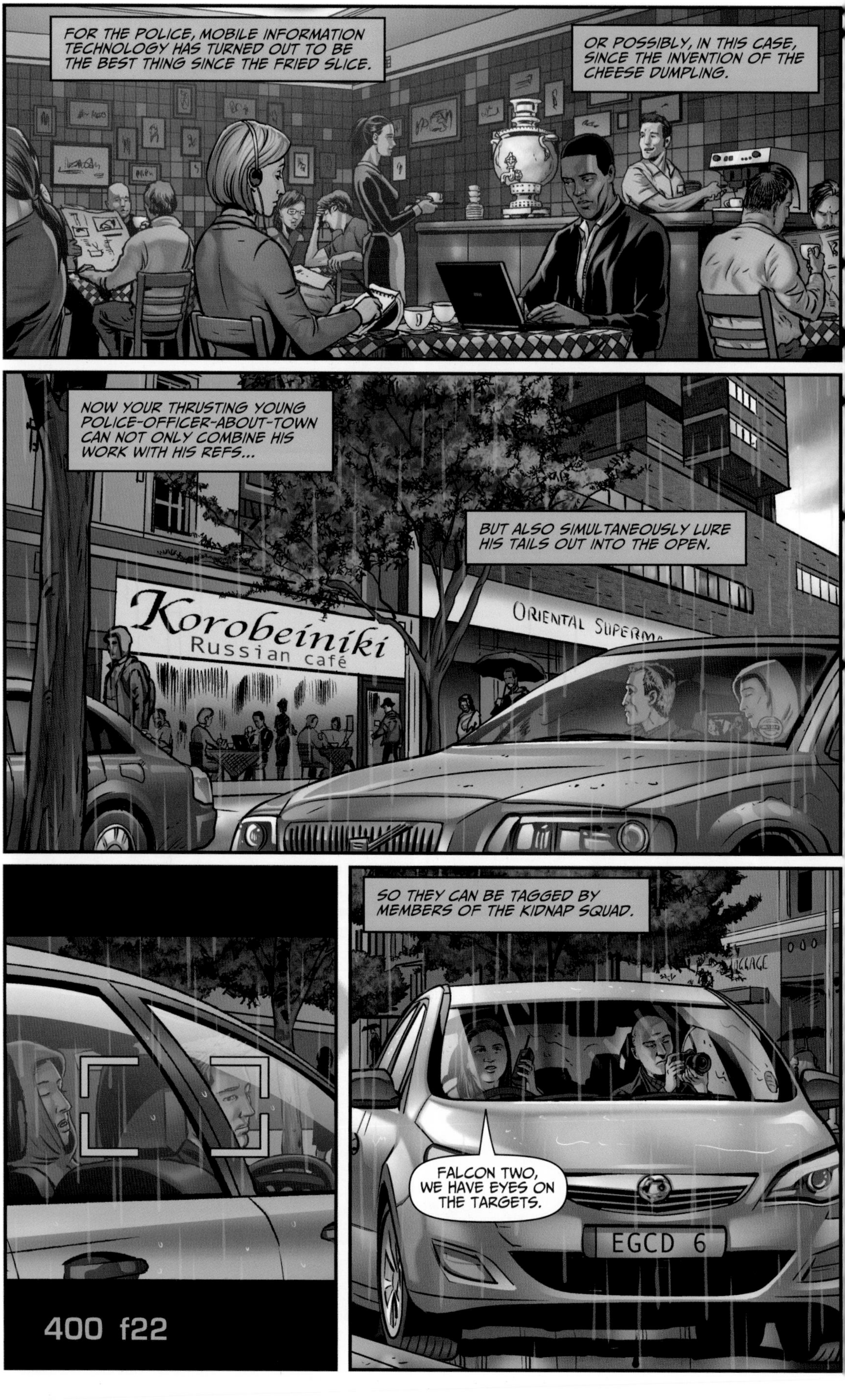
FOR THE POLICE, MOBILE INFORMATION TECHNOLOGY HAS TURNED OUT TO BE THE BEST THING SINCE THE FRIED SLICE.
OR POSSIBLY, IN THIS CASE, SINCE THE INVENTION OF THE CHEESE DUMPLING.
NOW YOUR THRUSTING YOUNG POLICE-OFFICER-ABOUT-TOWN CAN NOT ONLY COMBINE HIS WORK WITH HIS REFS...
BUT ALSO SIMULTANEOUSLY LURE HIS TAILS OUT INTO THE OPEN.
Korobeiniki
Russian café
ORIENTAL
400 f22
SO THEY CAN BE TAGGED BY MEMBERS OF THE KIDNAP SQUAD.
FALCON TWO, WE HAVE EYES ON THE TARGETS.
EGCD 6

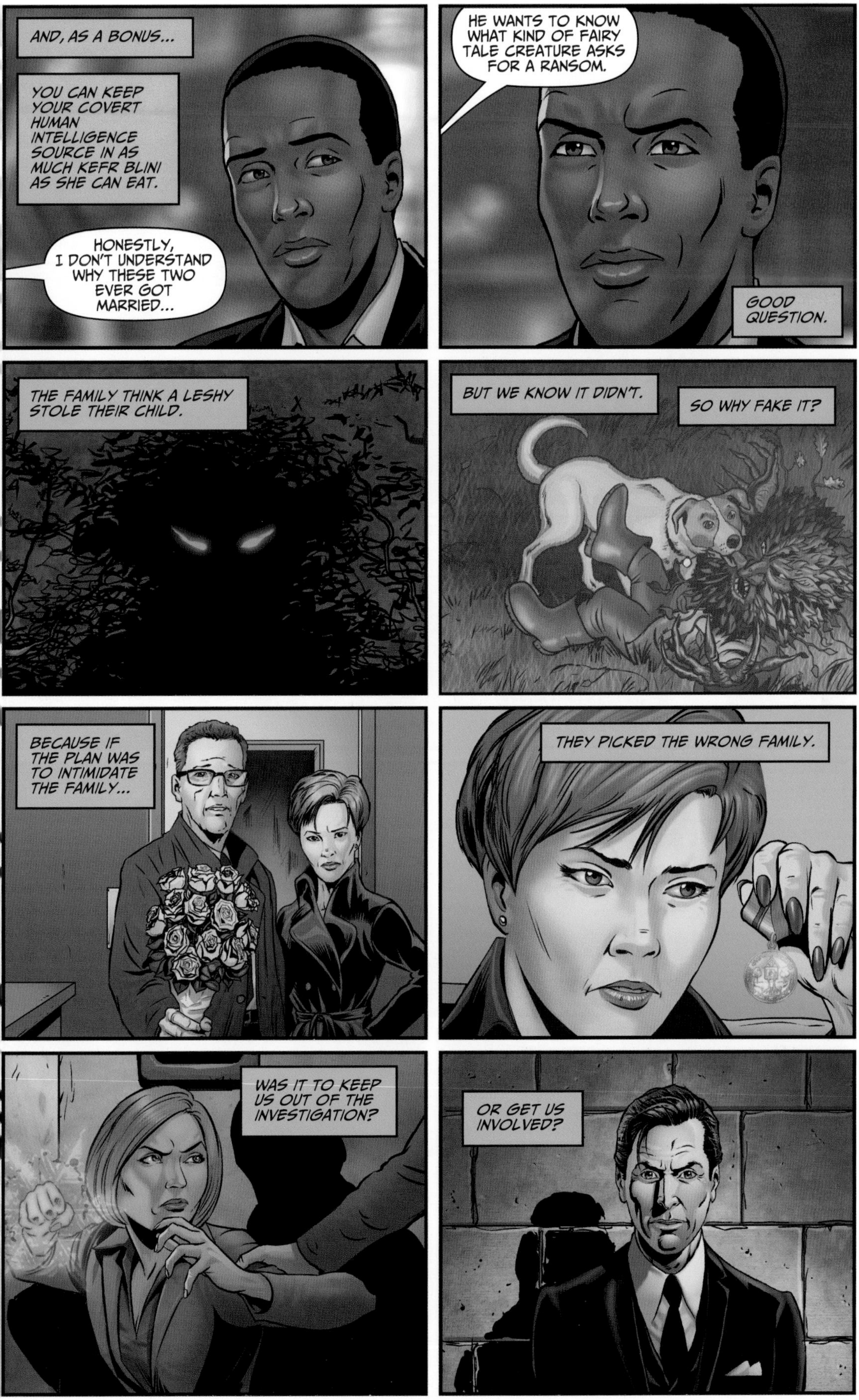
AND, AS A BONUS...
YOU CAN KEEP YOUR COVERT HUMAN INTELLIGENCE SOURCE IN AS MUCH KEFR BLINI AS SHE CAN EAT.
HONESTLY, I DON'T UNDERSTAND WHY THESE TWO EVER GOT MARRIED...
HE WANTS TO KNOW WHAT KIND OF FAIRY TALE CREATURE ASKS FOR A RANSOM.
GOOD QUESTION.
THE FAMILY THINK A LESHY STOLE THEIR CHILD.
BUT WE KNOW IT DIDN'T.
SO WHY FAKE IT?
BECAUSE IF THE PLAN WAS TO INTIMIDATE THE FAMILY...
THEY PICKED THE WRONG FAMILY.
WAS IT TO KEEP US OUT OF THE INVESTIGATION?
OR GET US INVOLVED?

AND IF SO...

WHO BENEFITS?

ARE WE READY FOR THE MOVE?

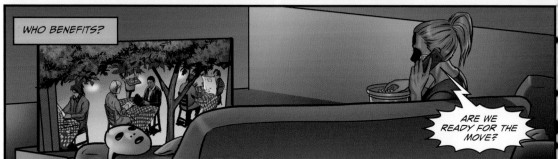

WE MIGHT WANT TO HOLD OFF A BIT.

I THINK PETER'S ABOUT TO DO SOMETHING HASTY.

HOW CAN YOU TELL?

"IT'S A MONTH WITH AN 'R' IN IT."

HAVE THEY SAID ANYTHING THAT PROVES THEY'RE HOLDING NIGHTINGALE?

I'M SORRY— NO.

I WISH I KNEW HOW THEY WERE HOLDING HIM.

HE'S NOT SOMEONE YOU CAN JUST KEEP IN A BOX.

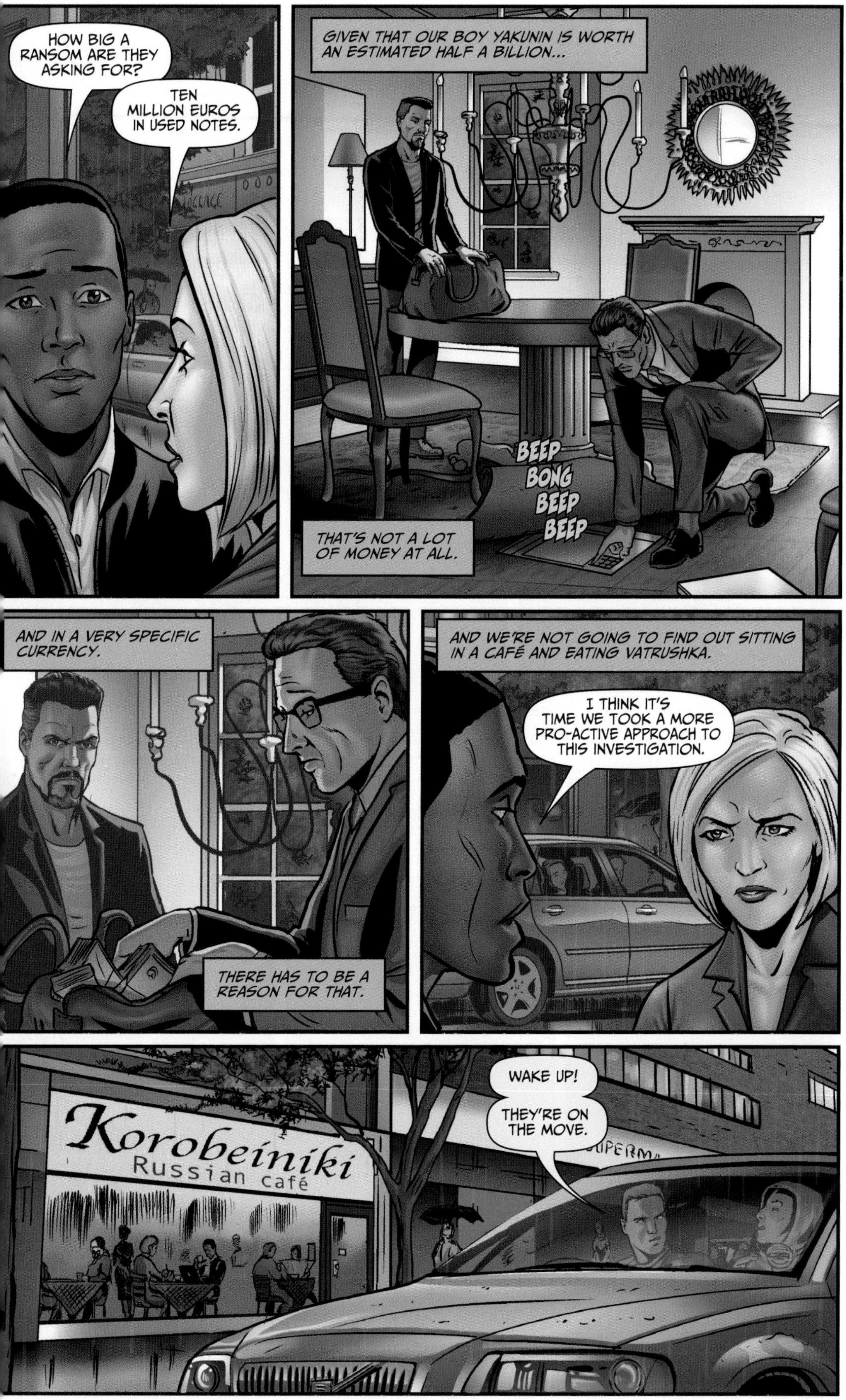
HOW BIG A RANSOM ARE THEY ASKING FOR?
TEN MILLION EUROS IN USED NOTES.
GIVEN THAT OUR BOY YAKUNIN IS WORTH AN ESTIMATED HALF A BILLION...
BEEP BONG BEEP BEEP
THAT'S NOT A LOT OF MONEY AT ALL.
AND IN A VERY SPECIFIC CURRENCY.
THERE HAS TO BE A REASON FOR THAT.
AND WE'RE NOT GOING TO FIND OUT SITTING IN A CAFÉ AND EATING VATRUSHKA.
I THINK IT'S TIME WE TOOK A MORE PRO-ACTIVE APPROACH TO THIS INVESTIGATION.
Korobeiniki
Russian café
WAKE UP!
THEY'RE ON THE MOVE.

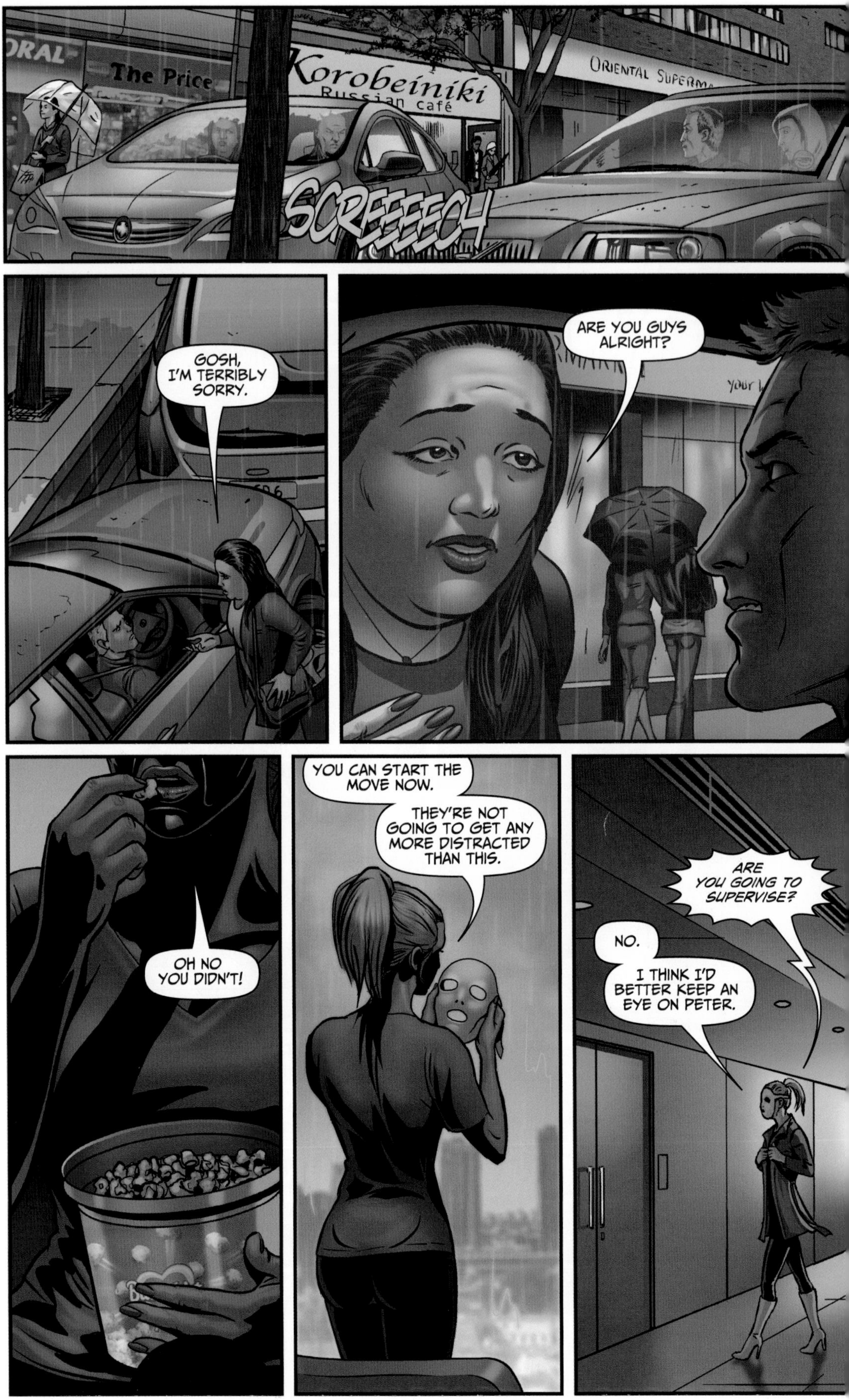

ORAL
The Price
Korobeiniki
Russian café
ORIENTAL SUPERM
SCREEEEECH
GOSH, I'M TERRIBLY SORRY.
ARE YOU GUYS ALRIGHT?
OH NO YOU DIDN'T!
YOU CAN START THE MOVE NOW.
THEY'RE NOT GOING TO GET ANY MORE DISTRACTED THAN THIS.
ARE YOU GOING TO SUPERVISE?
NO.
I THINK I'D BETTER KEEP AN EYE ON PETER.

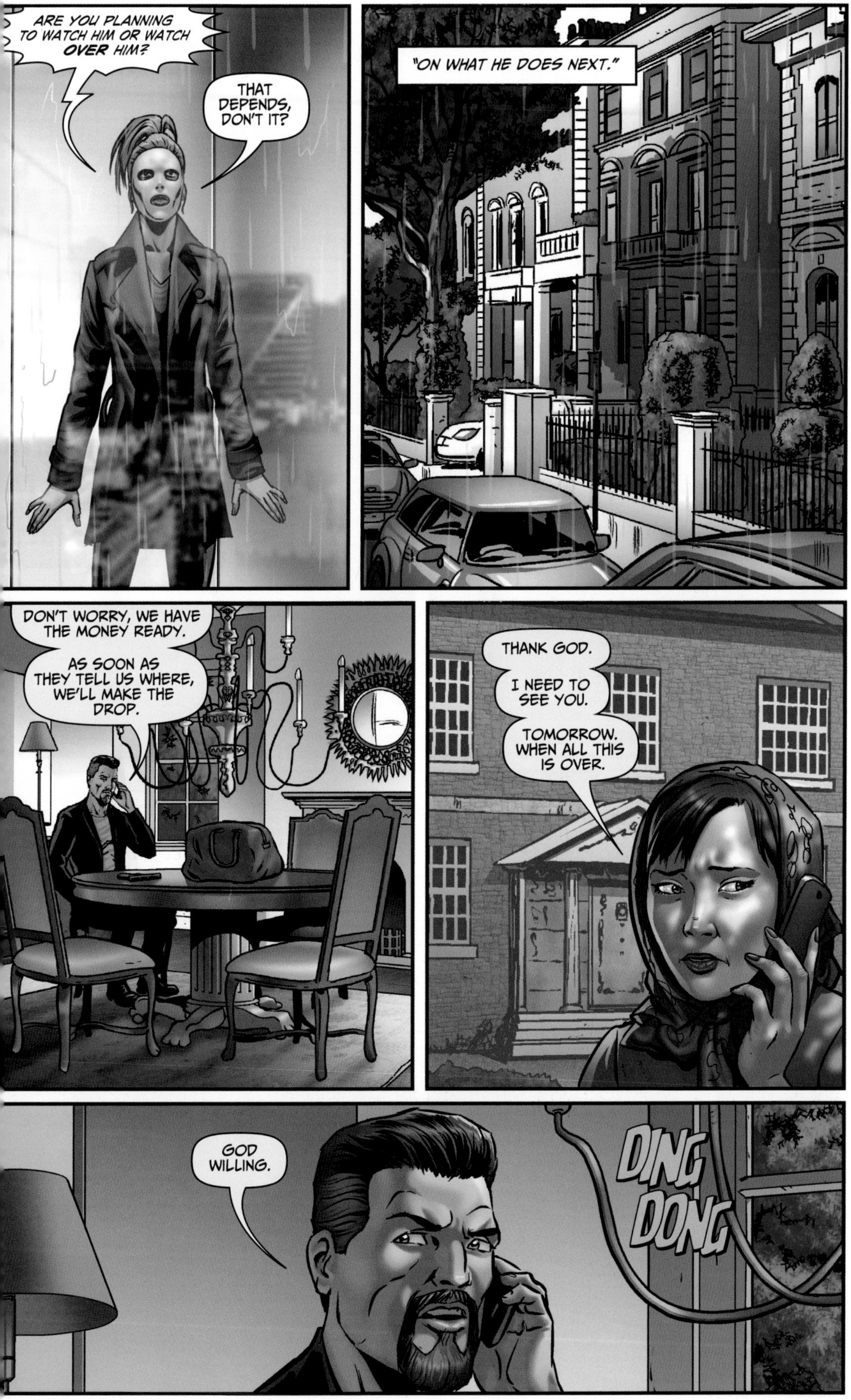
ARE YOU PLANNING TO WATCH HIM OR WATCH OVER HIM?
THAT DEPENDS, DON'T IT?
"ON WHAT HE DOES NEXT."
DON'T WORRY, WE HAVE THE MONEY READY.
AS SOON AS THEY TELL US WHERE, WE'LL MAKE THE DROP.
THANK GOD.
I NEED TO SEE YOU.
TOMORROW. WHEN ALL THIS IS OVER.
GOD WILLING.
DING DONG

DING DONG

IT'S ALWAYS EASIER DEALING WITH PROFESSIONAL CRIMINALS.

AMATEURS PANIC, REACT ON INSTINCT, BEHAVE STUPIDLY.

DING DONG

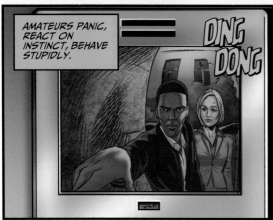

PROFESSIONALS THINK ABOUT THE CONSEQUENCES OF THEIR ACTIONS.

HI, MY NAME'S PETER GRANT, I'M WITH THE POLICE.

AND THIS IS VARVARA TAMONINA, MY DESIGNATED TRANSLATOR.

TRANSLATOR?

SHE'S FLUENT IN MORE THAN TWO MILLION FORMS OF COMMUNICATION.

WHAT CAN I DO FOR YOU?

WELL MR. ZHIDANOV.

I THOUGHT IT WAS ABOUT TIME WE STOPPED FUCKING AROUND.

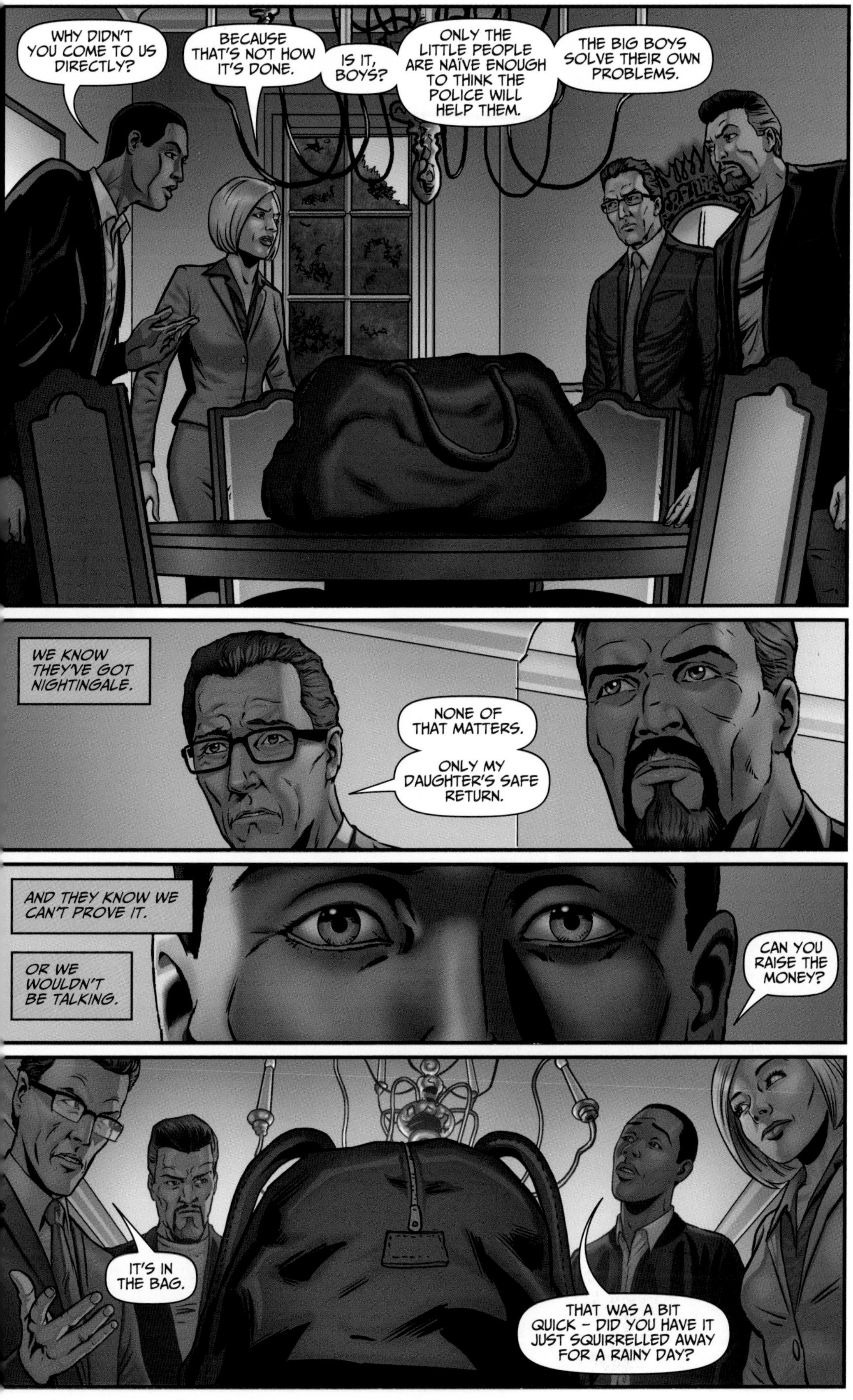
WHY DIDN'T YOU COME TO US DIRECTLY?
BECAUSE THAT'S NOT HOW IT'S DONE.
IS IT, BOYS?
ONLY THE LITTLE PEOPLE ARE NAÏVE ENOUGH TO THINK THE POLICE WILL HELP THEM.
THE BIG BOYS SOLVE THEIR OWN PROBLEMS.
WE KNOW THEY'VE GOT NIGHTINGALE.
NONE OF THAT MATTERS.
ONLY MY DAUGHTER'S SAFE RETURN.
AND THEY KNOW WE CAN'T PROVE IT.
OR WE WOULDN'T BE TALKING.
CAN YOU RAISE THE MONEY?
IT'S IN THE BAG.
THAT WAS A BIT QUICK - DID YOU HAVE IT JUST SQUIRRELLED AWAY FOR A RAINY DAY?

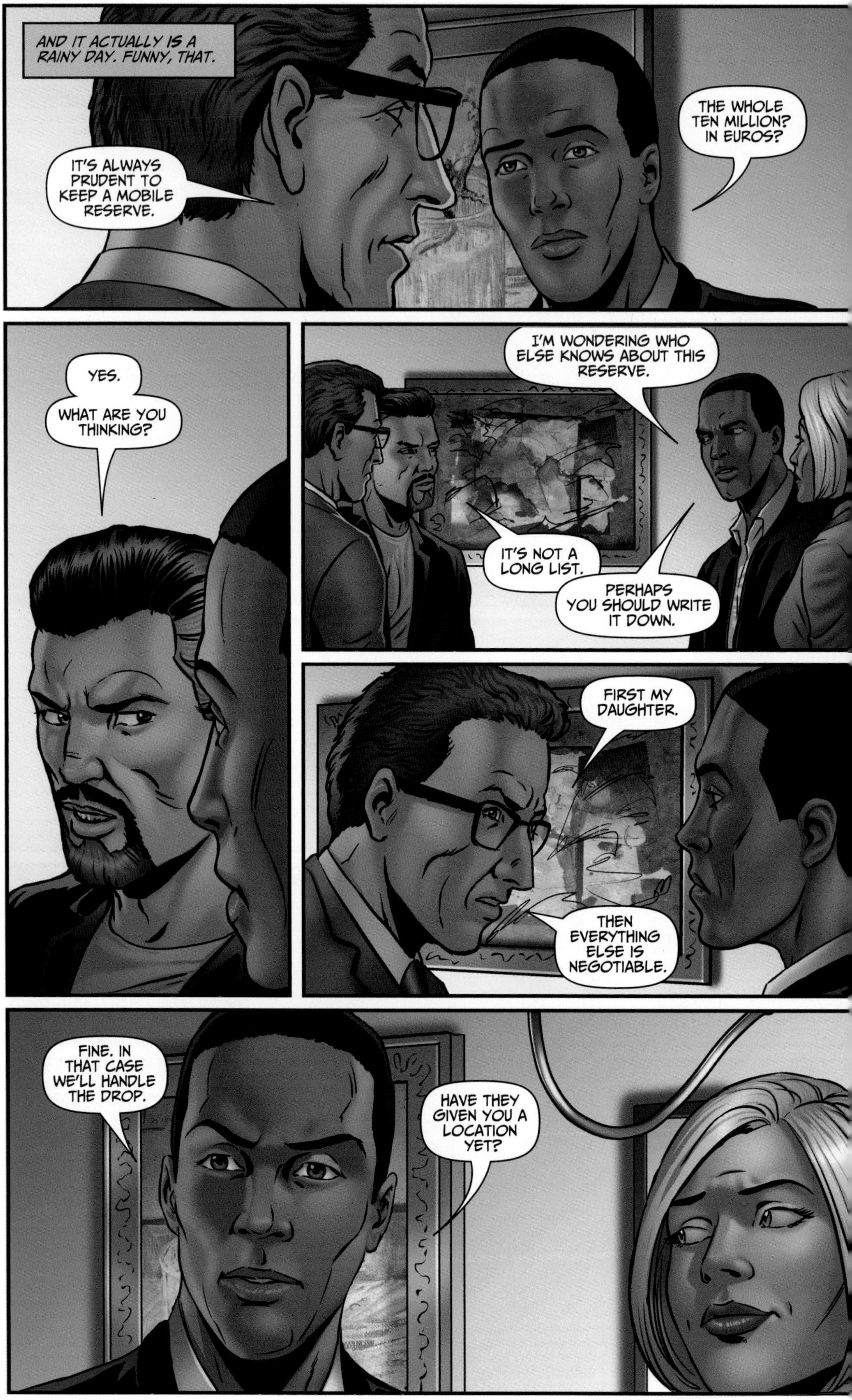
AND IT ACTUALLY IS A RAINY DAY. FUNNY, THAT.
IT'S ALWAYS PRUDENT TO KEEP A MOBILE RESERVE.
THE WHOLE TEN MILLION? IN EUROS?
YES.
WHAT ARE YOU THINKING?
I'M WONDERING WHO ELSE KNOWS ABOUT THIS RESERVE.
IT'S NOT A LONG LIST.
PERHAPS YOU SHOULD WRITE IT DOWN.
FIRST MY DAUGHTER.
THEN EVERYTHING ELSE IS NEGOTIABLE.
FINE. IN THAT CASE WE'LL HANDLE THE DROP.
HAVE THEY GIVEN YOU A LOCATION YET?

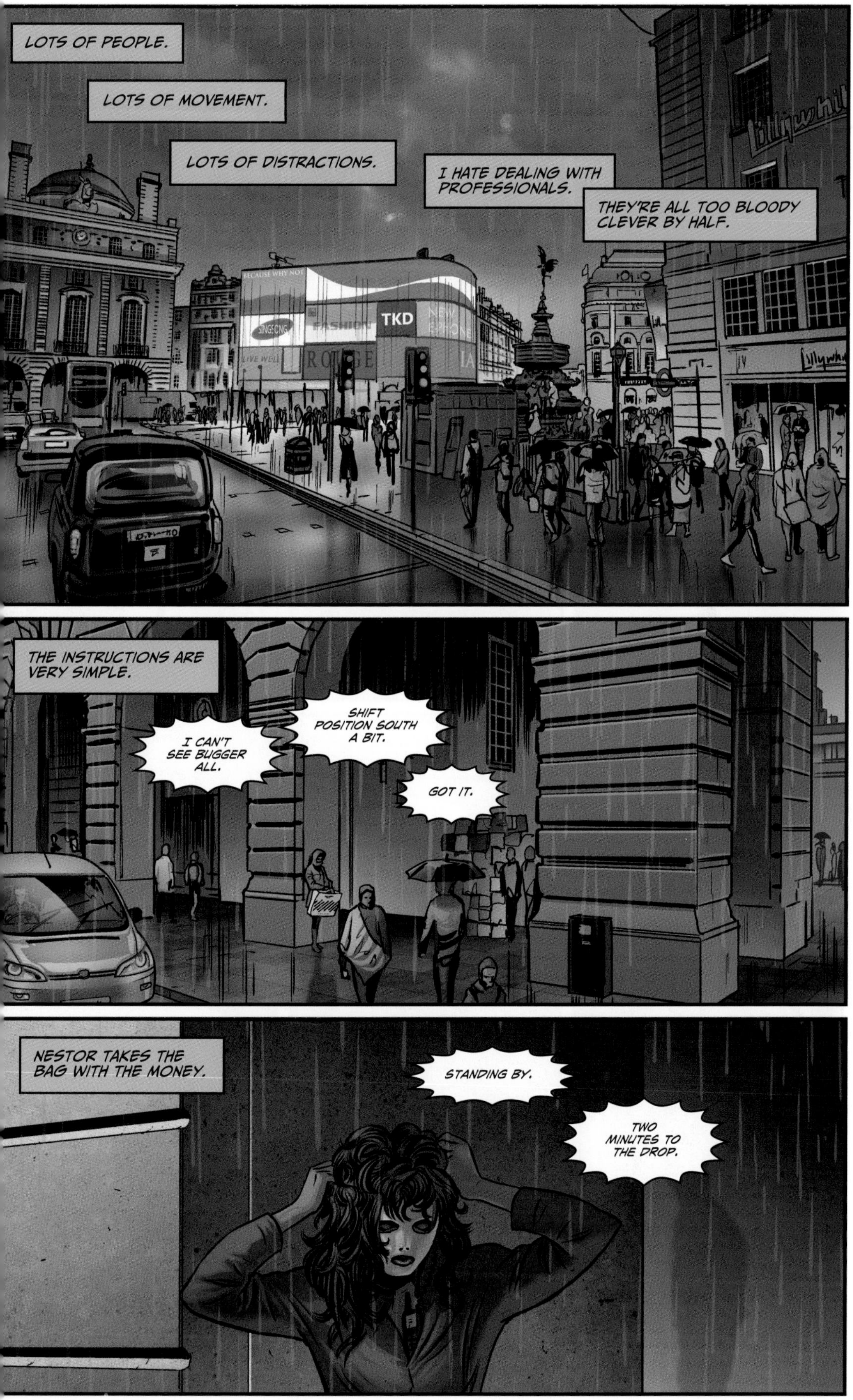
LOTS OF PEOPLE.
LOTS OF MOVEMENT.
LOTS OF DISTRACTIONS.
I HATE DEALING WITH PROFESSIONALS.
THEY'RE ALL TOO BLOODY CLEVER BY HALF.
THE INSTRUCTIONS ARE VERY SIMPLE.
I CAN'T SEE BUGGER ALL.
SHIFT POSITION SOUTH A BIT.
GOT IT.
NESTOR TAKES THE BAG WITH THE MONEY.
STANDING BY.
TWO MINUTES TO THE DROP.

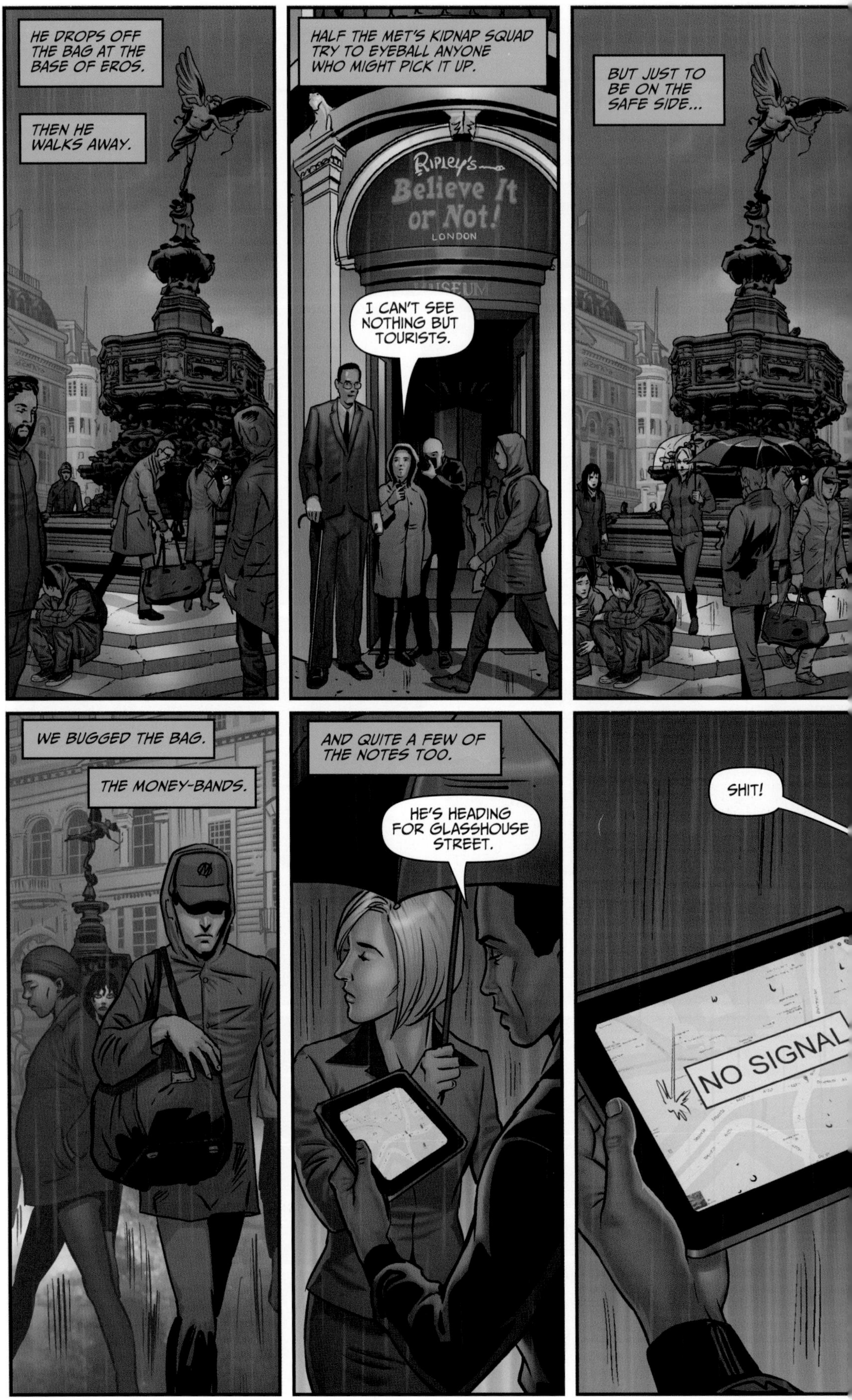
HE DROPS OFF THE BAG AT THE BASE OF EROS.
THEN HE WALKS AWAY.
HALF THE MET'S KIDNAP SQUAD TRY TO EYEBALL ANYONE WHO MIGHT PICK IT UP.
RIPLEY'S Believe It or Not! LONDON
I CAN'T SEE NOTHING BUT TOURISTS.
BUT JUST TO BE ON THE SAFE SIDE...
WE BUGGED THE BAG.
THE MONEY-BANDS.
AND QUITE A FEW OF THE NOTES TOO.
HE'S HEADING FOR GLASSHOUSE STREET.
SHIT!
NO SIGNAL

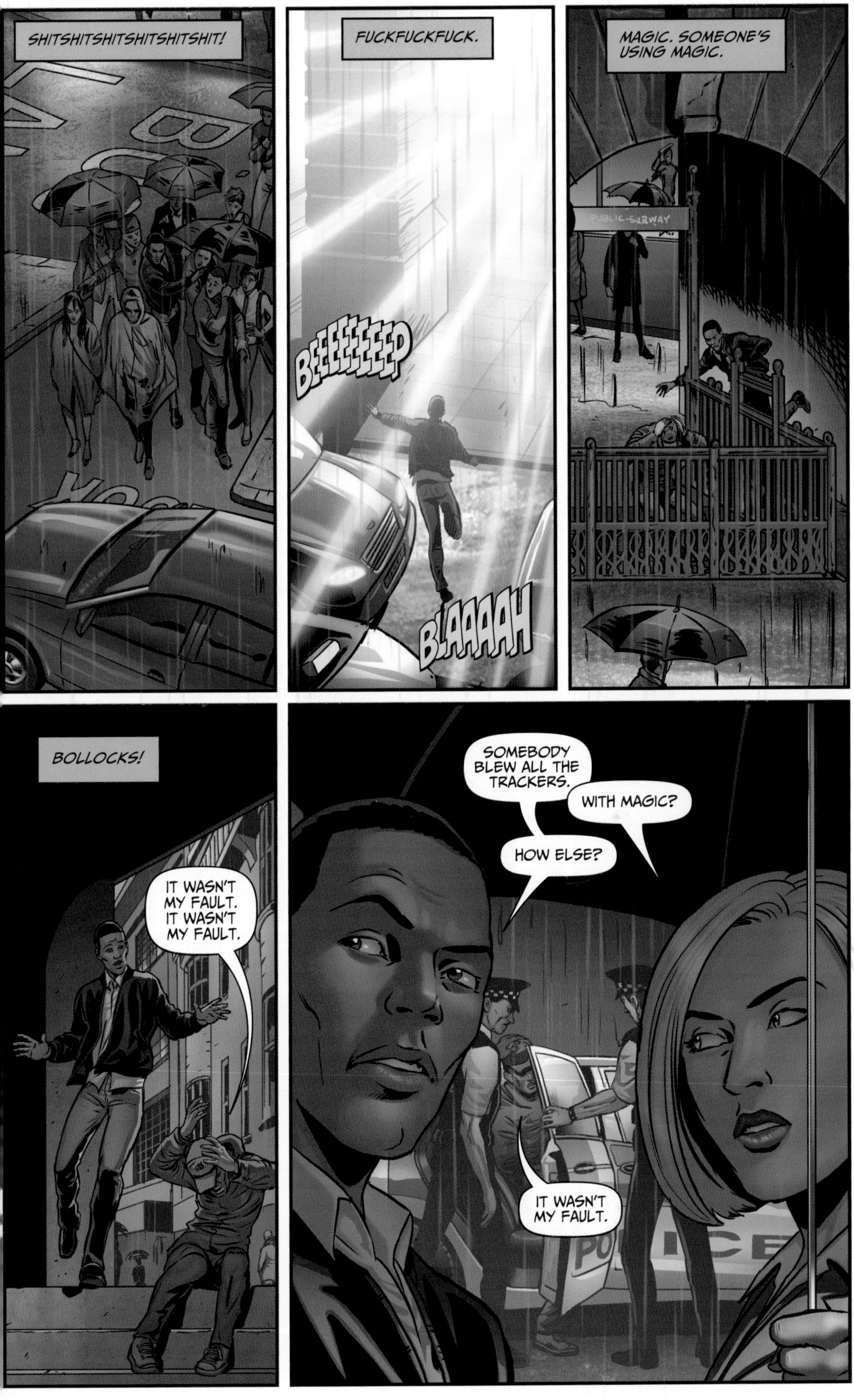
SHITSHITSHITSHITSHITSHIT!
FUCKFUCKFUCK.
BEEEEEEEP
BLAAAAH
MAGIC. SOMEONE'S USING MAGIC.
PUBLIC SUBWAY
BOLLOCKS!
IT WASN'T MY FAULT. IT WASN'T MY FAULT.
SOMEBODY BLEW ALL THE TRACKERS.
WITH MAGIC?
HOW ELSE?
IT WASN'T MY FAULT.
POLICE

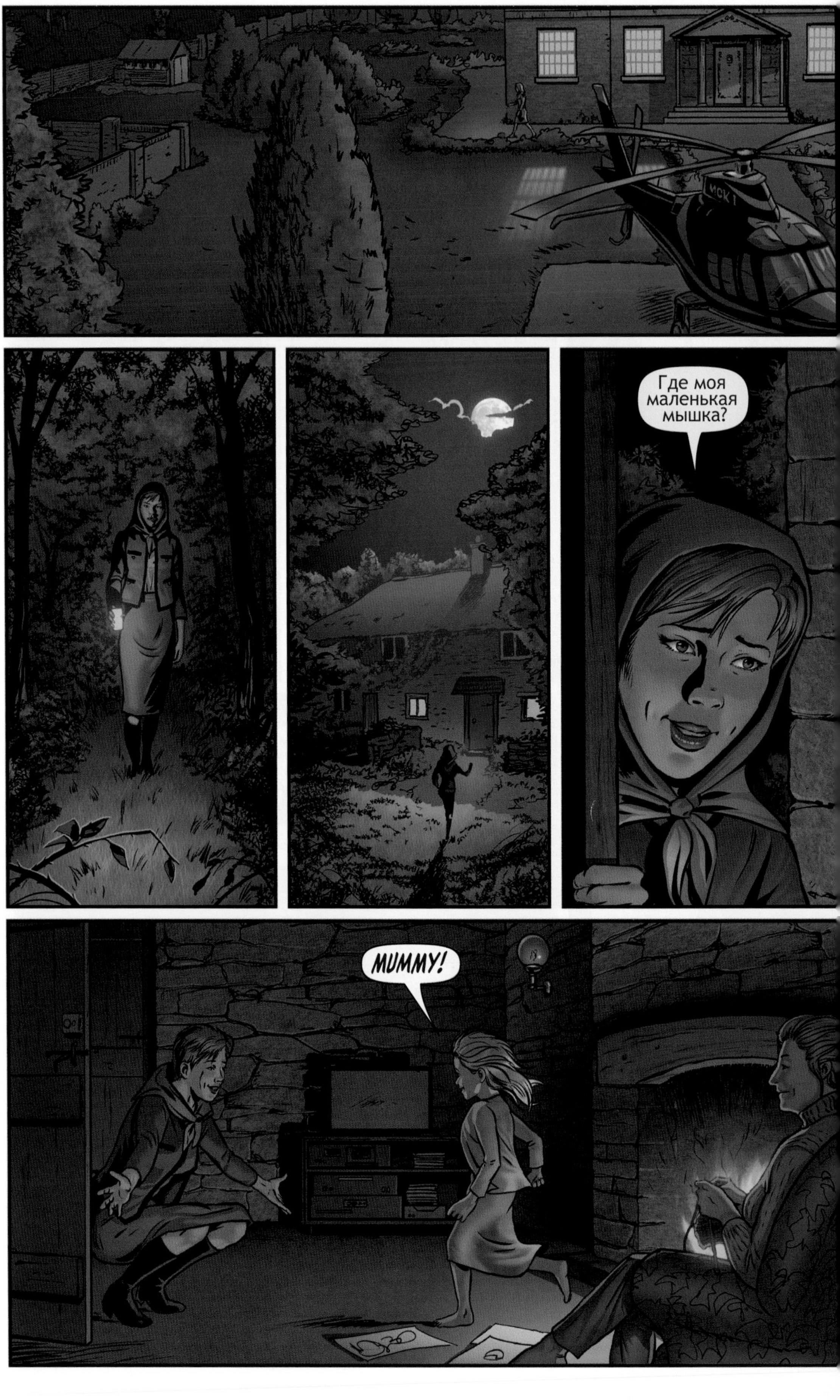
Где моя маленькая мышка?
MUMMY!

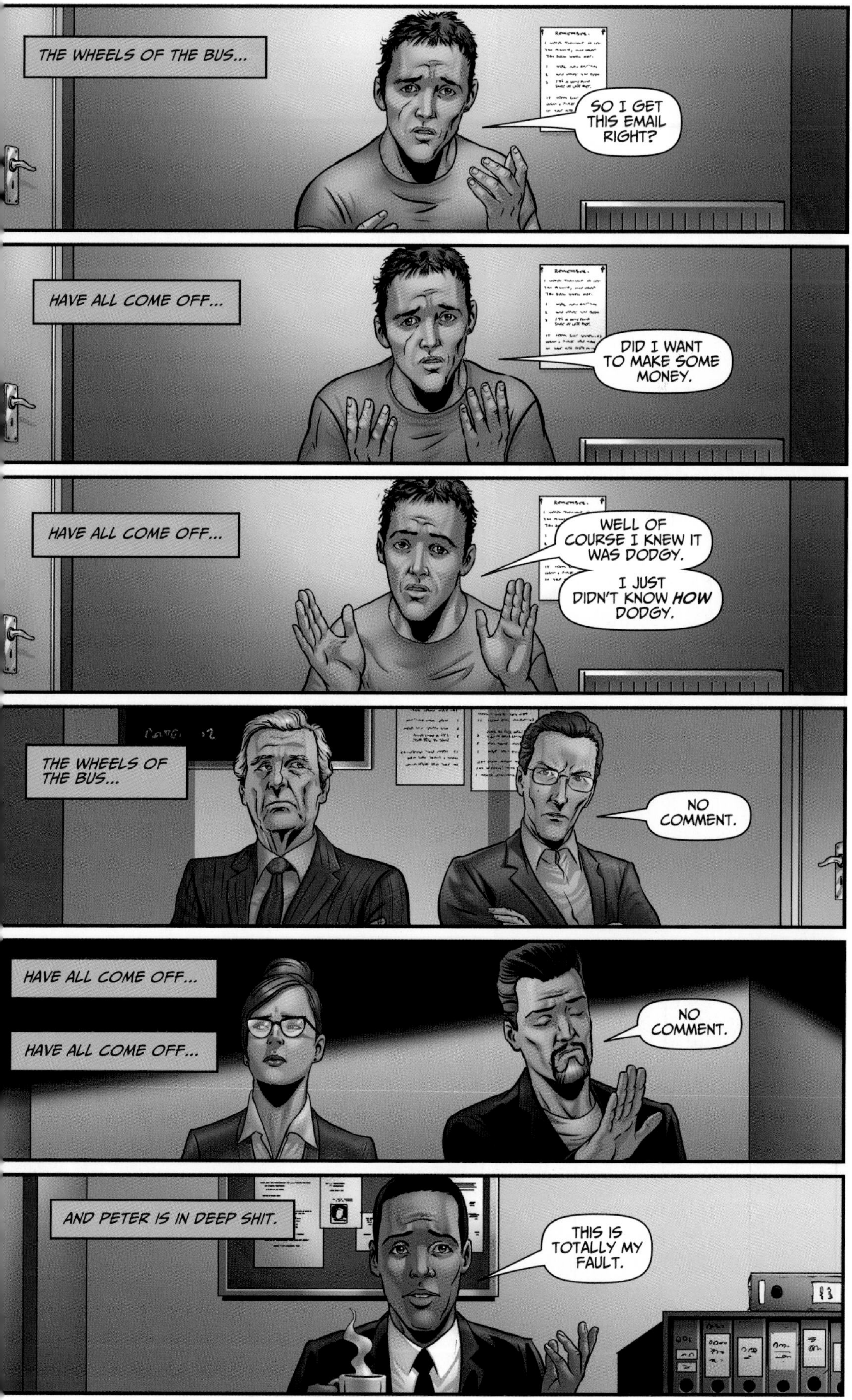
THE WHEELS OF THE BUS...
SO I GET THIS EMAIL RIGHT?
HAVE ALL COME OFF...
DID I WANT TO MAKE SOME MONEY.
HAVE ALL COME OFF...
WELL OF COURSE I KNEW IT WAS DODGY.
I JUST DIDN'T KNOW HOW DODGY.
THE WHEELS OF THE BUS...
NO COMMENT.
HAVE ALL COME OFF...
HAVE ALL COME OFF...
NO COMMENT.
AND PETER IS IN DEEP SHIT.
THIS IS TOTALLY MY FAULT.

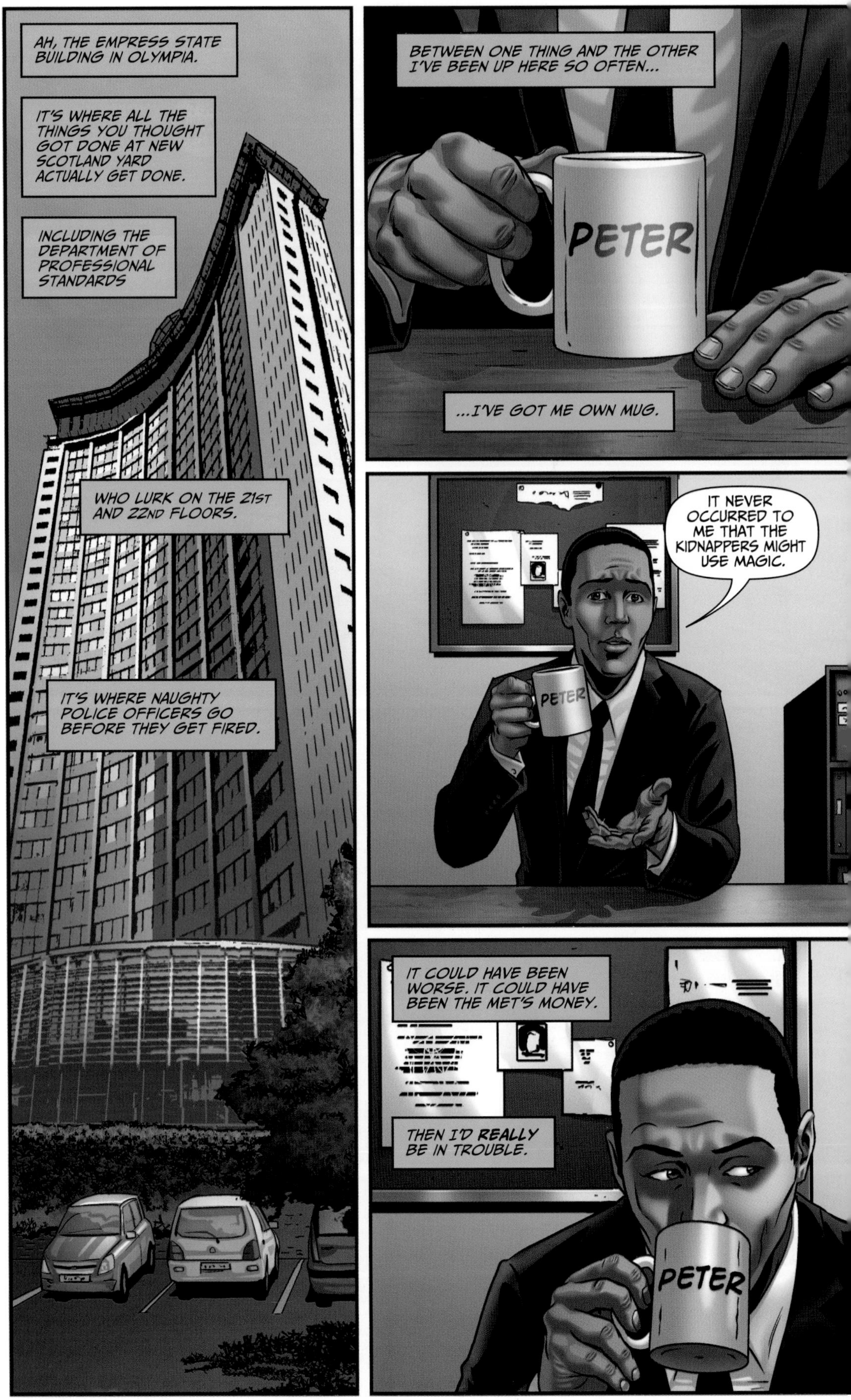
AH, THE EMPRESS STATE BUILDING IN OLYMPIA.
IT'S WHERE ALL THE THINGS YOU THOUGHT GOT DONE AT NEW SCOTLAND YARD ACTUALLY GET DONE.
INCLUDING THE DEPARTMENT OF PROFESSIONAL STANDARDS
WHO LURK ON THE 21ST AND 22ND FLOORS.
IT'S WHERE NAUGHTY POLICE OFFICERS GO BEFORE THEY GET FIRED.
BETWEEN ONE THING AND THE OTHER I'VE BEEN UP HERE SO OFTEN...
PETER
...I'VE GOT ME OWN MUG.
IT NEVER OCCURRED TO ME THAT THE KIDNAPPERS MIGHT USE MAGIC.
PETER
IT COULD HAVE BEEN WORSE. IT COULD HAVE BEEN THE MET'S MONEY.
THEN I'D REALLY BE IN TROUBLE.
PETER

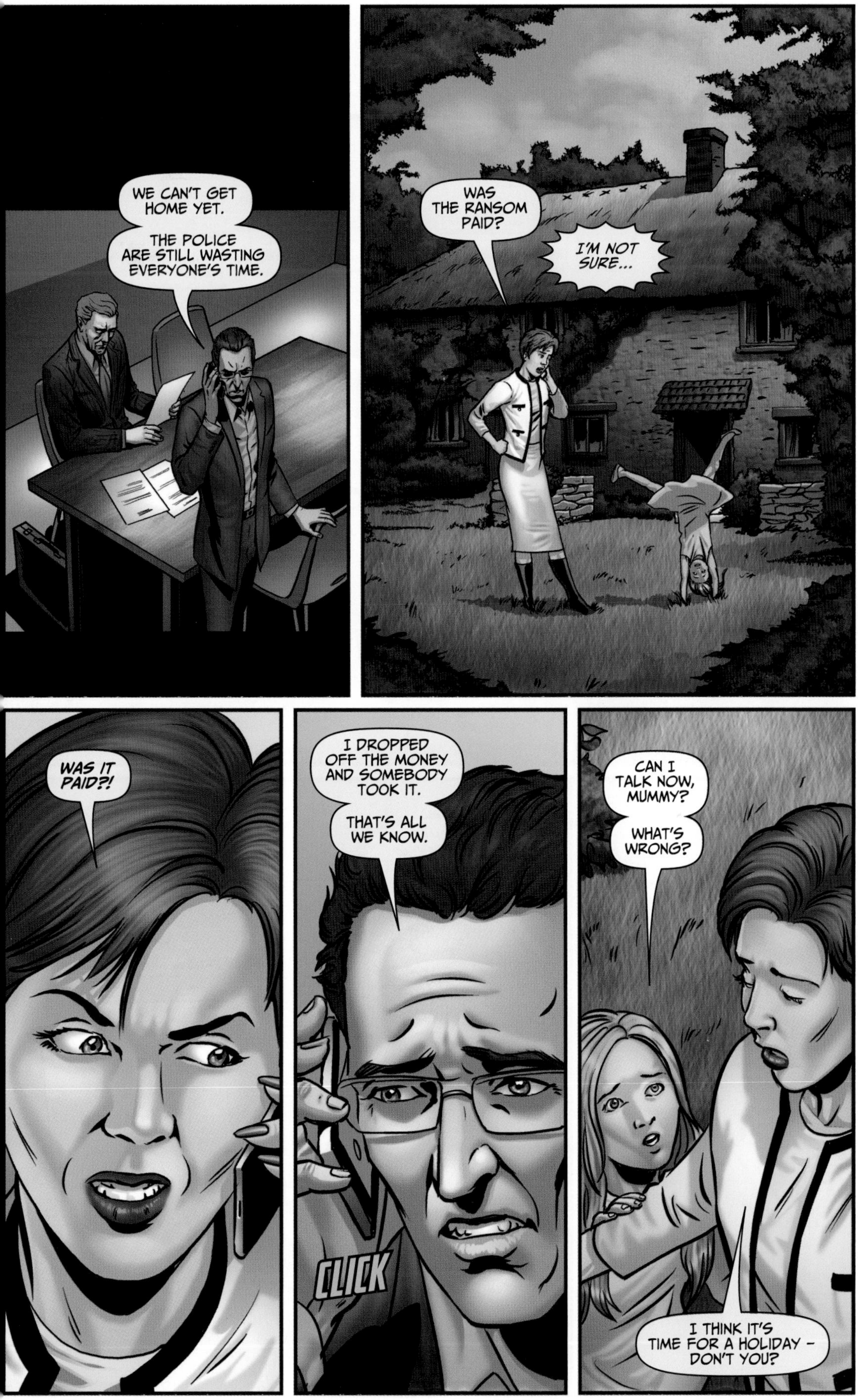
WE CAN'T GET HOME YET.
THE POLICE ARE STILL WASTING EVERYONE'S TIME.
WAS THE RANSOM PAID?
I'M NOT SURE...
WAS IT PAID?!
I DROPPED OFF THE MONEY AND SOMEBODY TOOK IT.
THAT'S ALL WE KNOW.
CLICK
CAN I TALK NOW, MUMMY?
WHAT'S WRONG?
I THINK IT'S TIME FOR A HOLIDAY – DON'T YOU?

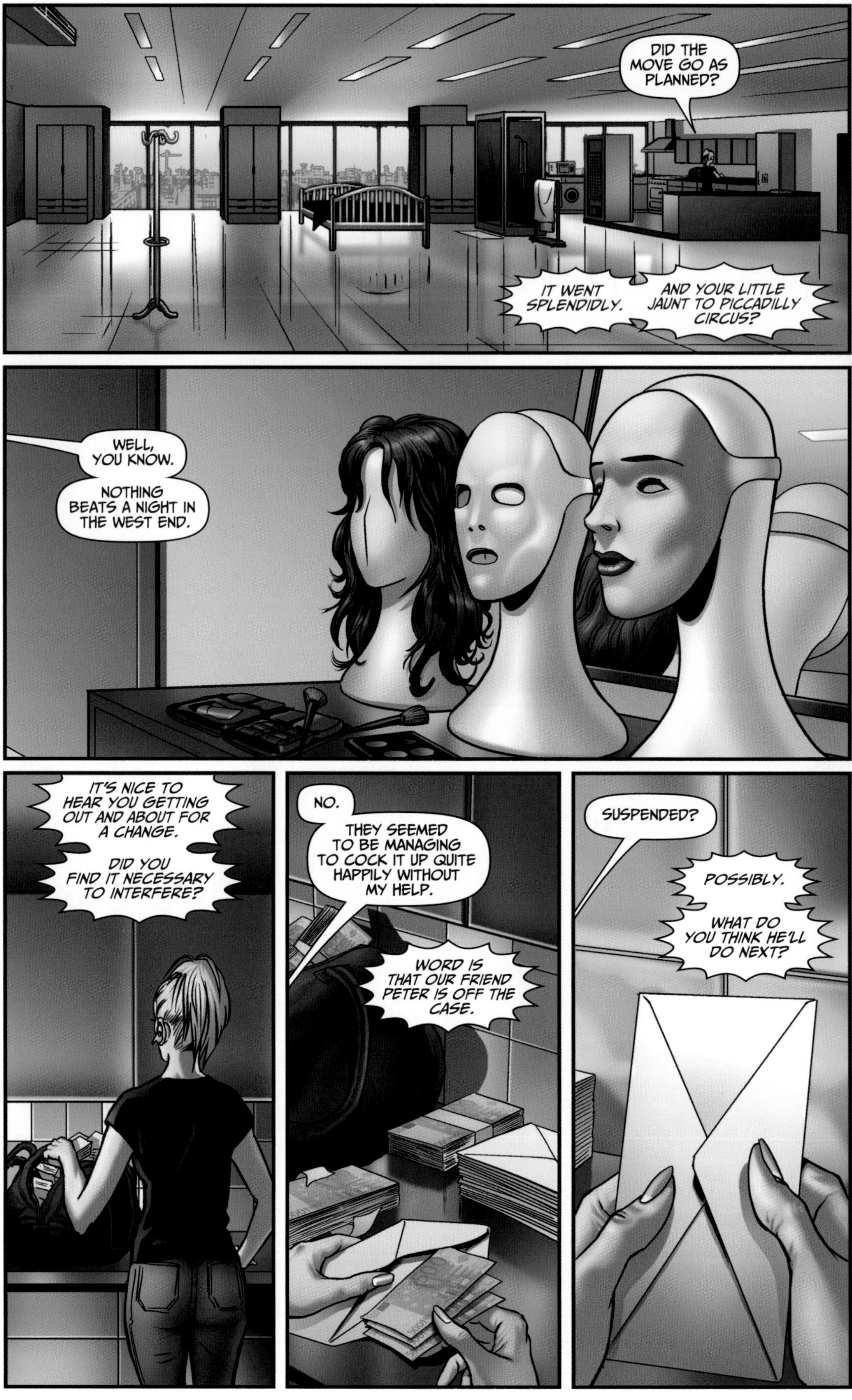
DID THE MOVE GO AS PLANNED?
IT WENT SPLENDIDLY.
AND YOUR LITTLE JAUNT TO PICCADILLY CIRCUS?
WELL, YOU KNOW.
NOTHING BEATS A NIGHT IN THE WEST END.
IT'S NICE TO HEAR YOU GETTING OUT AND ABOUT FOR A CHANGE.
DID YOU FIND IT NECESSARY TO INTERFERE?
NO.
THEY SEEMED TO BE MANAGING TO COCK IT UP QUITE HAPPILY WITHOUT MY HELP.
WORD IS THAT OUR FRIEND PETER IS OFF THE CASE.
SUSPENDED?
POSSIBLY.
WHAT DO YOU THINK HE'LL DO NEXT?

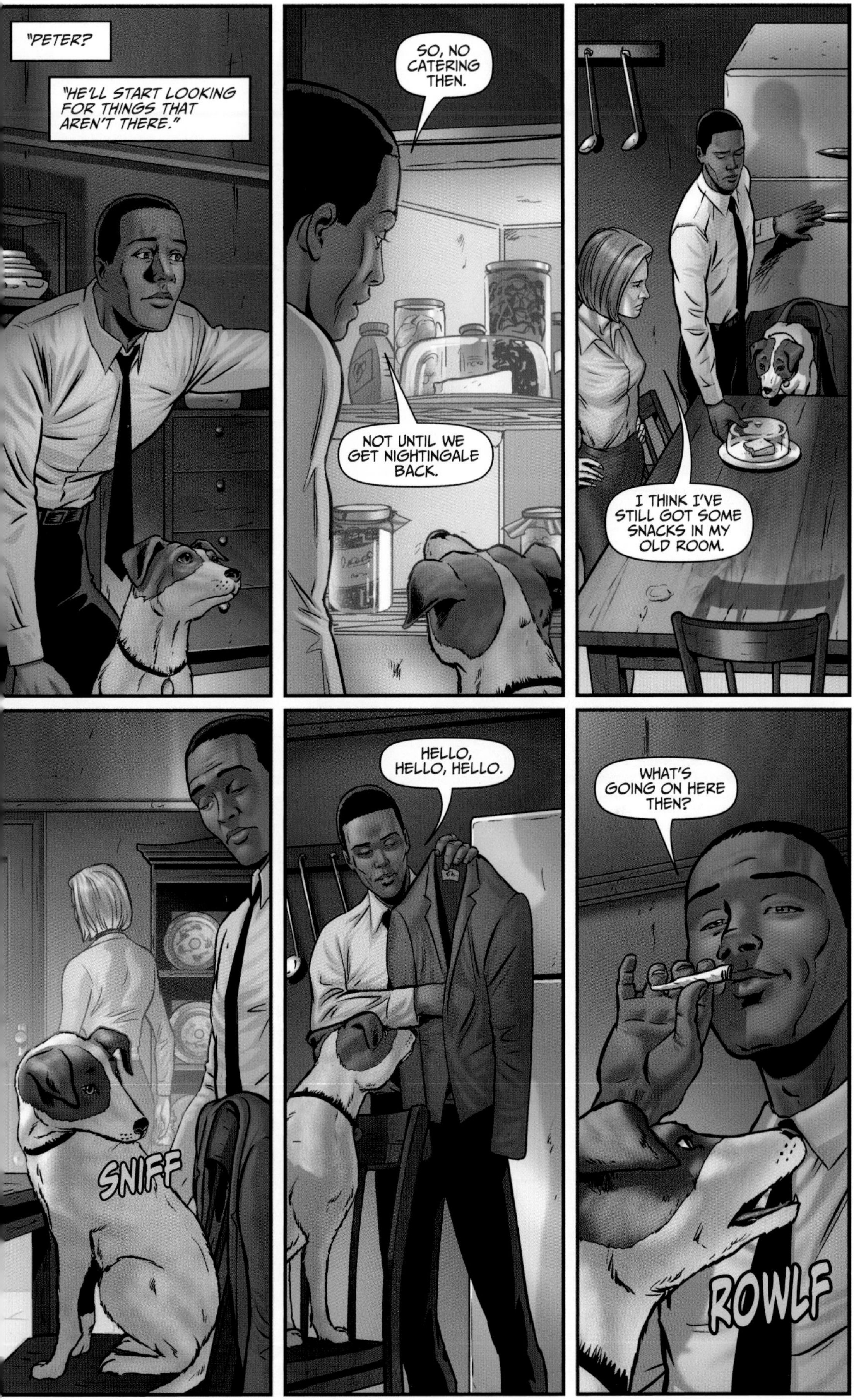
"PETER?
"HE'LL START LOOKING FOR THINGS THAT AREN'T THERE."
SO, NO CATERING THEN.
NOT UNTIL WE GET NIGHTINGALE BACK.
I THINK I'VE STILL GOT SOME SNACKS IN MY OLD ROOM.
SNIFF
HELLO, HELLO, HELLO.
WHAT'S GOING ON HERE THEN?
ROWLF

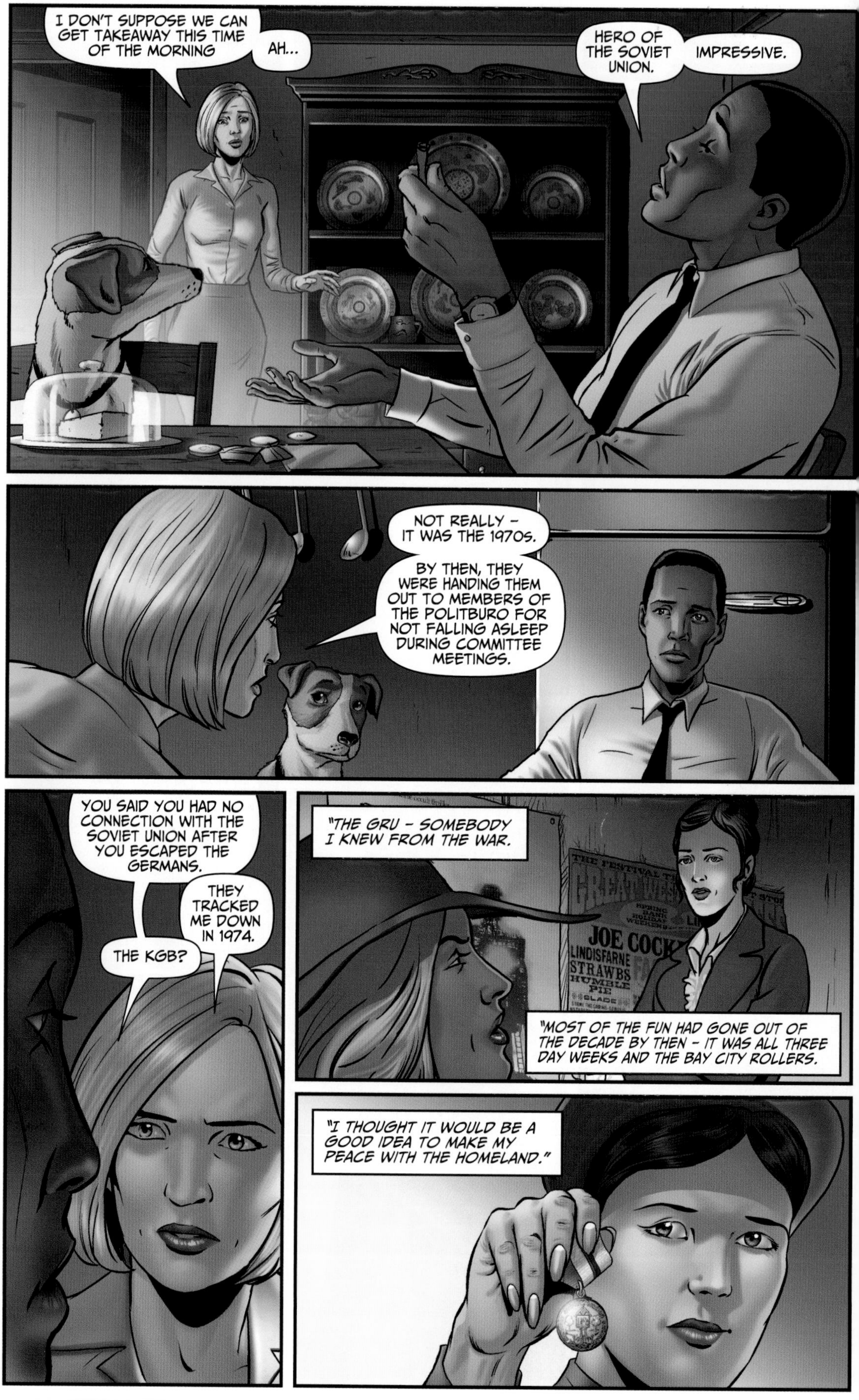
I DON'T SUPPOSE WE CAN GET TAKEAWAY THIS TIME OF THE MORNING
AH...
HERO OF THE SOVIET UNION.
IMPRESSIVE.
NOT REALLY – IT WAS THE 1970s.
BY THEN, THEY WERE HANDING THEM OUT TO MEMBERS OF THE POLITBURO FOR NOT FALLING ASLEEP DURING COMMITTEE MEETINGS.
YOU SAID YOU HAD NO CONNECTION WITH THE SOVIET UNION AFTER YOU ESCAPED THE GERMANS.
THEY TRACKED ME DOWN IN 1974.
THE KGB?
"THE GRU – SOMEBODY I KNEW FROM THE WAR.
LINDISFARNE
STRAWBS
HUMBLE PIE
"MOST OF THE FUN HAD GONE OUT OF THE DECADE BY THEN – IT WAS ALL THREE DAY WEEKS AND THE BAY CITY ROLLERS.
"I THOUGHT IT WOULD BE A GOOD IDEA TO MAKE MY PEACE WITH THE HOMELAND."

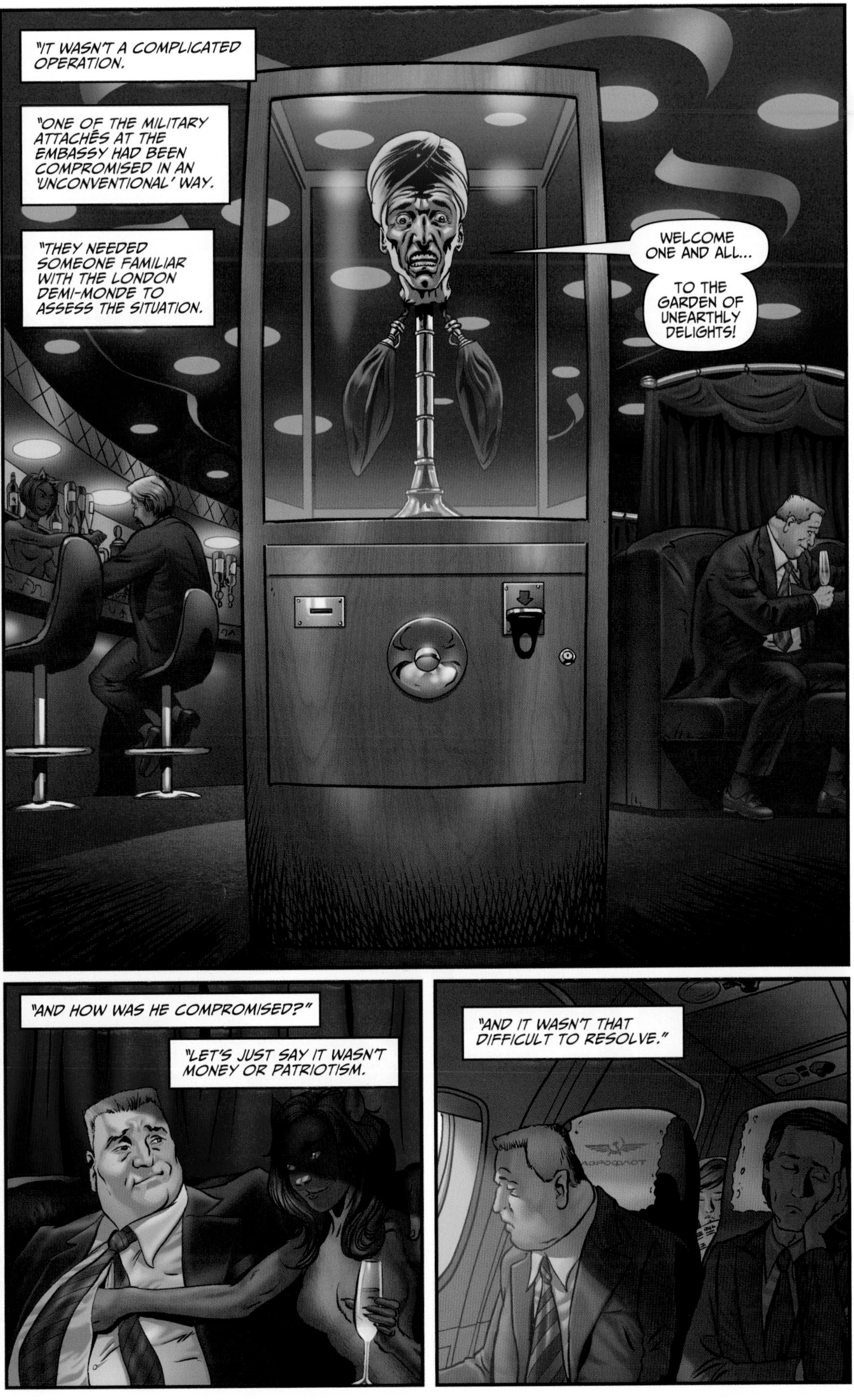
"IT WASN'T A COMPLICATED OPERATION.
"ONE OF THE MILITARY ATTACHÉS AT THE EMBASSY HAD BEEN COMPROMISED IN AN 'UNCONVENTIONAL' WAY.
"THEY NEEDED SOMEONE FAMILIAR WITH THE LONDON DEMI-MONDE TO ASSESS THE SITUATION.
WELCOME ONE AND ALL...
TO THE GARDEN OF UNEARTHLY DELIGHTS!
"AND HOW WAS HE COMPROMISED?"
"LET'S JUST SAY IT WASN'T MONEY OR PATRIOTISM.
"AND IT WASN'T THAT DIFFICULT TO RESOLVE."

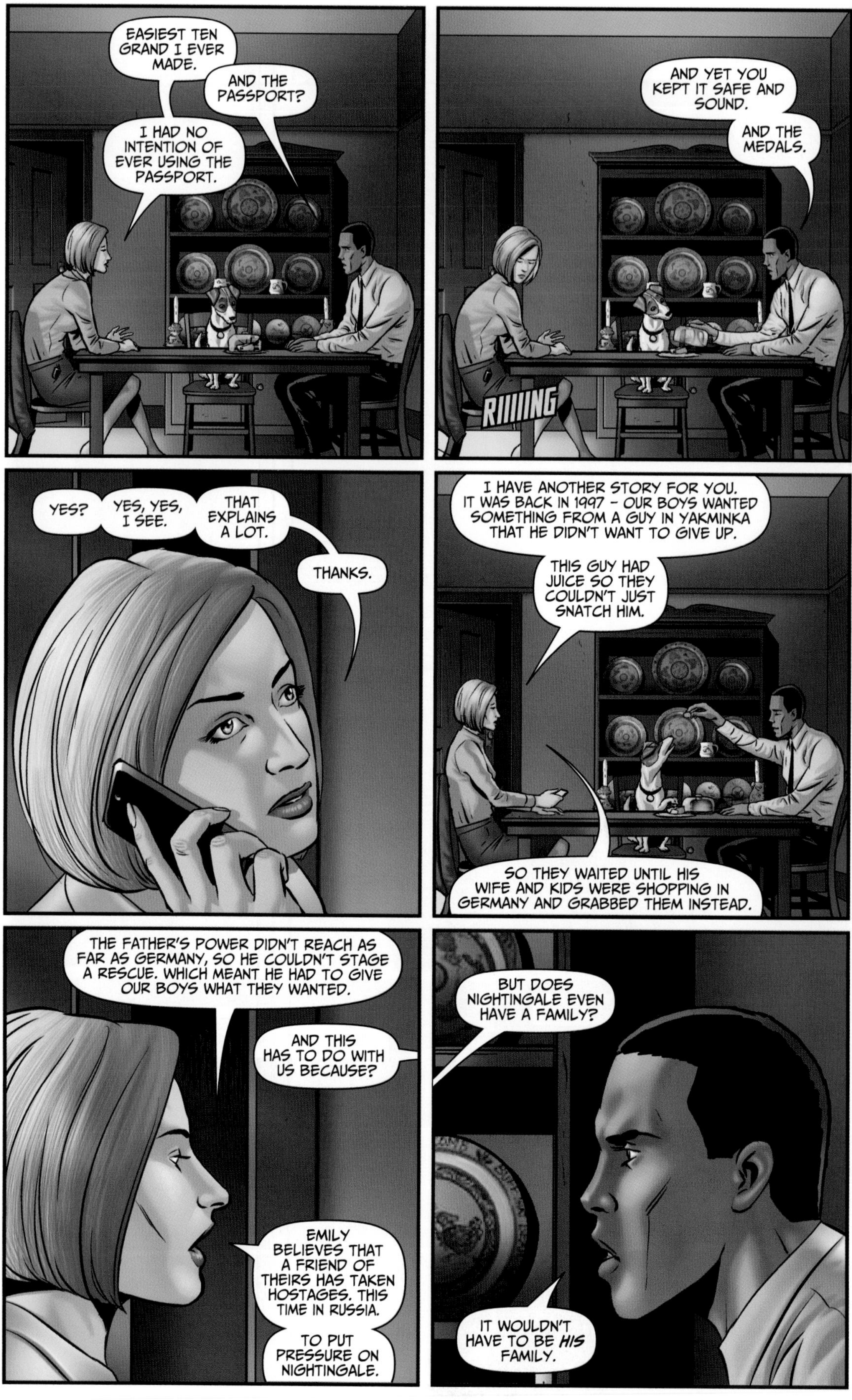

EASIEST TEN GRAND I EVER MADE.
AND THE PASSPORT?
I HAD NO INTENTION OF EVER USING THE PASSPORT.
AND YET YOU KEPT IT SAFE AND SOUND.
AND THE MEDALS.
RIIIIING
YES?
YES, YES, I SEE.
THAT EXPLAINS A LOT.
THANKS.
I HAVE ANOTHER STORY FOR YOU. IT WAS BACK IN 1997 - OUR BOYS WANTED SOMETHING FROM A GUY IN YAKMINKA THAT HE DIDN'T WANT TO GIVE UP.
THIS GUY HAD JUICE SO THEY COULDN'T JUST SNATCH HIM.
SO THEY WAITED UNTIL HIS WIFE AND KIDS WERE SHOPPING IN GERMANY AND GRABBED THEM INSTEAD.
THE FATHER'S POWER DIDN'T REACH AS FAR AS GERMANY, SO HE COULDN'T STAGE A RESCUE. WHICH MEANT HE HAD TO GIVE OUR BOYS WHAT THEY WANTED.
AND THIS HAS TO DO WITH US BECAUSE?
EMILY BELIEVES THAT A FRIEND OF THEIRS HAS TAKEN HOSTAGES. THIS TIME IN RUSSIA.
TO PUT PRESSURE ON NIGHTINGALE.
BUT DOES NIGHTINGALE EVEN HAVE A FAMILY?
IT WOULDN'T HAVE TO BE *HIS* FAMILY.

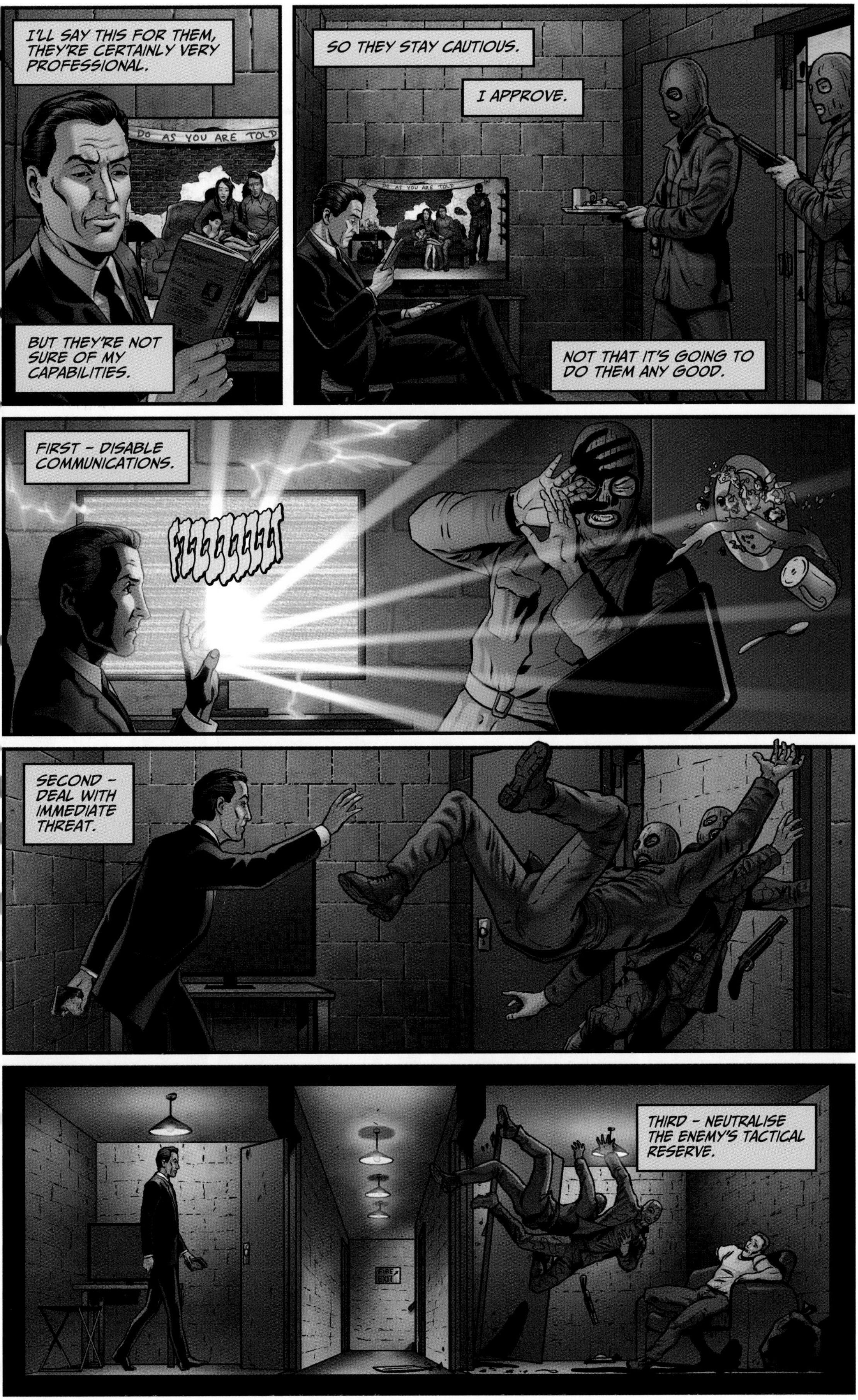

I'LL SAY THIS FOR THEM, THEY'RE CERTAINLY VERY PROFESSIONAL.
DO AS YOU ARE TOLD
BUT THEY'RE NOT SURE OF MY CAPABILITIES.
SO THEY STAY CAUTIOUS.
I APPROVE.
DO AS YOU ARE TOLD
NOT THAT IT'S GOING TO DO THEM ANY GOOD.
FIRST - DISABLE COMMUNICATIONS.
FZZZZZZT
SECOND - DEAL WITH IMMEDIATE THREAT.
THIRD - NEUTRALISE THE ENEMY'S TACTICAL RESERVE.
FIRE EXIT

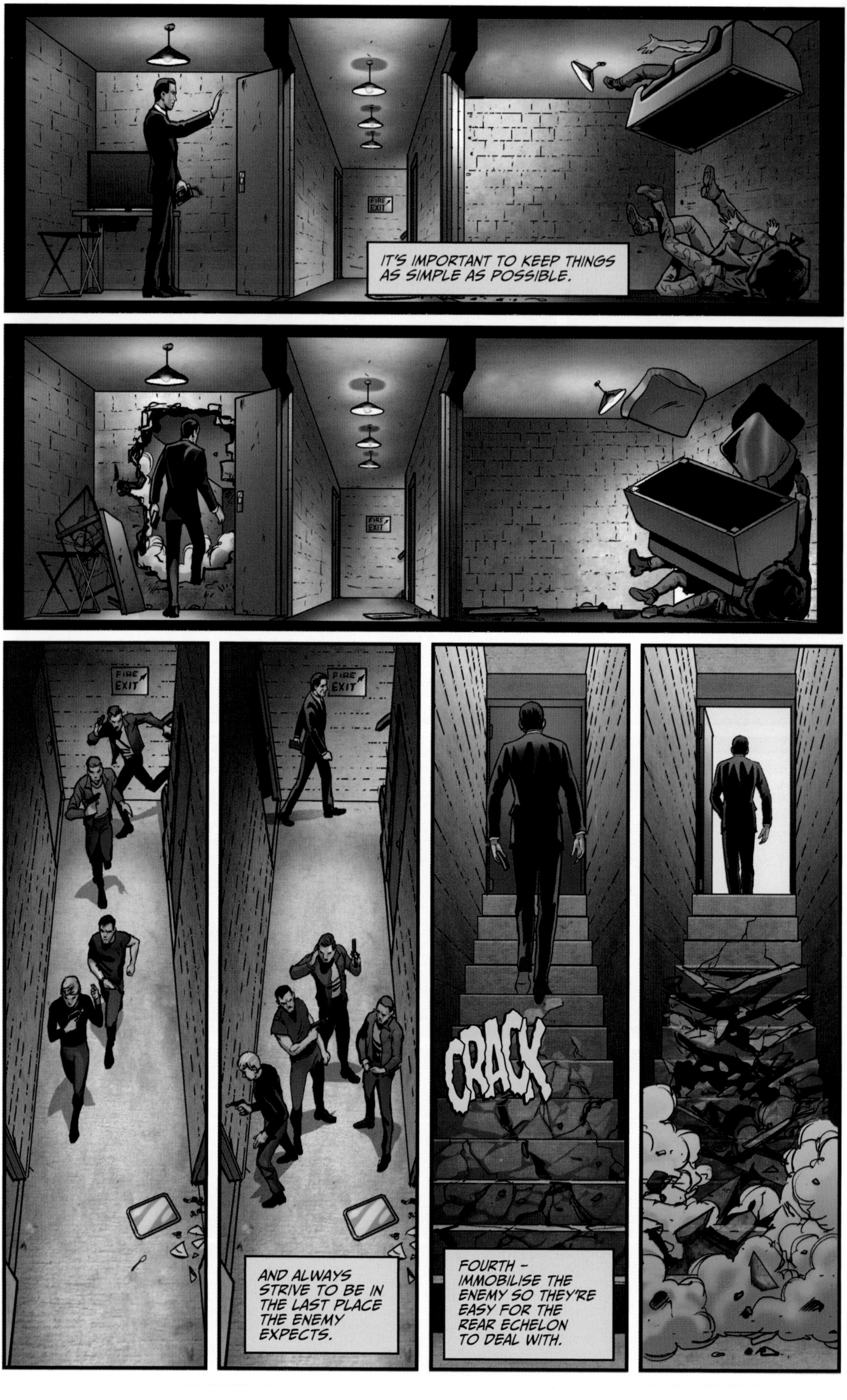

IT'S IMPORTANT TO KEEP THINGS AS SIMPLE AS POSSIBLE.
FIRE EXIT
FIRE EXIT
FIRE EXIT
FIRE EXIT
AND ALWAYS STRIVE TO BE IN THE LAST PLACE THE ENEMY EXPECTS.
CRACK
FOURTH – IMMOBILISE THE ENEMY SO THEY'RE EASY FOR THE REAR ECHELON TO DEAL WITH.

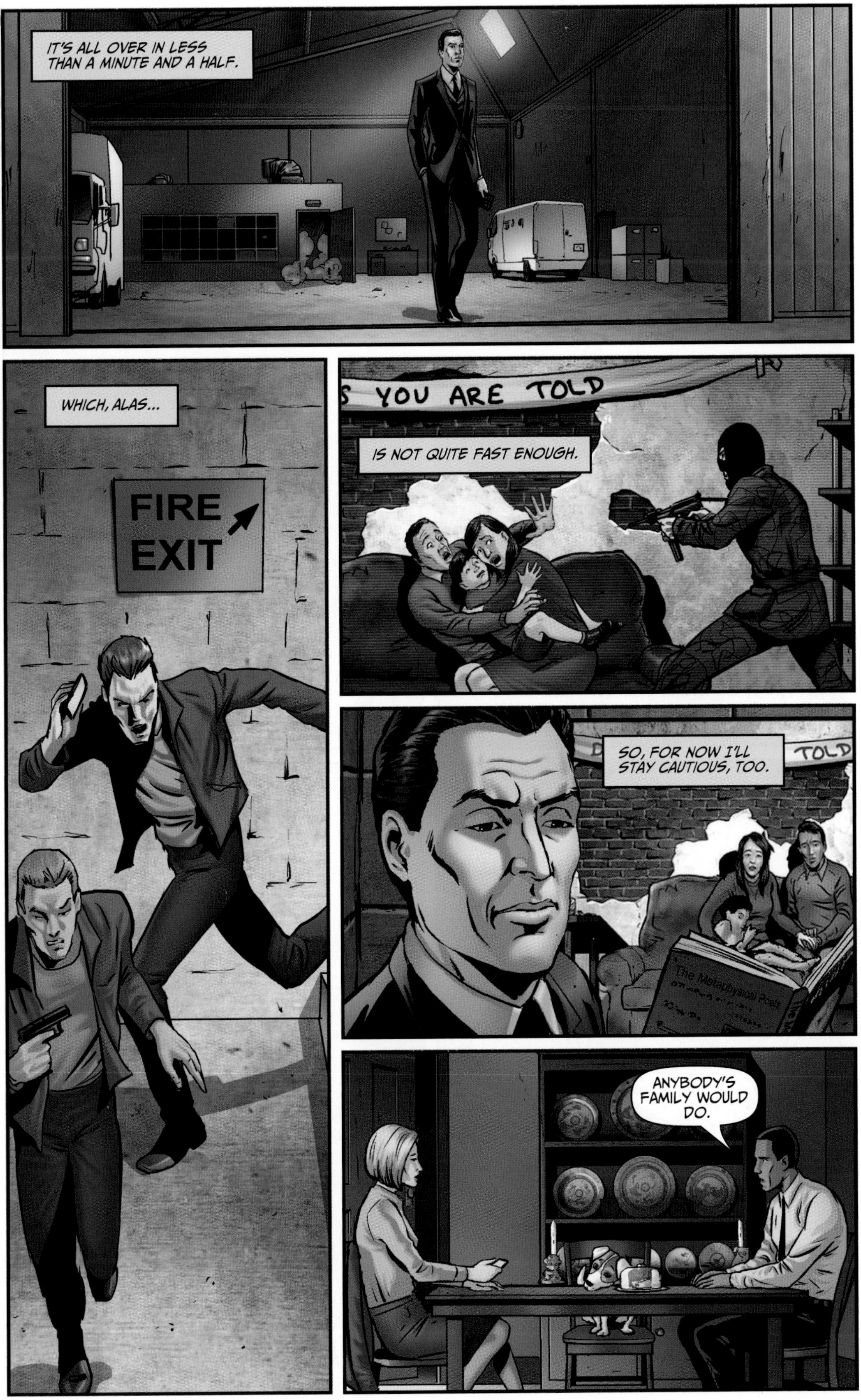
IT'S ALL OVER IN LESS THAN A MINUTE AND A HALF.
WHICH, ALAS...
FIRE EXIT
YOU ARE TOLD
IS NOT QUITE FAST ENOUGH.
SO, FOR NOW I'LL STAY CAUTIOUS, TOO.
TOLD
The Metaphysical Poets
ANYBODY'S FAMILY WOULD DO.

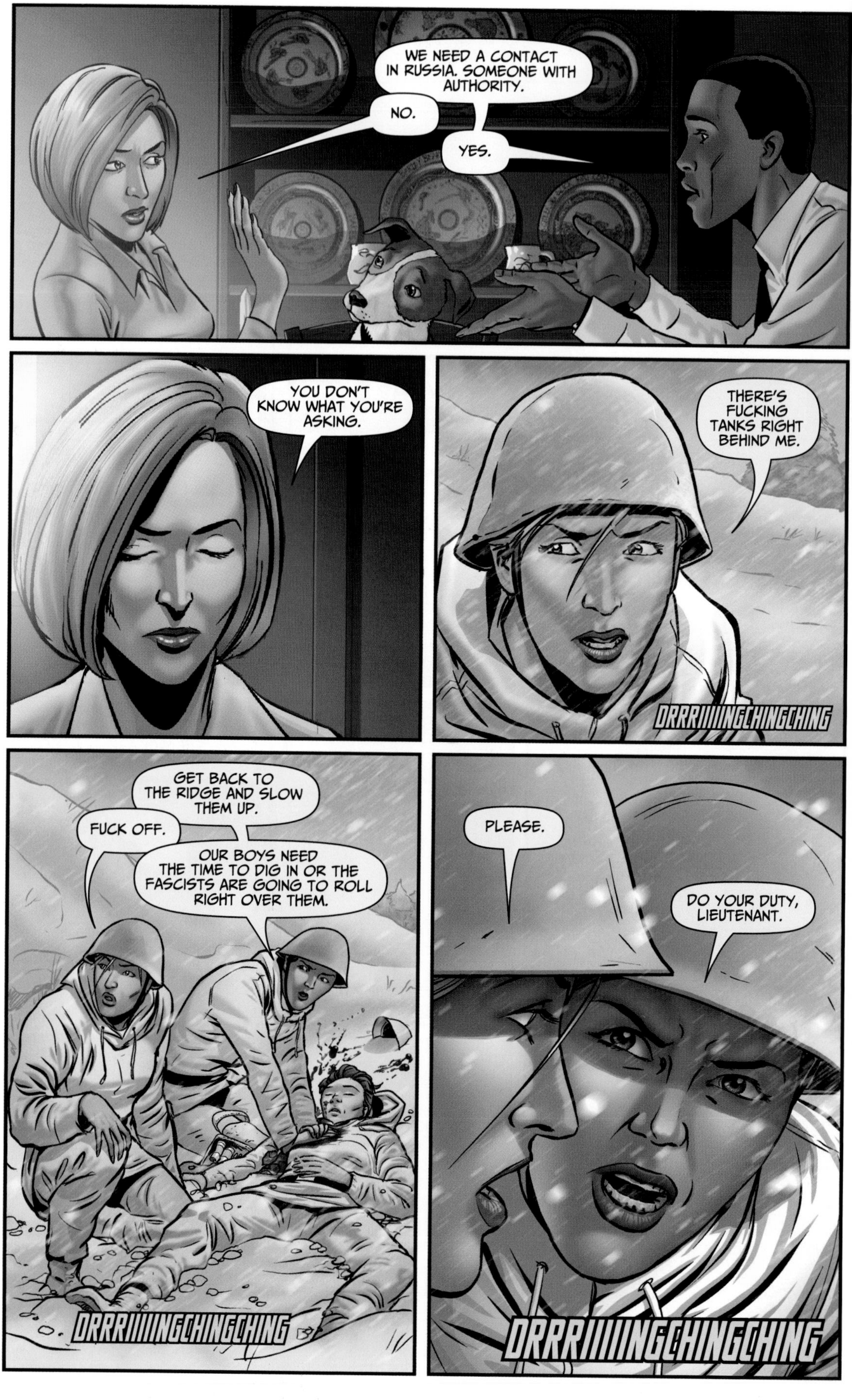
WE NEED A CONTACT IN RUSSIA. SOMEONE WITH AUTHORITY.
NO.
YES.
YOU DON'T KNOW WHAT YOU'RE ASKING.
THERE'S FUCKING TANKS RIGHT BEHIND ME.
DRRRIIIIINGCHINGCHING
GET BACK TO THE RIDGE AND SLOW THEM UP.
FUCK OFF.
OUR BOYS NEED THE TIME TO DIG IN OR THE FASCISTS ARE GOING TO ROLL RIGHT OVER THEM.
DRRRIIIIINGCHINGCHING
PLEASE.
DO YOUR DUTY, LIEUTENANT.
DRRRIIIIINGCHINGCHING

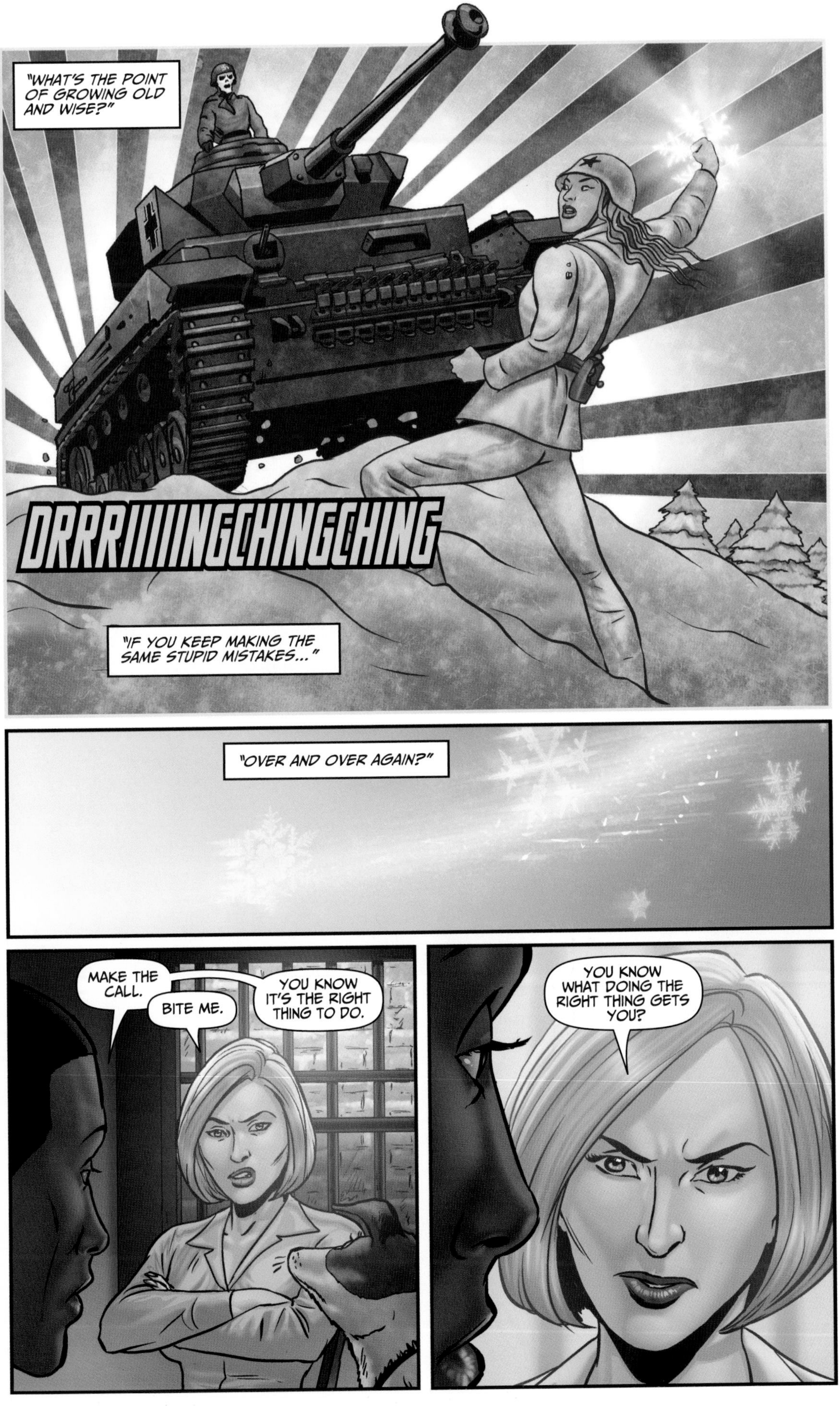
"WHAT'S THE POINT OF GROWING OLD AND WISE?"
DRRRIIIIINGCHINGCHING
"IF YOU KEEP MAKING THE SAME STUPID MISTAKES..."
"OVER AND OVER AGAIN?"
MAKE THE CALL.
BITE ME.
YOU KNOW IT'S THE RIGHT THING TO DO.
YOU KNOW WHAT DOING THE RIGHT THING GETS YOU?

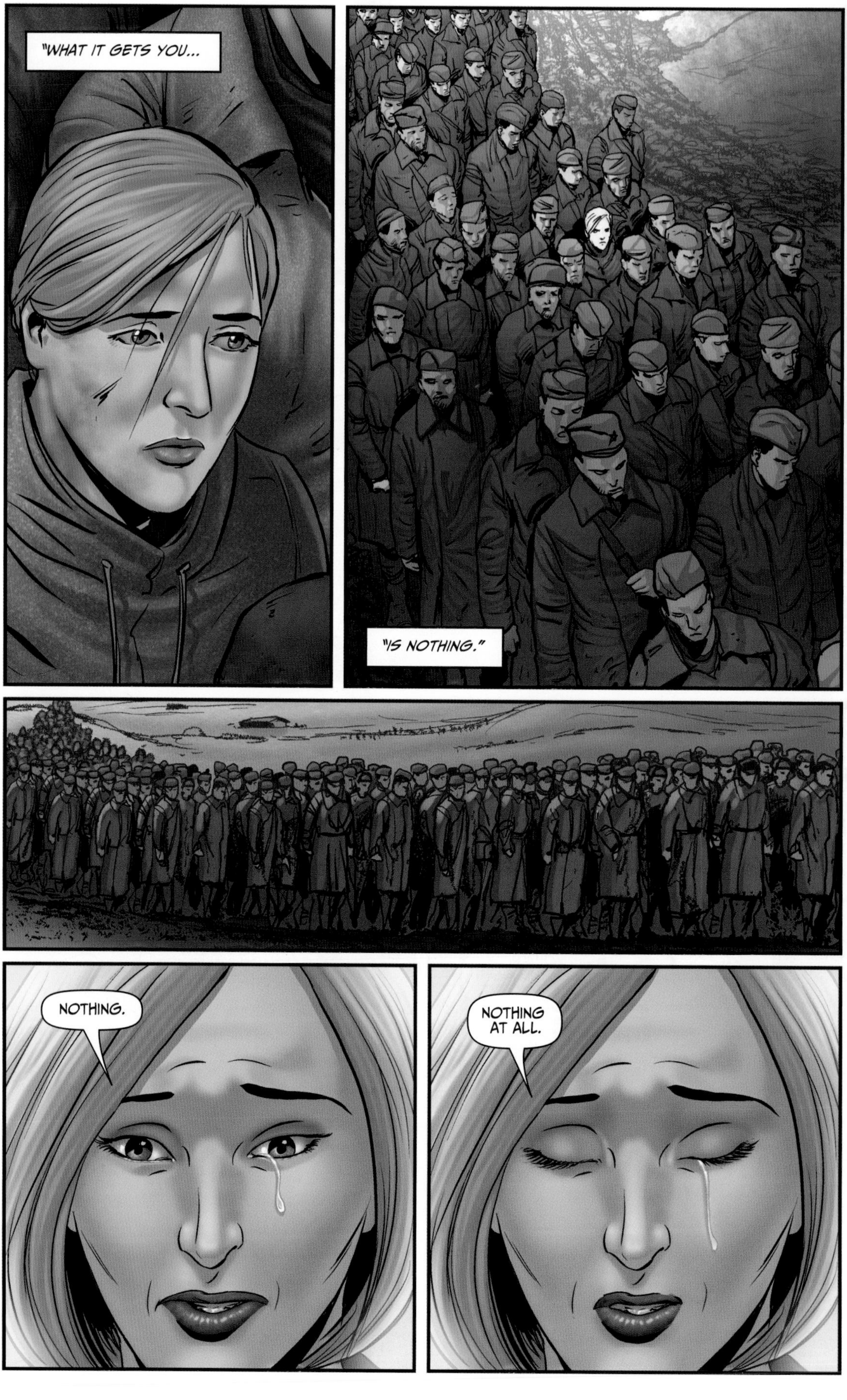
"WHAT IT GETS YOU...
"IS NOTHING."
NOTHING.
NOTHING AT ALL.

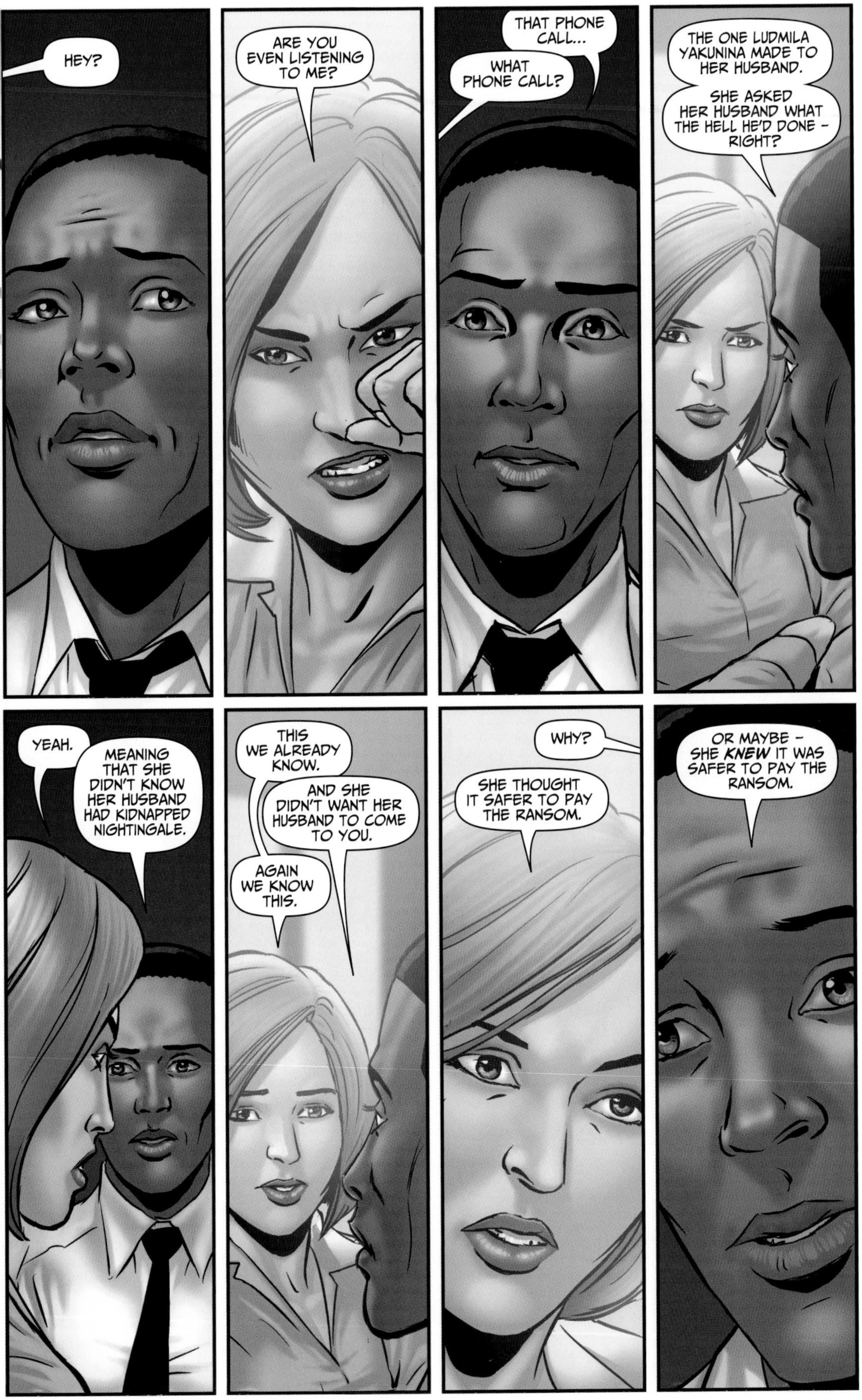
HEY?
ARE YOU EVEN LISTENING TO ME?
THAT PHONE CALL...
WHAT PHONE CALL?
THE ONE LUDMILA YAKUNINA MADE TO HER HUSBAND.
SHE ASKED HER HUSBAND WHAT THE HELL HE'D DONE - RIGHT?
YEAH.
MEANING THAT SHE DIDN'T KNOW HER HUSBAND HAD KIDNAPPED NIGHTINGALE.
THIS WE ALREADY KNOW.
AND SHE DIDN'T WANT HER HUSBAND TO COME TO YOU.
AGAIN WE KNOW THIS.
WHY?
SHE THOUGHT IT SAFER TO PAY THE RANSOM.
OR MAYBE - SHE KNEW IT WAS SAFER TO PAY THE RANSOM.

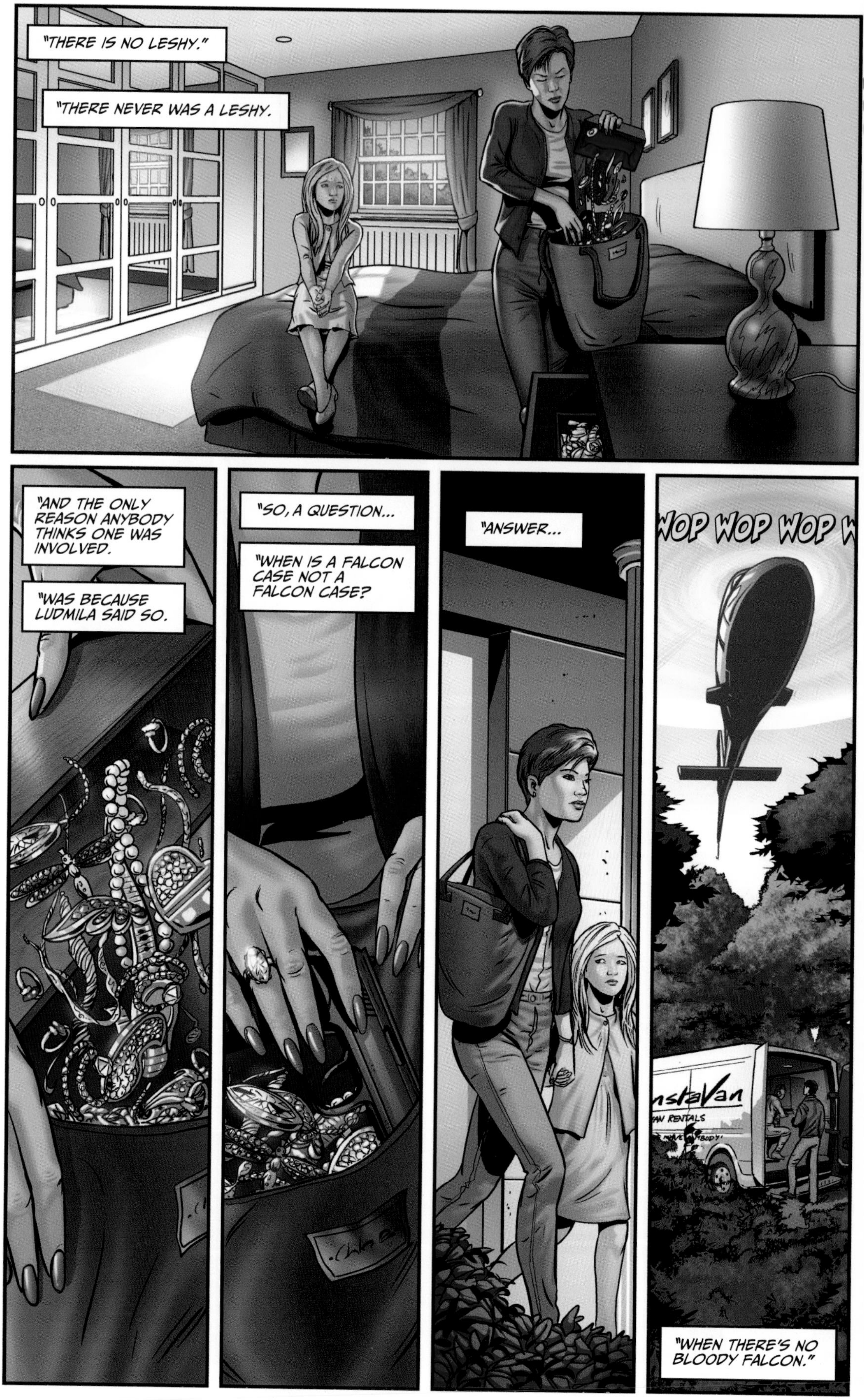
"THERE IS NO LESHY."
"THERE NEVER WAS A LESHY.
"AND THE ONLY REASON ANYBODY THINKS ONE WAS INVOLVED.
"WAS BECAUSE LUDMILA SAID SO.
"SO, A QUESTION...
"WHEN IS A FALCON CASE NOT A FALCON CASE?
"ANSWER...
WOP WOP WOP
"WHEN THERE'S NO BLOODY FALCON."

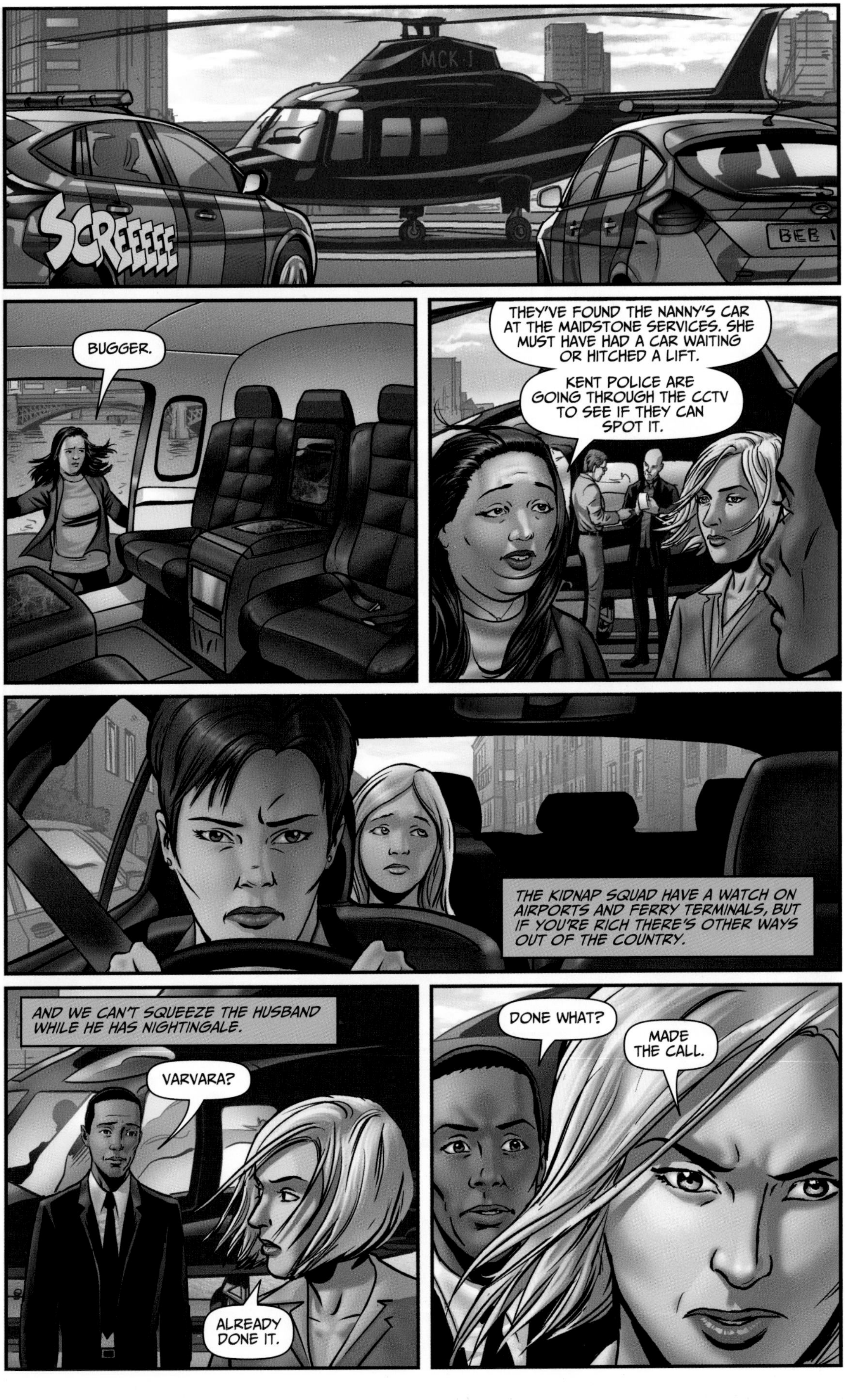
SCREEEEEE
BEB
BUGGER.
THEY'VE FOUND THE NANNY'S CAR AT THE MAIDSTONE SERVICES. SHE MUST HAVE HAD A CAR WAITING OR HITCHED A LIFT.
KENT POLICE ARE GOING THROUGH THE CCTV TO SEE IF THEY CAN SPOT IT.
THE KIDNAP SQUAD HAVE A WATCH ON AIRPORTS AND FERRY TERMINALS, BUT IF YOU'RE RICH THERE'S OTHER WAYS OUT OF THE COUNTRY.
AND WE CAN'T SQUEEZE THE HUSBAND WHILE HE HAS NIGHTINGALE.
VARVARA?
ALREADY DONE IT.
DONE WHAT?
MADE THE CALL.

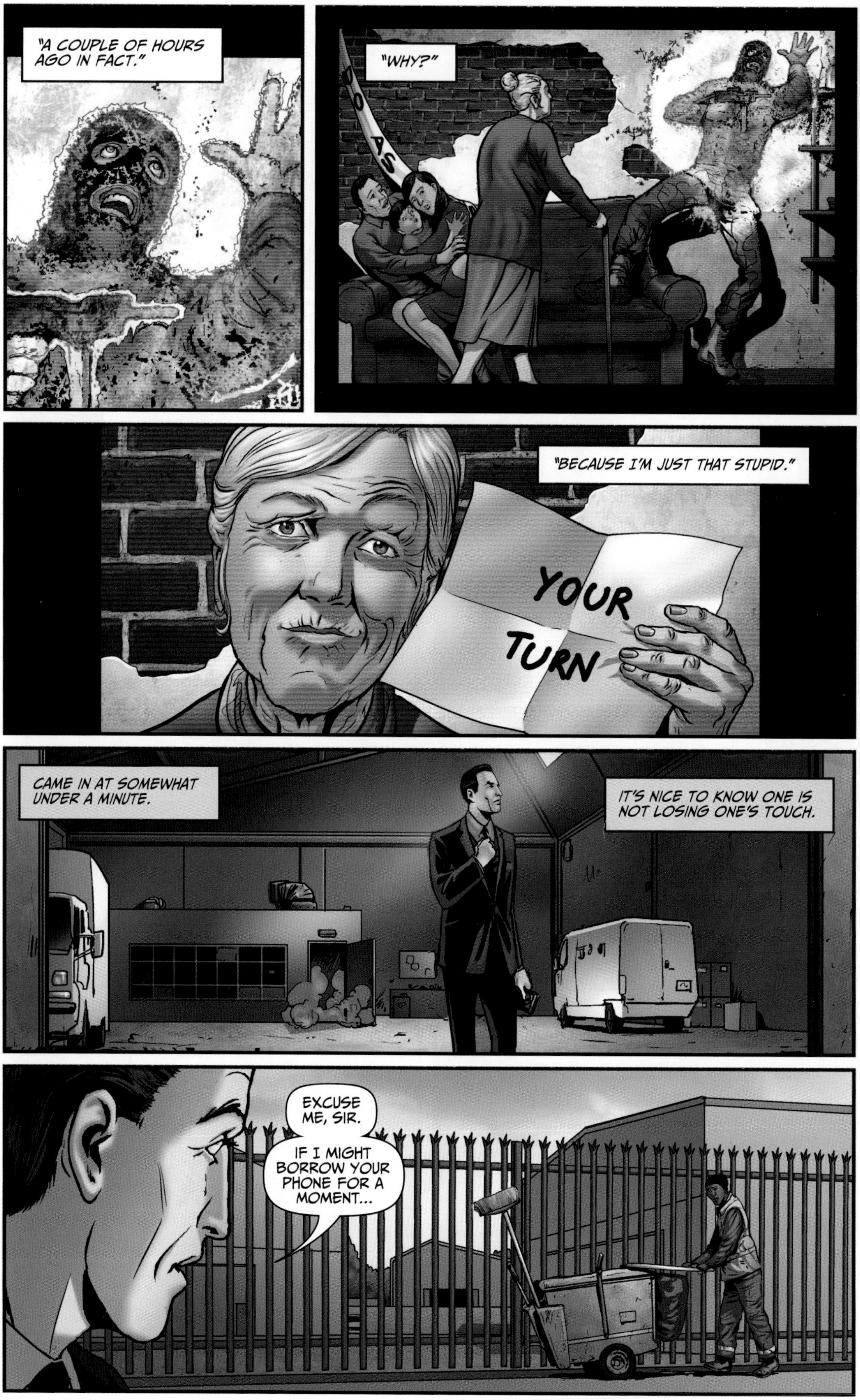
"A COUPLE OF HOURS AGO IN FACT."
"WHY?"
"BECAUSE I'M JUST THAT STUPID."
YOUR TURN
CAME IN AT SOMEWHAT UNDER A MINUTE.
IT'S NICE TO KNOW ONE IS NOT LOSING ONE'S TOUCH.
EXCUSE ME, SIR.
IF I MIGHT BORROW YOUR PHONE FOR A MOMENT...

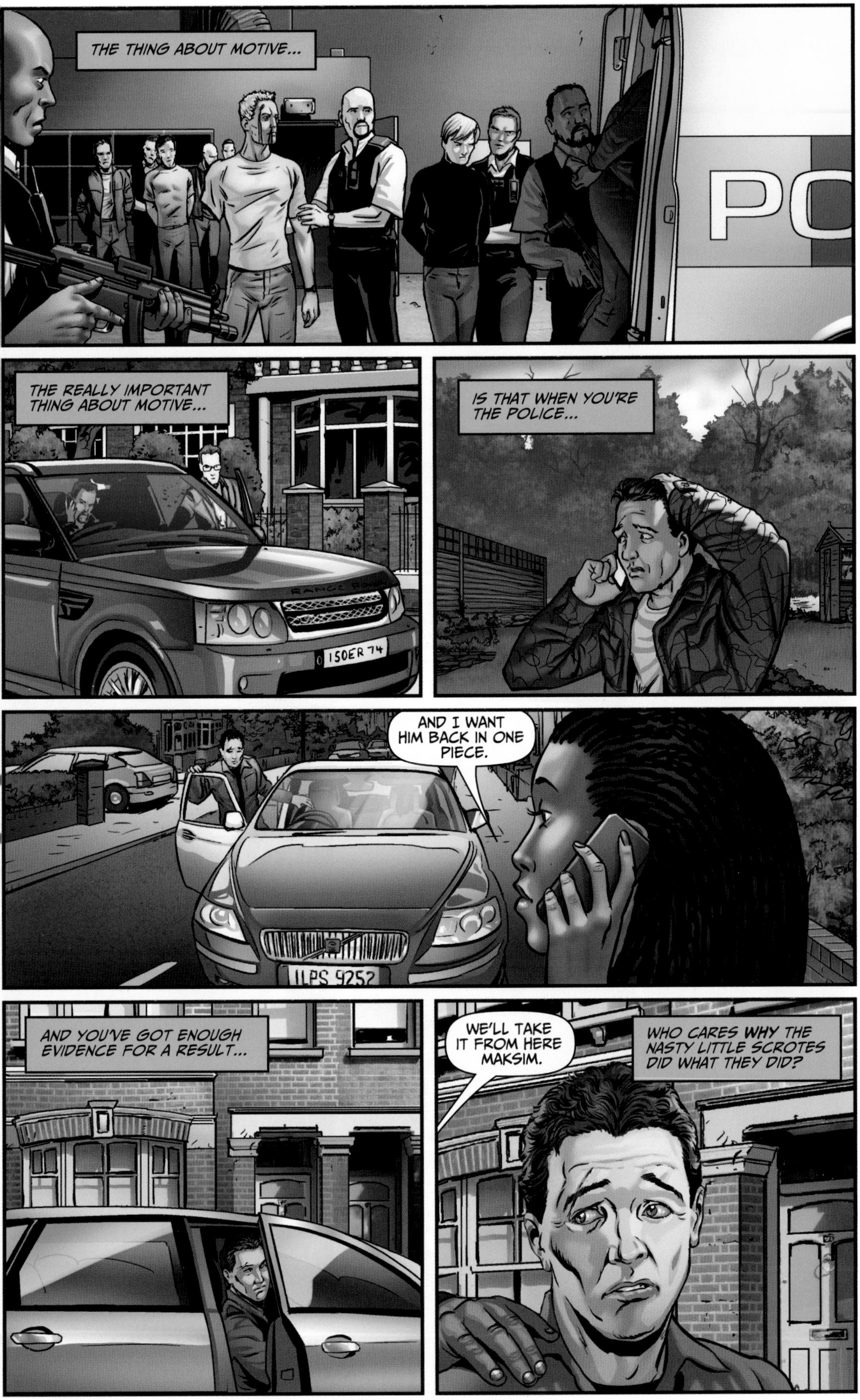
THE THING ABOUT MOTIVE...
PO
THE REALLY IMPORTANT THING ABOUT MOTIVE...
IS1OER 74
IS THAT WHEN YOU'RE THE POLICE...
AND I WANT HIM BACK IN ONE PIECE.
AND YOU'VE GOT ENOUGH EVIDENCE FOR A RESULT...
WE'LL TAKE IT FROM HERE MAKSIM.
WHO CARES **WHY** THE NASTY LITTLE SCROTES DID WHAT THEY DID?

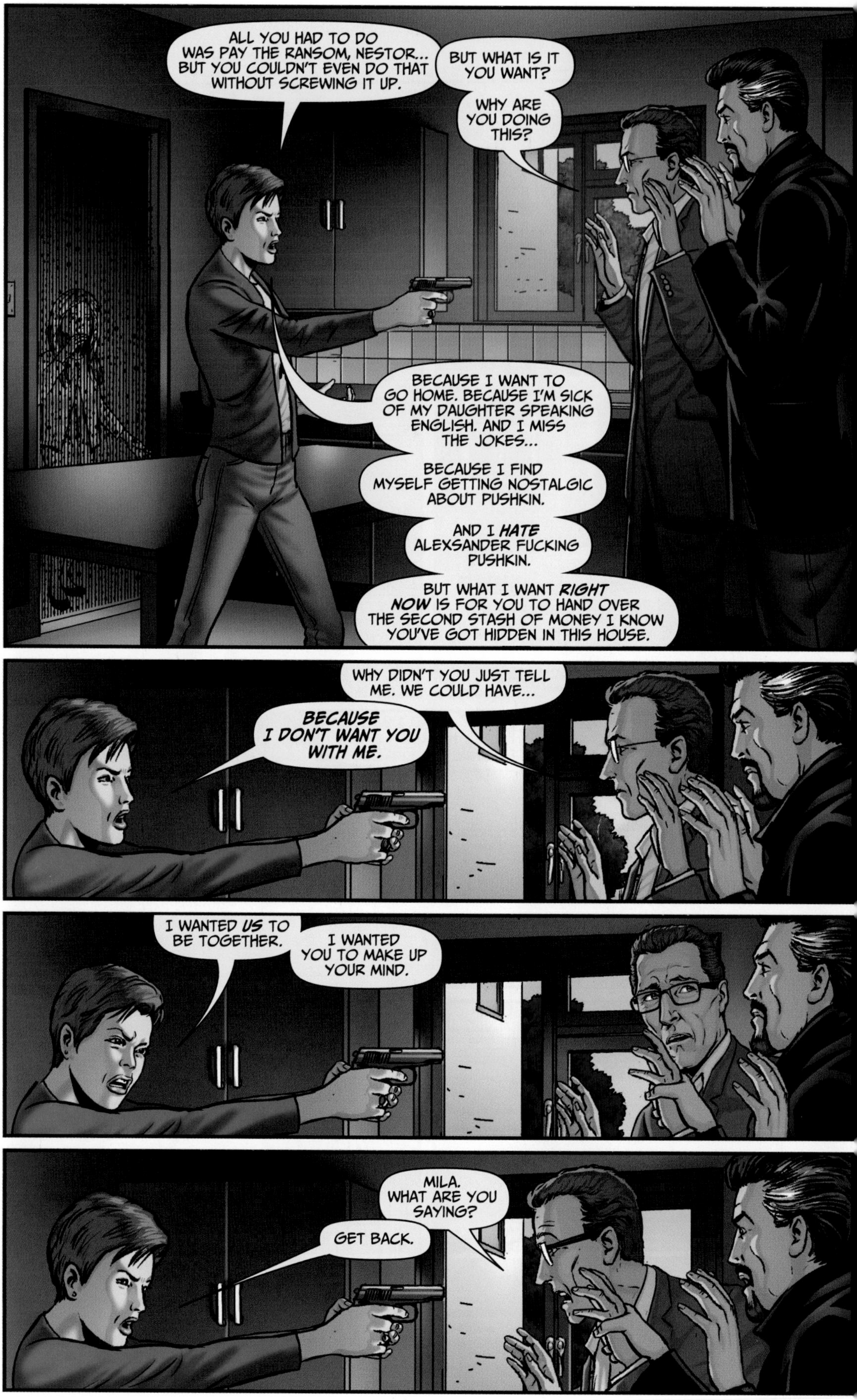
ALL YOU HAD TO DO WAS PAY THE RANSOM, NESTOR... BUT YOU COULDN'T EVEN DO THAT WITHOUT SCREWING IT UP.
BUT WHAT IS IT YOU WANT?
WHY ARE YOU DOING THIS?
BECAUSE I WANT TO GO HOME. BECAUSE I'M SICK OF MY DAUGHTER SPEAKING ENGLISH. AND I MISS THE JOKES...
BECAUSE I FIND MYSELF GETTING NOSTALGIC ABOUT PUSHKIN.
AND I *HATE* ALEXSANDER FUCKING PUSHKIN.
BUT WHAT I WANT *RIGHT NOW* IS FOR YOU TO HAND OVER THE SECOND STASH OF MONEY I KNOW YOU'VE GOT HIDDEN IN THIS HOUSE.
WHY DIDN'T YOU JUST TELL ME. WE COULD HAVE...
BECAUSE I DON'T WANT YOU WITH ME.
I WANTED *US* TO BE TOGETHER.
I WANTED YOU TO MAKE UP YOUR MIND.
MILA. WHAT ARE YOU SAYING?
GET BACK.

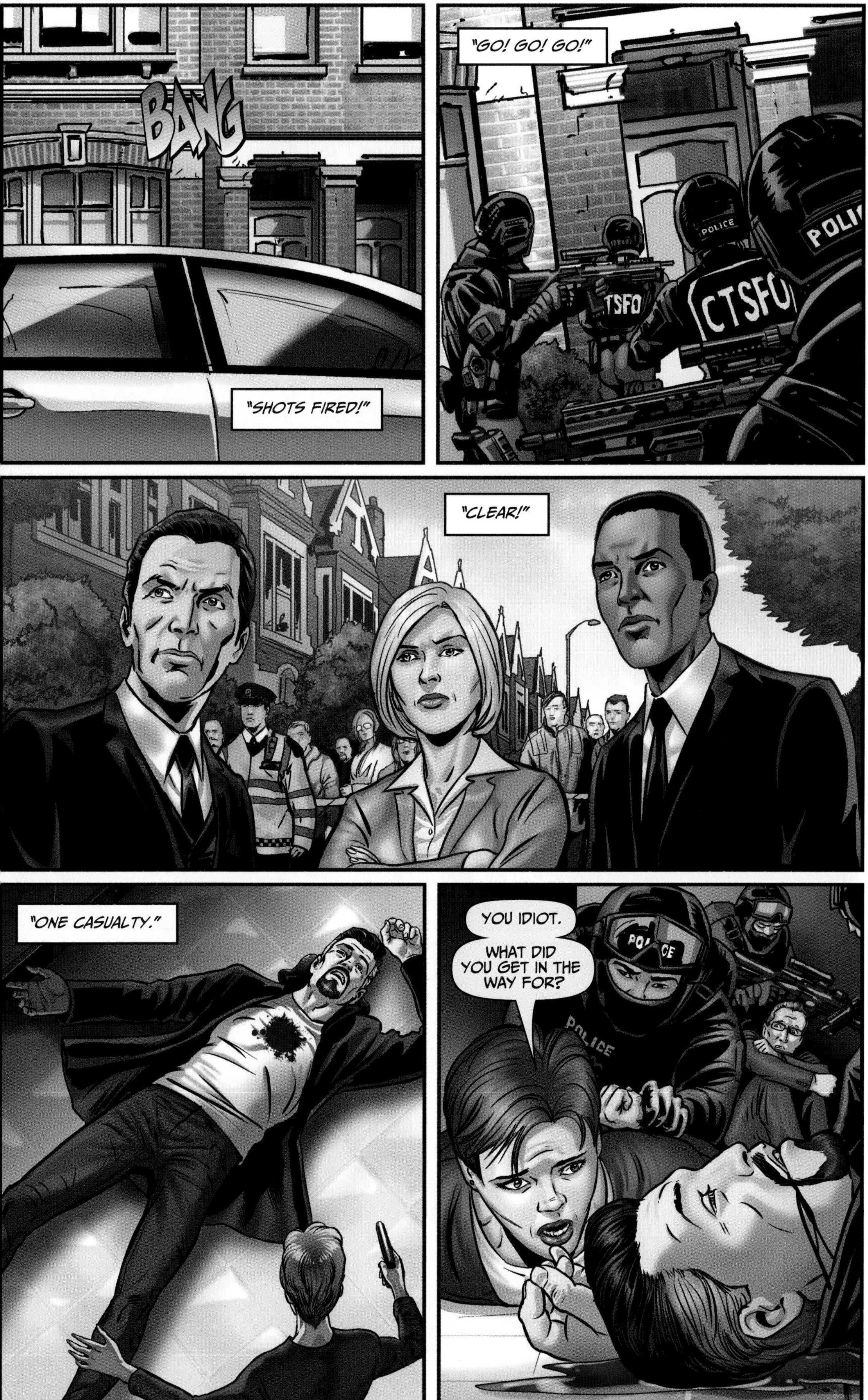
BANG
"SHOTS FIRED!"
"GO! GO! GO!"
POLICE
POLIC
CTSFO
CTSFO
"CLEAR!"
"ONE CASUALTY."
YOU IDIOT.
WHAT DID YOU GET IN THE WAY FOR?
POLICE
POLICE

WHAT WERE YOU EXPECTING?

WE DON'T RUSH INTO ARMED CONFRONTATIONS.

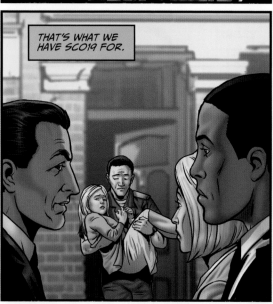

THAT'S WHAT WE HAVE SCO19 FOR.

ONE QUESTION, THOUGH...

IF LUDMILA DIDN'T HAVE THE RANSOM...

"WHO DOES?"

THE END

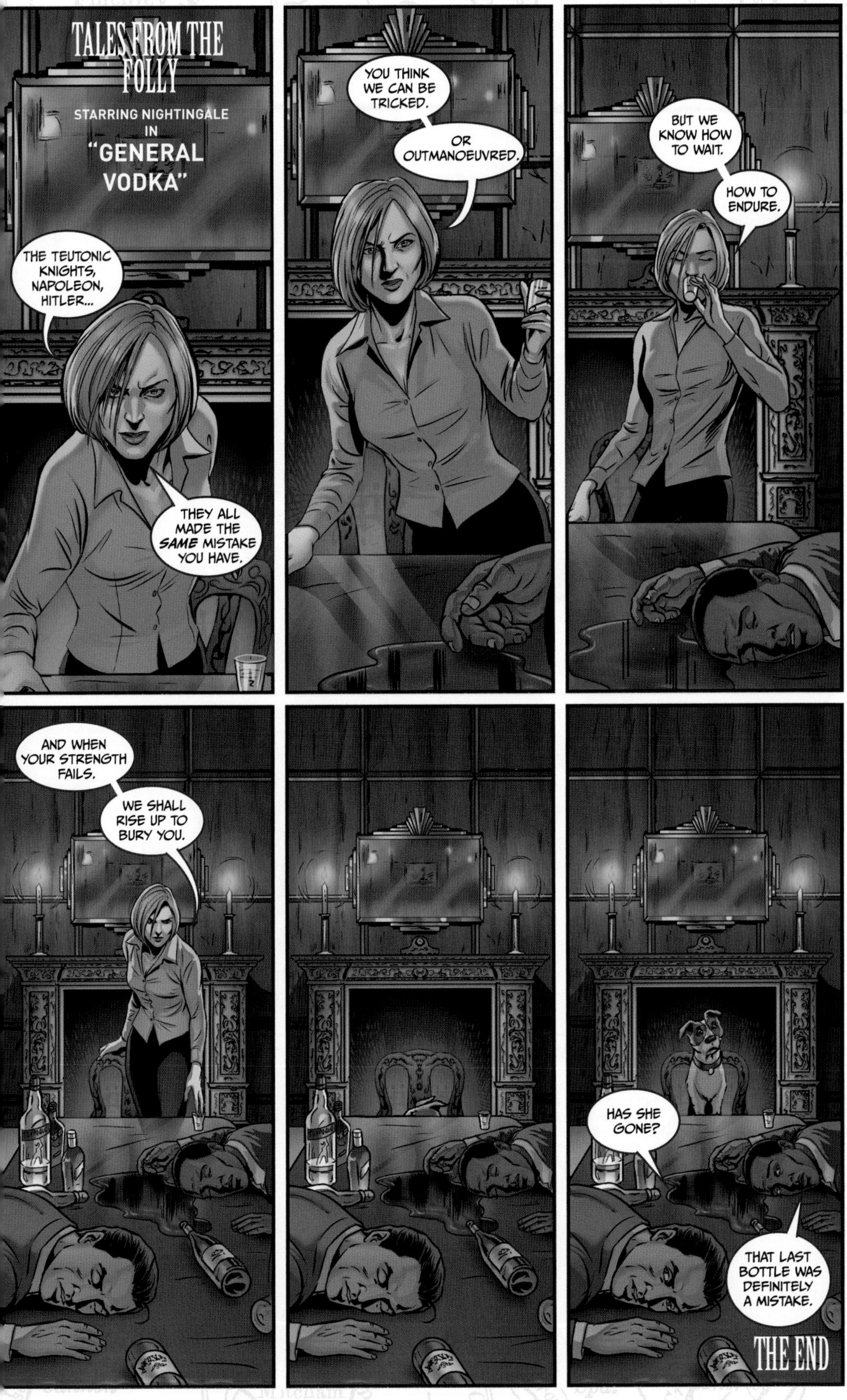
TALES FROM THE FOLLY
STARRING NIGHTINGALE IN
"GENERAL VODKA"
THE TEUTONIC KNIGHTS, NAPOLEON, HITLER...
THEY ALL MADE THE *SAME* MISTAKE YOU HAVE.
YOU THINK WE CAN BE TRICKED.
OR OUTMANOEUVRED.
BUT WE KNOW HOW TO WAIT.
HOW TO ENDURE.
AND WHEN YOUR STRENGTH FAILS.
WE SHALL RISE UP TO BURY YOU.
HAS SHE GONE?
THAT LAST BOTTLE WAS DEFINITELY A MISTAKE.
THE END

TALES FROM THE FOLLY
STARRING NICKY
IN
"THESE AREN'T THE GODS YOU'RE LOOKING FOR."
ODEON
ODEON
STAR WARS
BRING ME AN ICE CREAM.
GIVE ME YOUR AUTOGRAPH.
AUTO GRAPHS
GIVE ME YOUR AUTOGRAPH.
AND ALSO, MARRY ME AND COME AND LIVE IN MY RIVER AND NEVER EVER LEAVE...
NICKY!
WE'VE TALKED ABOUT WHY DOING THIS IS WRONG.
YOU DON'T KNOW THE POWER OF THE DARK SIDE.
THE END

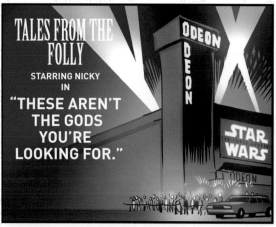

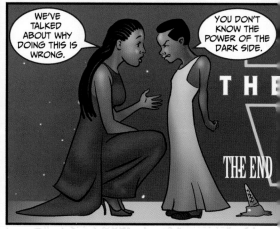

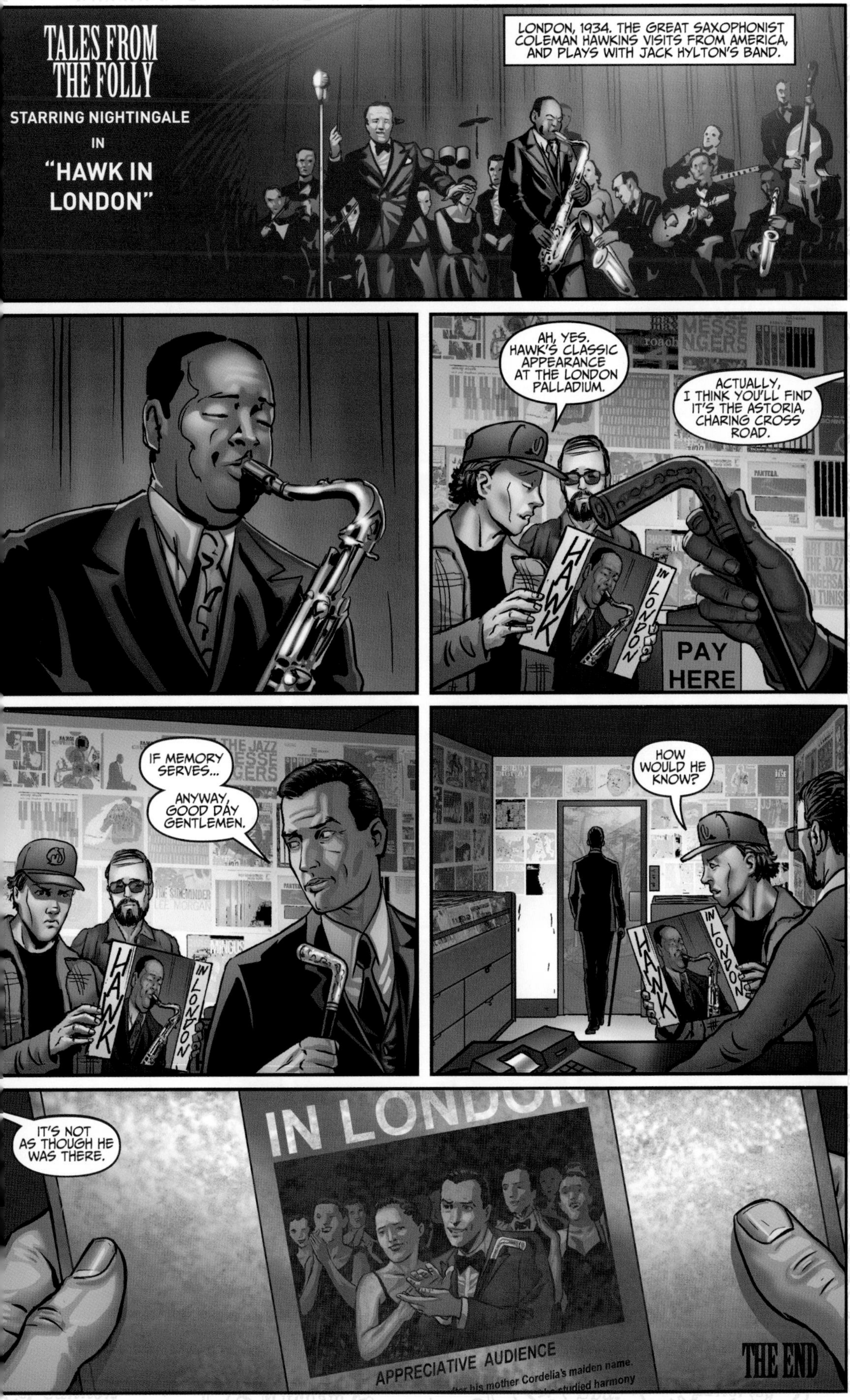
TALES FROM THE FOLLY
STARRING NIGHTINGALE
IN
"HAWK IN LONDON"
LONDON, 1934. THE GREAT SAXOPHONIST COLEMAN HAWKINS VISITS FROM AMERICA, AND PLAYS WITH JACK HYLTON'S BAND.
AH, YES. HAWK'S CLASSIC APPEARANCE AT THE LONDON PALLADIUM.
ACTUALLY, I THINK YOU'LL FIND IT'S THE ASTORIA, CHARING CROSS ROAD.
HAWK
IN LONDON
PAY HERE
IF MEMORY SERVES...
ANYWAY, GOOD DAY GENTLEMEN.
HOW WOULD HE KNOW?
IT'S NOT AS THOUGH HE WAS THERE.
IN LONDON
APPRECIATIVE AUDIENCE
THE END

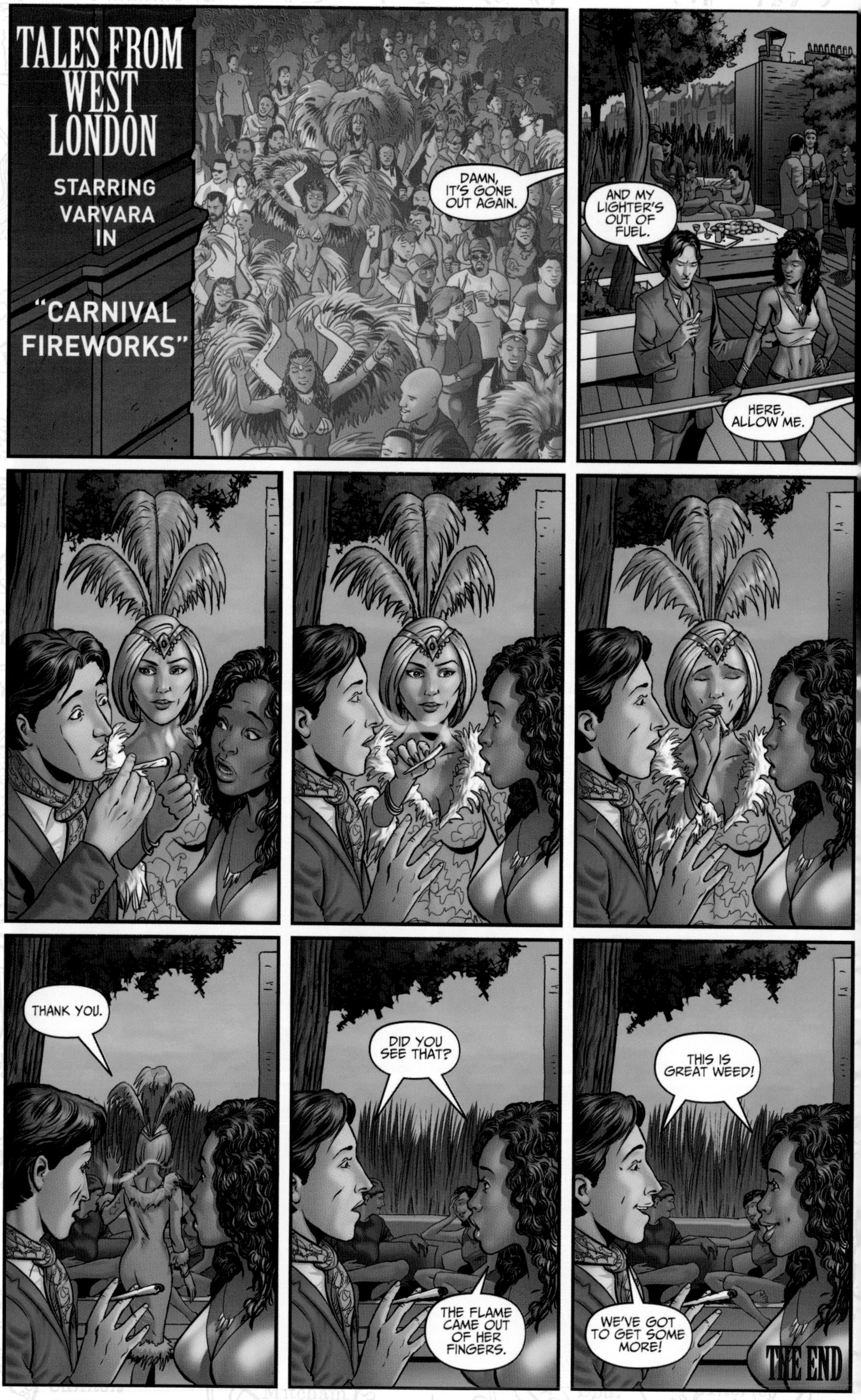
TALES FROM WEST LONDON
STARRING VARVARA IN
"CARNIVAL FIREWORKS"
DAMN, IT'S GONE OUT AGAIN.
AND MY LIGHTER'S OUT OF FUEL.
HERE, ALLOW ME.
THANK YOU.
DID YOU SEE THAT?
THE FLAME CAME OUT OF HER FINGERS.
THIS IS GREAT WEED!
WE'VE GOT TO GET SOME MORE!
THE END

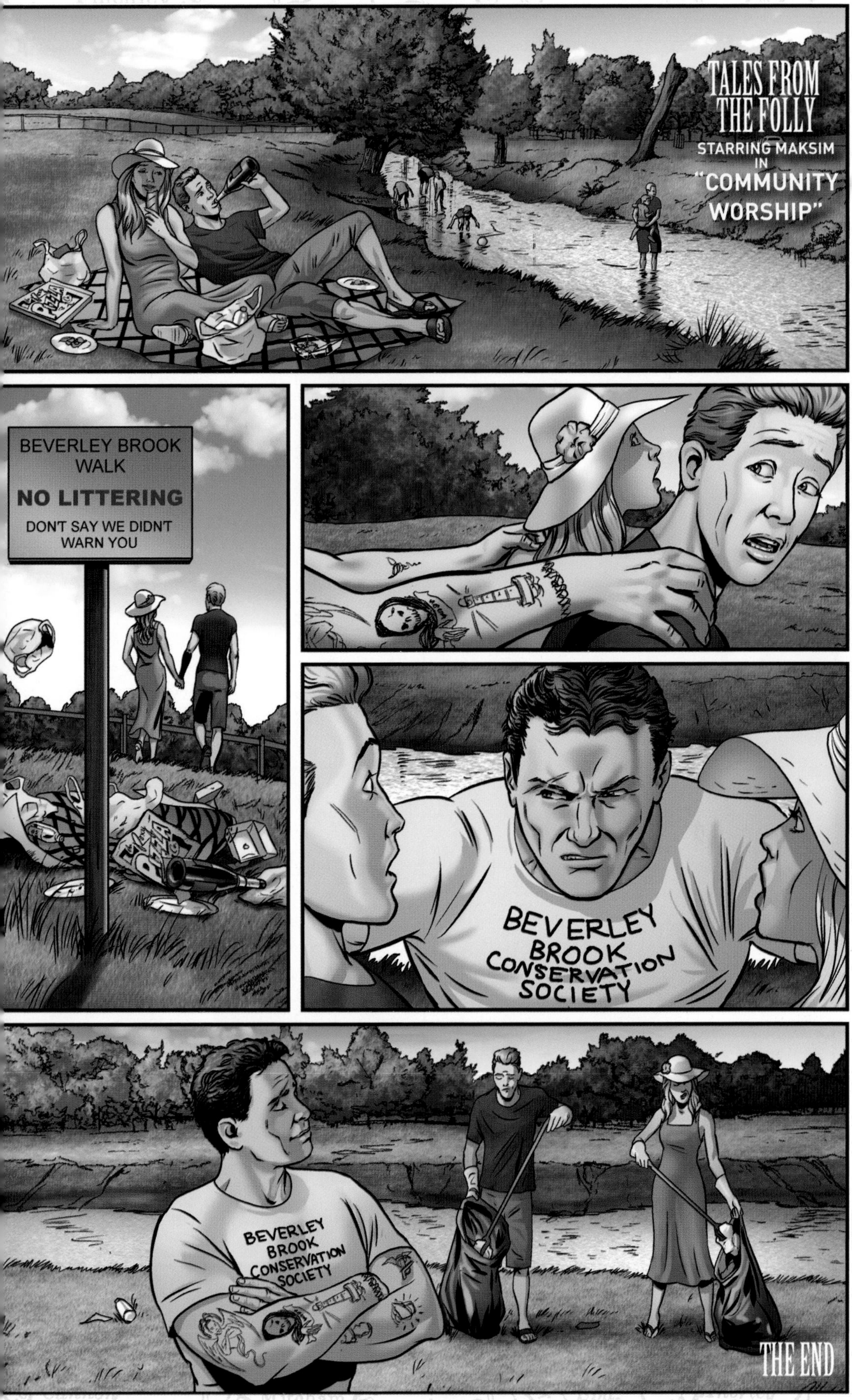
TALES FROM THE FOLLY
STARRING MAKSIM
IN
"COMMUNITY WORSHIP"
BEVERLEY BROOK WALK
NO LITTERING
DON'T SAY WE DIDN'T WARN YOU
BEVERLEY BROOK CONSERVATION SOCIETY
BEVERLEY BROOK CONSERVATION SOCIETY
THE END

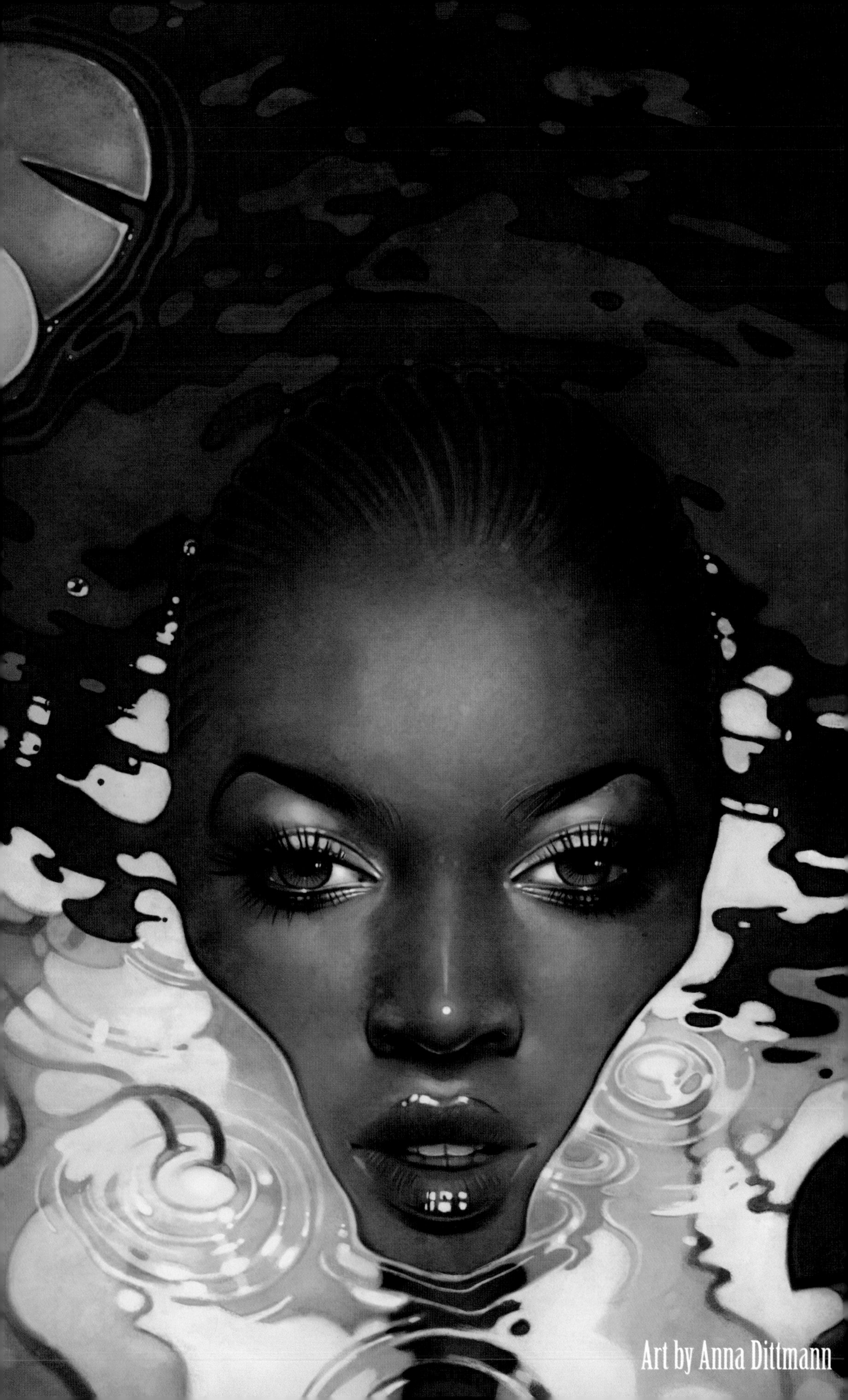
Art by Anna Dittmann

COVERS GALLERY

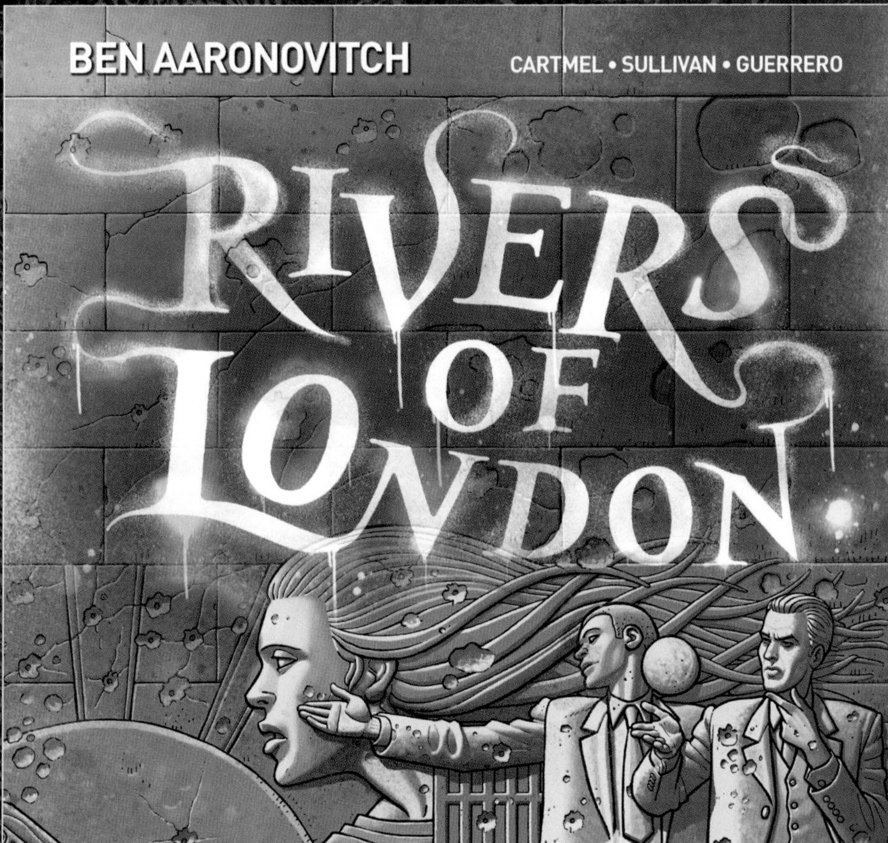

BEN AARONOVITCH

CARTMEL • SULLIVAN • GUERRERO

RIVERS OF LONDON

Ночные Колдуньи

Titan
COMICS

ISSUE 1 – Cover A   Paul McCaffrey

BEN AARONOVITCH
CARTMEL • SULLIVAN • GUERRERO
RIVERS OF LONDON
Ночные Колдуньи
TITAN COMICS

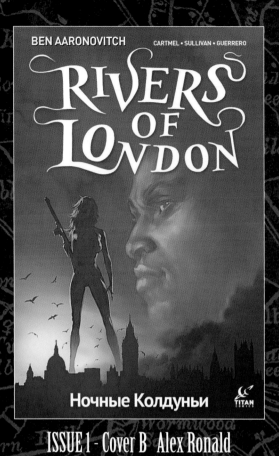

ISSUE 1 - Cover B Alex Ronald

BEN AARONOVITCH
CARTMEL • SULLIVAN • GUERRERO
RIVERS OF LONDON
Ночные Колдуньи
TITAN COMICS

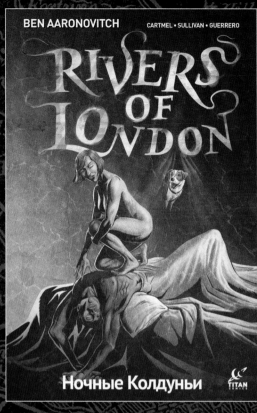

ISSUE 1 - Cover C Lee Sullivan & Luis Guerrero

RIVERS OF LONDON
BEVERLEY BROOK'S
Cop
BEN AARONOVITCH
ANDREW CARTMEL
LEE SULLIVAN
LUIS GUERRERO
COVER: BEN OLIVER
SUGGESTED FOR MATURE READERS
Ночные Колдуньи
$3.99 APR 2016
COVER D
#01
FORBIDDEN PLANET.COM
JETPACK EXCLUSIVE
TITAN COMICS

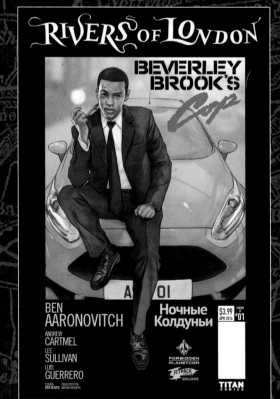

ISSUE 1 - Forbidden Planet/Jetpack Exclusive Ben Oliver

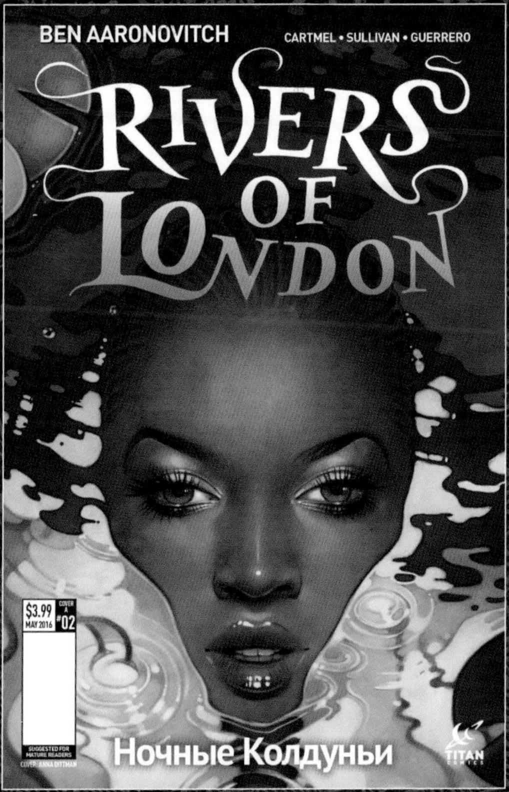
BEN AARONOVITCH
CARTMEL • SULLIVAN • GUERRERO
RIVERS OF LONDON
$3.99 COVER A MAY 2016 #02
SUGGESTED FOR MATURE READERS
COVER: ANNA DITTMANN
Ночные Колдуньи
TITAN COMICS

ISSUE 2 - Cover A Anna Dittmann

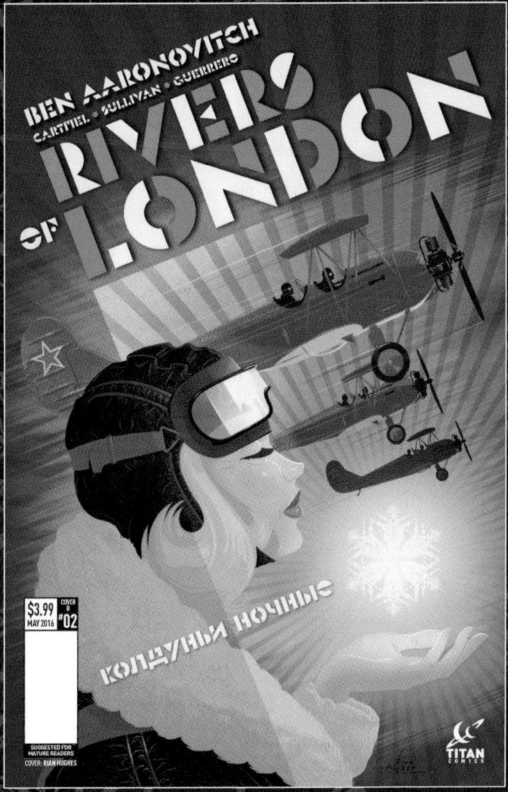
BEN AARONOVITCH
CARTMEL • SULLIVAN • GUERRERO
RIVERS OF LONDON
$3.99 COVER B MAY 2016 #02
КОЛДУНЬИ НОЧНЫЕ
SUGGESTED FOR MATURE READERS
COVER: RIAN HUGHES
TITAN COMICS

ISSUE 2 - Cover B Rian Hughes

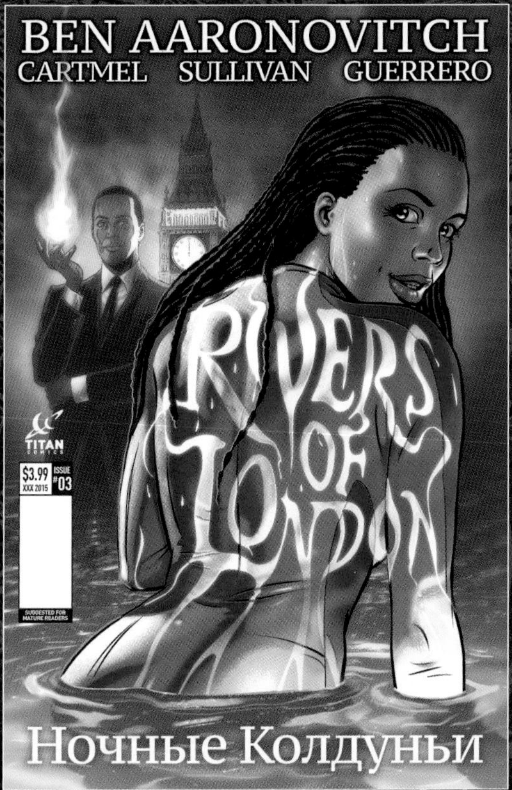
BEN AARONOVITCH
CARTMEL SULLIVAN GUERRERO
RIVERS OF LONDON
TITAN COMICS
$3.99 ISSUE XXX 2015 #03
SUGGESTED FOR MATURE READERS
Ночные Колдуньи

ISSUE 3 - Cover A Lee Sullivan & Luis Guerrero

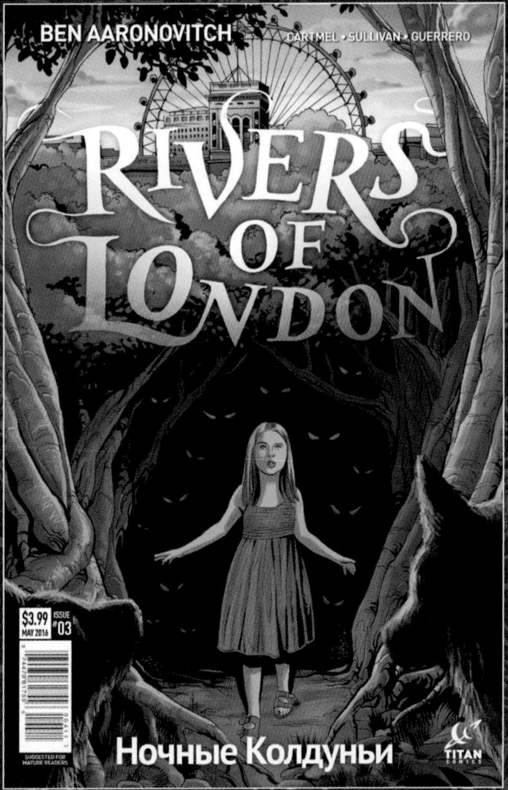
BEN AARONOVITCH
CARTMEL • SULLIVAN • GUERRERO
RIVERS OF LONDON
$3.99 ISSUE MAY 2016 #03
SUGGESTED FOR MATURE READERS
Ночные Колдуньи
TITAN COMICS

ISSUE 3 - Cover B Mariano Laclaustra

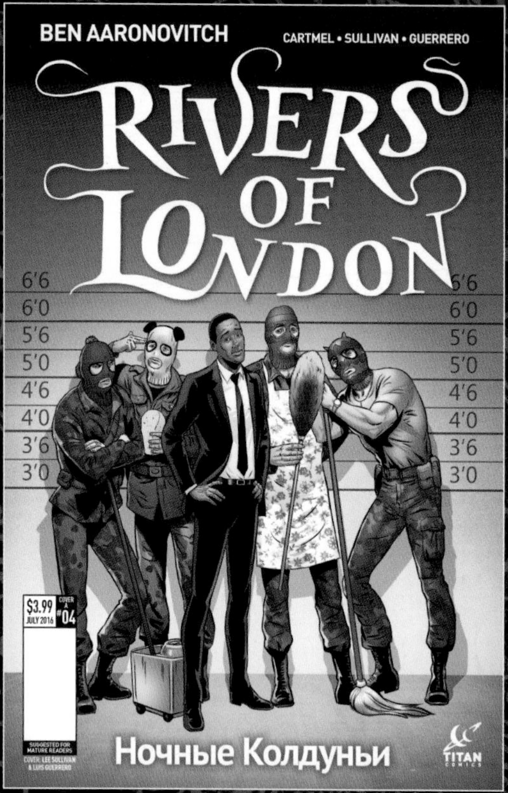
BEN AARONOVITCH
CARTMEL • SULLIVAN • GUERRERO
RIVERS OF LONDON
$3.99 COVER A #04
JULY 2016
SUGGESTED FOR MATURE READERS
COVER: LEE SULLIVAN & LUIS GUERRERO
Ночные Колдуньи
TITAN

ISSUE 4 - Cover A Lee Sullivan & Luis Guerrero

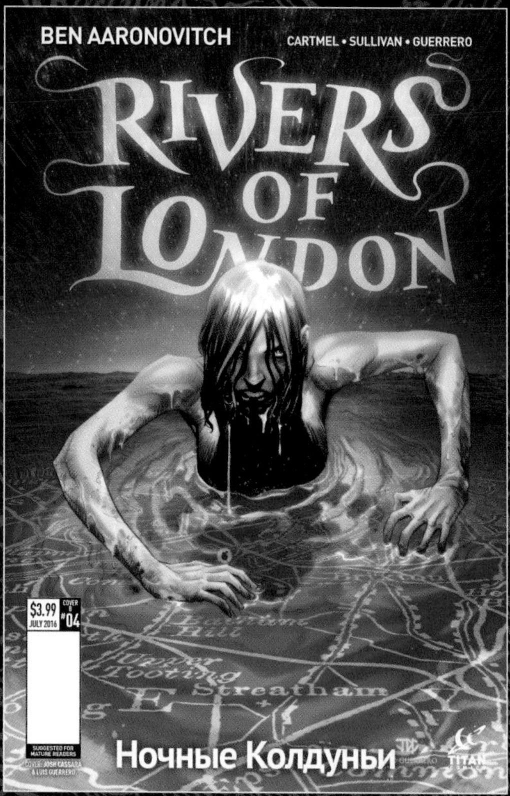
BEN AARONOVITCH
CARTMEL • SULLIVAN • GUERRERO
RIVERS OF LONDON
Upper Tooting
Streatham
$3.99 COVER B #04
JULY 2016
SUGGESTED FOR MATURE READERS
COVER: JOSH CASSARA & LUIS GUERRERO
Ночные Колдуньи
TITAN

ISSUE 4 - Cover B Joshua Cassara & Luis Guerrero

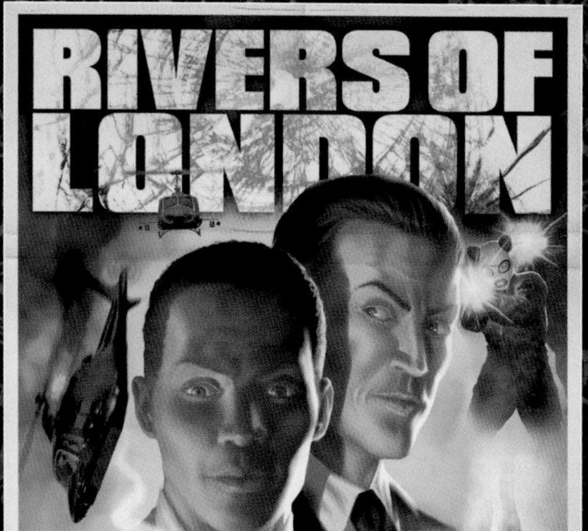
RIVERS OF LONDON
$3.99 COVER A #05
SEPT 2016
TITAN COMICS presents an AARONOVITCH/CARTMEL production LEE SULLIVAN comic
PETER GRANT THOMAS NIGHTINGALE BEVERLEY BROOK LUIS GUERRERO coloring ROB STEEN lettering STEVE WHITE director
НОЧНЫЕ КОЛДУНЬИ
NIGHT WITCH
COMING THIS FALL
SUGGESTED FOR MATURE READERS
COVER: LEE SULLIVAN & LUIS GUERRERO

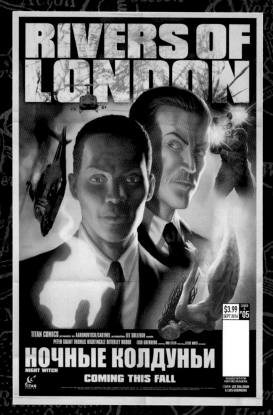

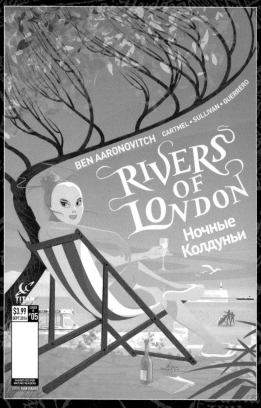

ISSUE 5 - Cover A Lee Sullivan & Luis Guerrero

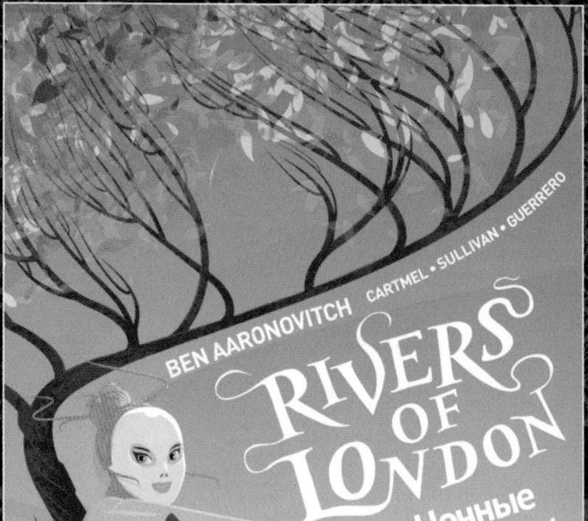
BEN AARONOVITCH
CARTMEL • SULLIVAN • GUERRERO
RIVERS OF LONDON
Ночные Колдуньи
$3.99 COVER B #05
SEPT 2016
SUGGESTED FOR MATURE READERS
COVER: RIAN HUGHES

ISSUE 5 - Cover B Rian Hughes

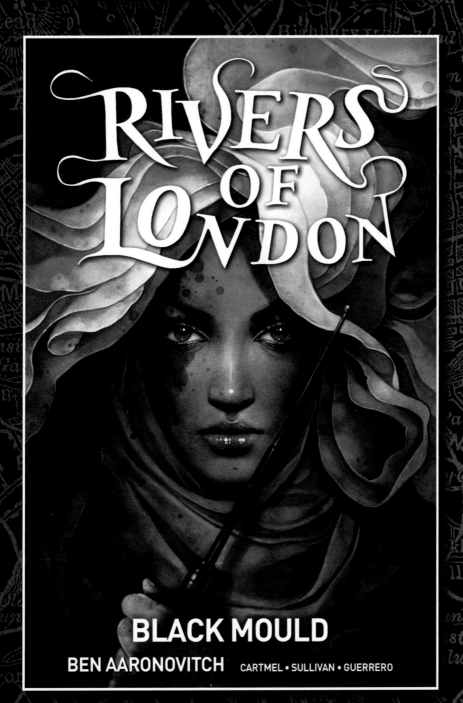

CREATOR BIOGRAPHIES

ANDREW CARTMEL

began a long and varied career in TV and publishing when he was hired as script editor on *Doctor Who* in 1986. He had a major (and very positive) impact on the final years of the original run of the TV show, after which he worked as script editor on *Casualty*. He is also writing the *Vinyl Detective* series of crime novels for Titan Books; the first, *Written on Dead Wax*, is available now. In his spare time, he likes to do stand-up comedy.

LEE SULLIVAN

began his comics career at Marvel UK, drawing *Transformers*, *Thundercats* and *Robocop* – but it is with *Doctor Who* that he is most closely associated. He remains a huge fan of the show, and has continued to draw the Doctor for a variety of publishers.

He played saxophone in a Roxy Music tribute band for a decade. He has dotted various Roxy Music-related gags through this series!

LUIS GUERRERO

Unlike the grizzled veterans above, Luis is a relative newcomer to comics. A native of Mexico, his earliest published work was for Big Dog Ink's 2012 series, *Ursa Minor*. Since then, he has been a regular fixture at Titan Comics, coloring interiors and covers for a number of series including *Doctor Who, The Troop,* and *Man Plus*, as well as *Rivers of London*.

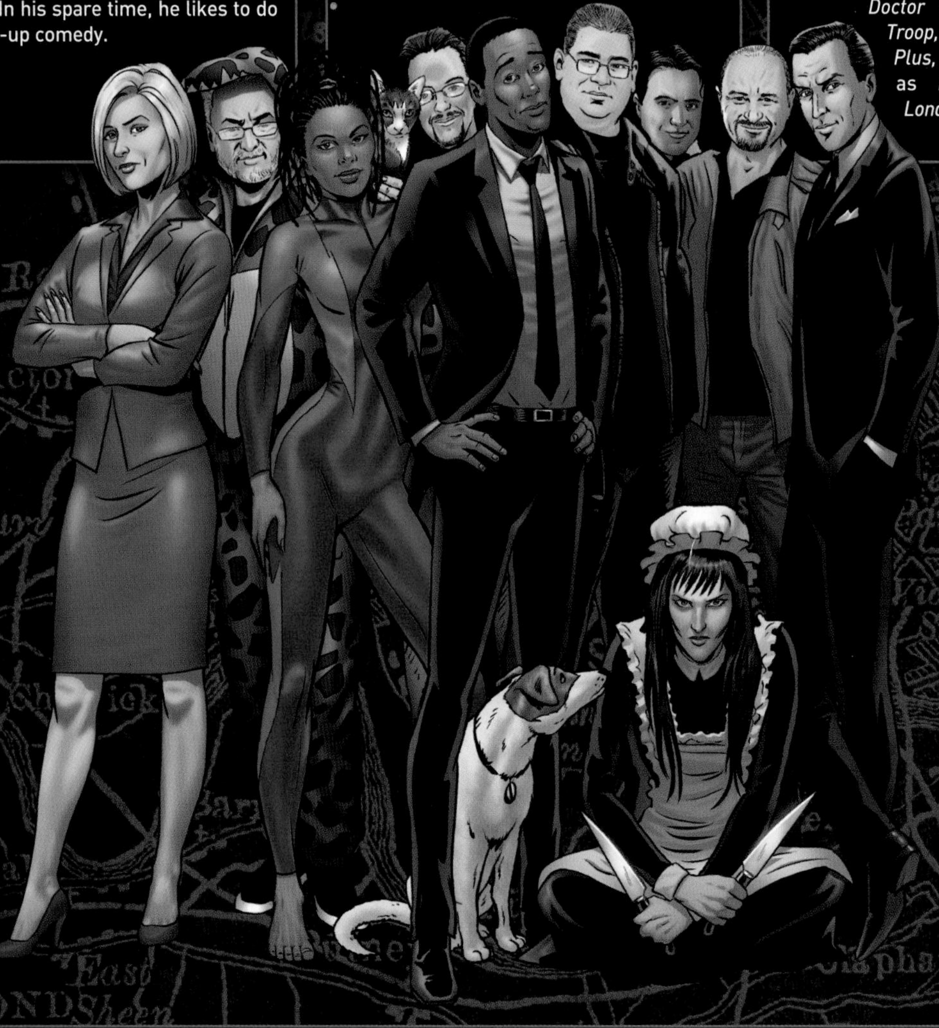

BEN AARONOVITCH

Ben is perhaps best known for his series of Peter Grant novels, which began with *Rivers of London*, released in 2011. Mixing police procedural with urban fantasy and London history, these novels have now sold over a million copies worldwide; the latest, *The Hanging Tree*, is released in 2017.

Ben is also known for his TV writing, especially on *Doctor Who*, where he wrote fan-favorites *Remembrance of the Daleks* and *Battlefield*. He also wrote an episode of long-running BBC hospital drama, *Casualty*, and contributed to cult British sci-fi show, *Jupiter Moon*.

Ben was born, raised and lives in London, and says he will leave the city when they prise it out of his cold, dead fingers.